# Consumer Credit Act Manual

## F A R Bennion
### MA (Oxon), Barrister

Formerly one of the Parliamentary Counsel
(draftsmen of UK Government legislation)

## Third Edition

Longman

© Longman Group UK Limited 1981, 1986

*Published by*
Longman
21–27 Lamb's Conduit Street
London WC1N 3NJ

*Associated offices*
Australia, Hong Kong, Malaysia, Singapore, USA

*British Library Cataloguing in Publication Data*
Bennion, F. A. R.
The Consumer Credit Act manual.—3rd ed.
—(Longman professional practitioner
series)
1. Great Britain. Consumer Credit Act 1974
2. Consumer credit—Law and legislation
—Great Britain
I. Title
344.106′73     KD1755.A3/

ISBN 0–85121–100–3

LR 82438

Printed in Great Britain by Biddles of Guildford Ltd.

# Contents

# CONTENTS

# CONTENTS

# CONTENTS

# Publisher's Note

In earlier editions, this book, written by the draftsman of the Consumer Credit Act 1974, was presented mainly as a working manual for business executives. In response to demands from legal practitioners and law students, the scope has been widened in this edition so as to cater fully for them also. Nevertheless for greater clarity citations and footnote references are, as before, kept to the minimum.

*The Consumer Credit Act Manual* is a distillation of the same author's four-volume loose-leaf work *Consumer Credit Control* (Longman). Case references to 'CCLR' refer to the Consumer Credit Law Reports published in Volume 3 of that work. As a distillation only, this book does not attempt to reproduce the full complexity of the system of control imposed by the Act. It aims to give the essential outline, but for fuller details readers are referred to the main work.

The basic method of *The Consumer Credit Act Manual* is to present separately provisions affecting each type of business, so that the reader concerned with a particular business need not read material which is of no interest to him.

The publishers gratefully acknowledge the permission of Her Majesty's Stationery Office to reproduce the extract from the OFT's booklet *Regulated and Exempt Agreements*.

This book states the law as at 1 April 1986.

# Introduction

## 1 Scope of this book

The Consumer Credit Act profoundly affects more than one hundred thousand businesses throughout the United Kingdom. They include firms which consist of, or are engaged in:

Accountancy
Advertising agencies
Banking
Building societies
Check trading
Consumer advice services
Credit brokerage
Credit card operations
Credit rating
Credit reference agencies
Debt adjusting
Debt collecting
Debt counselling
Department stores
Estate agency
Finance house operations
Hire-purchase and credit sales
Hiring of goods
Hotels and restaurants
House building, maintenance and improvement
Insurance broking
Life assurance
Loan societies and clubs
Mail order trading
Moneylending
Mortgage broking
Motor trading
Pawnbroking
Plant hire
Publishing
Retail selling
Service industries
Solicitors
Television rental
Travel
Vehicle hire
Vending machine operations

This book is primarily designed as a guide for those operating such businesses. It requires no legal knowledge. Although in summarised form, it keeps closely to the statutory provisions. The aim is that it should be at the same time concise, reliable and

1

informative in relation to this important Act which was passed on 31 July 1974 and took eleven years to become fully operative.

Although in terms the book is addressed to those carrying on the businesses affected by the Act, it can be equally well read and applied by others—for example officials, students and indeed members of the general public. Since however it is primarily designed as an aid for business executives, its main chapters describe directly the Act's impact on their operations. Chapter 1 deals with the main category of business affected, called by the Act a 'consumer credit business'. Succeeding chapters are addressed in turn to persons who operate consumer hire businesses, credit (or hire) brokerage businesses, debt counselling or debt adjusting businesses, debt collecting businesses, credit reference agencies and advertising agencies (together with publishers of advertisements). Then follows a chapter giving a general account of the licensing system, which is the keystone of the Act's control structure. The final chapter describes the enforcement machinery, while seven appendices contain various items of useful information. The Act coins a large number of new terms and a dictionary of these is given in Appendix 1 (terms appearing in the dictionary are printed in bold type where they occur in the body of the book). Appendix 2 lists the names of credit businesses which by Ministerial order have been exempted from regulation by the Act. Other appendices list regulations, orders etc made under the Act, addresses and telephone numbers of relevant organisations, and details of official publications. Finally, Appendix 7 gives a comprehensive guide to the dates on which various provisions of the Act came into force and corresponding provisions of earlier legislation were repealed.

## 2 Objects of the Consumer Credit Act

The basic philosophy of the Act is to give uniform protection to individuals (including sole traders and partnerships, but not limited companies) who incur debts not exceeding £15,000, though there are numerous exceptions. The Act aims to operate in the same way whatever the reason for the indebtedness. This is logical, for all debtors face the same risk of not being able to pay and therefore suffering legal proceedings and the seizure of property. Moreover the consumer, whatever transaction he enters into, may be led to incur excessive obligations for interest or other charges, and the trader may be content to leave him in ignorance of the true extent and nature of those obligations.

The Act replaces the Hire-Purchase, Moneylenders and Pawn-brokers Acts as well as filling in the many gaps left by those measures. It is based on the report of a committee headed by the late Lord Crowther. This found that the greatest weakness of the existing law was the failure to look behind the *form* of a credit transaction and deal with its *substance*. Thus distinctions were drawn between one type of transaction and another which were based on legal abstractions and were regarded by the commercial world as unrealistic. For example, hire-purchase, although in substance a form of sale in which the vendor retains, by way of security, a right of property in the goods, was not treated as such by the law. On the contrary, it was treated (and indeed still is under the 1974 Act) as a kind of hiring coupled with a deferred option to purchase. (This is one of the few cases where, for practical reasons, the new Act did not succeed in living up to the intentions of the Crowther Committee.)

As the Crowther Committee pointed out, an individual desiring to obtain goods, services or property without paying out the full price at once can either pay the supplier by instalments under some arrangement such as a hire-purchase agreement, budget account or rental agreement or he can pay the supplier in full using money borrowed from a third party. The economic and social effects are broadly the same, though there may be differences in the creditor's security protection. Either way the consumer acquires immediately the goods, services or property he wants, while incurring indebtedness corresponding to the price (plus interest) less what he puts down in cash out of his own resources. It follows that the protection he needs is much the same regardless of the *legal* nature of the transaction and the type of business carried on by the person who provides finance (whether the supplier of the goods, services or property, or a third party).

It is the aim of the Consumer Credit Act to provide this uniform protection, and at the same time free the credit and hire industries from arbitrary and selective restrictions. The Act is designed indeed to encourage competition between different forms of commercial activity and the development of new forms of business. Its controls fall into two categories: trading control and agreement control.

## 3 Trading control

General regulation of the trading methods of those credit and hire businesses which are not exempted from the Act's provisions is in the hands of the Office of Fair Trading (OFT). The OFT is subject to supervision by the Secretary of State for Trade and Industry. In turn it supervises the local enforcement authorities (trading standards departments), who carry out detailed inspection and control of businesses.

Trading control operates mainly through the licensing system. An OFT licence is required to enable the business to be carried on (so far as it falls within the purview of the Act). Up to the end of 1985, the number of standard licences issued amounted (by categories) to 311,967. These were divided as follows:

| | |
|---|---:|
| Category A (consumer credit business) | 62,302 |
| Category B (consumer hire business) | 34,572 |
| Category C (credit brokerage) | 144,889 |
| Category D (debt counselling and debt adjusting) | 48,929 |
| Category E (debt collecting) | 16,489 |
| Category F (credit reference agency) | 4,786 |
| Canvassing authorisations | 56,011 |

Many licences included more than one category, the total number of licences being 180,446. A licence will not be granted to a trader with a bad record. If a licensee transgresses, his licence can be suspended or withdrawn. This potent threat gives the enforcement authorities very effective disciplinary powers.

A further aspect of trading control is the extensive power conferred by the Act to regulate methods of seeking business. Close restrictions are placed on doorstep selling and other face-to-face canvassing off trade premises. Distribution of circulars to persons under 18 is penalised, as is the delivery of unsolicited **credit-tokens**. Advertisements and quotations must conform to complex requirements.

## 4 Agreement control

Whereas trading control looks to the general way a business is conducted, agreement control is concerned with individual credit and hire agreements (and any **security** given in connection with them). While trading control is largely administrative, being operated by the OFT and other public authorities, agreement control (at least so far as its enforcement is concerned) is in the hands of the court. Except in Scotland (where the sheriff courts are responsible), the court in question is the county court.

Agreement control is the legacy of the Hire-Purchase Acts. The Consumer Credit Act has largely proceeded by extending and elaborating the system worked out by successive Hire-Purchase Acts since Ellen Wilkinson's pioneering Act of 1938.

Agreement control specifies the information which must be supplied to consumers *before* they commit themselves to entering a contract. Where the consumer wishes to withdraw before contract but has already committed himself to a **linked transaction**, it permits him to free himself from this. It lays down in detail the form and content of credit and hire agreements, with the object of ensuring that the consumer is fully aware of what he is committing himself to and of his rights. Where there has been face-to-face canvassing, it may confer rights of cancellation within a brief period after the contract is made.

Once the contract has become fully operative, agreement control deals with matters arising during the currency of the contract. It requires the consumer to be kept informed of facts affecting him (for example that the trader intends to exercise a right adverse to the consumer). It gives the consumer the right to obtain information about his contract. If another person misuses his credit or hire facility, it limits his liability. It protects him from overcharging where he wishes to terminate the contract prematurely. If he dies during its currency, it protects his relatives from harassment.

Agreement control closely regulates the trader's rights where the consumer defaults on his obligations. It also ensures that **sureties** are fully aware of their position and are protected from unfair treatment. (The Act cannot be evaded by taking security.)

Where agreement control provisions are not complied with by the trader, or the consumer is in difficulties, the court is given a discretion to make orders which combine fairness (to both sides) with practical expediency. A general principle of relief is that the court is always able to allow the consumer an extension of time. An important power given to the court enables it to reopen **extortionate** credit bargains. Here the usual £15,000 limit does not apply and any credit agreement with an **individual**, however large the amount, is subject to review.

## 5 Ancillary credit and hire traders

In addition to the control of ordinary credit and hire traders and their transactions, the Act also brings under supervision certain businesses which form a subsidiary part of the credit and hire industry:

*Brokers:*      In general, any business which effects introductions of **individuals** desiring loans or other credit, or goods on hire, to traders offering such facilities is what the Act calls a 'credit broker' and subject to trading control. Since this term covers a great many department stores, retailers and other dealers (as well as more obvious broking traders such as mortgage brokers) it goes very wide (see Chapter 3).

*Debt counsellors and debt adjusters:*      Trading control also extends to these, when operating by way of business (see Chapter 4).

*Debt collectors:*      Oppressive methods used by some firms led to these being included (see Chapter 5).

*Credit reference agencies:*      These agencies are included in the Act's system of controls mainly to check breach of privacy and the spreading of incorrect or misleading information about consumers (see Chapter 6).

*Advertising agencies and publishers:*      The legislation renders these liable for breaches in connection with credit and hire advertisements in all media (see Chapter 7).


## 6 European Communities

The Commission of the European Communities propose to make a directive for securing uniformity in the consumer credit legislation of member states. The latest draft of the directive, dated 23 February 1979, has been presented by the Commission to the Council of Ministers, who in turn have referred it to the European Parliament and the Economic and Social Committee for their views. On 11 February 1983 the European Parliament proposed a large number of amendments to the draft. The draft, with proposed amendments, is to be referred to a working group of member states. The general approach of the British Government is that the requirements of the directive, when finally made, should not go beyond the Consumer Credit Act (which was first in the field in Europe).

# Chapter 1

# The Consumer Credit Business

## 1 What a 'consumer credit business' is

The Act uses the term 'consumer credit business' to describe the main type of business affected by its provisions. The following are likely to fall within the definition of consumer credit business: shops selling on **credit**, hire-purchase traders, moneylenders, pawnbrokers, mail-order firms, check traders, finance houses, clearing banks, merchant banks, building societies, life assurance companies and credit card issuers. So also are service industries such as hotels, restaurants, garages and travel agencies.

### The definition

The statutory definition of 'consumer credit business' states that the term includes any **business** so far as it comprises or relates to the provision of **credit** under regulated consumer credit agreements. With some exceptions, any agreement providing an **individual** with credit not exceeding £15,000 is a regulated consumer credit agreement. The precise spelling out of the definition of such agreements is a matter of some complexity however (see section 3 below). To fall within the definition of consumer credit business, the business actually has to provide credit, whether in the form of cash loans, hire-purchase, credit sales or otherwise.

## 2 How the Act affects your business

If you carry on a consumer credit business the Act affects you in numerous ways. Furthermore the Act may affect you if your business, while not within the definition of a consumer credit business, nevertheless grants credit to individuals. For example, the advertising restrictions apply to some land mortgages

7

exceeding £15,000 (see section 8 below) and the court's power to reopen **extortionate** credit bargains applies even where the credit exceeds £15,000 (see section 18 below).

If your business is or includes a consumer credit business the following controls operate:

You must have a licence issued by the OFT unless you are an **individual** and do not grant credit exceeding £30.

You are restricted in the way you canvass for business.

You must comply with the requirements governing advertisements and quotations.

You must give information about credit status inquiries made by you.

You may be liable for statements by dealers, retailers and negotiators.

You must supply customers with relevant basic information before they commit themselves to an agreement.

Withdrawal of a customer from a prospective credit agreement will cancel any **linked transaction**.

Your agreements, and any security taken, must comply with the documentation requirements.

Most agreements are cancellable by the customer if the **antecedent negotiations** included face-to-face representations made off trade premises.

Customers with a claim against a **supplier** may have a similar claim against you.

Your agreements may be reopened if the court finds them extortionate.

If you issue two- or three-party credit cards, trading checks or other **credit-tokens** you are subject to special rules.

You must give the prescribed notice when enforcing or varying an agreement.

Restrictions are placed on your ability to enforce contractual terms. Your customers have the right to terminate an agreement, or settle ahead of time subject to remission of unaccrued charges.

All these provisions, and others of less importance, are explained in the present chapter.

### 3  What credit agreements are regulated by the Act

Agreements which are subject to the general system of control imposed by the Act are called '**regulated agreements**'. They may be either **consumer credit agreements** or **consumer hire agreements**. The latter are described in Chapter 2 (page 115). Note that a word of mouth arrangement is an 'agreement' even if not reduced to writing.

### (a) The 'consumer credit agreement'

This is defined as an agreement between an **individual** (called the debtor) and any other person (called the creditor) by which the creditor provides the debtor with **credit** not exceeding £15,000. Although on the face of it this appears straightforward, it may not always be easy to determine whether the credit does or does not exceed £15,000. The following rules apply in answering this question:

(1) Disregard any sum falling within the **total charge for credit**. It does not count as credit even though time is allowed for its payment.

(2) Disregard any deposit (including any form of down-payment). Since this is provided by the debtor himself it does not count as credit.

(3) In the case of a **hire-purchase agreement** (which the Act treats as credit and not hire) or a **conditional sale agreement**, the credit equals the total price *less* the aggregate of any deposit and all amounts falling within the total charge for credit.

(4) In the case of **running-account credit** where there is a stated credit limit, the credit provided is taken to be equal to the amount of the limit, unless the limit exceeds £15,000 and the anti-avoidance provisions in paragraph (6) apply.

(5) In the case of running-account credit where there is no stated credit limit, the credit provided is taken to exceed £15,000 unless the anti-avoidance provisions in paragraph (6) apply.

(6) Running-account credit it taken not to exceed £15,000 if:

    (a) the **debtor** is not able to draw credit exceeding £15,000 at any one time; or

    (b) on the debit balance rising above a stated figure not exceeding £15,000, the interest rate increases or any other condition favouring the creditor or an **associate** of his comes into operation; or

    (c) at the time the **credit agreement** is made it is probable that the debit balance will never rise above £15,000.

Note that the effect of rules (1) and (2) above is that a transaction appearing at first sight to be well over the £15,000 limit may in fact be within it.

> **Example 1** A sole trader buys a truck on credit-sale for a price of £21,000 plus credit charges of £3,600, a total of £24,600. He pays a deposit of £7,500 towards the £21,000 and agrees to pay the remaining £17,100 by equal instalments over a period of two years. This is a **consumer credit agreement**. The deposit of £7,500 does not count towards the £15,000 limit. Nor does the credit charge of £3,600, even though the trader is given time to pay it. The credit therefore is £24,600 − (£7,500 + £3,600) = £13,500. (Note however that if the down-payment of £7,500 were stated to consist of £3,900 towards the price with the remainder discharging the credit charges in full it would *not* be a consumer credit agreement. The credit advanced would then be £21,000 − £3,900 = £17,100, which is over the £15,000 limit.)

The £15,000 limit was raised from £5,000 on 20 May 1985. The increase is not retrospective. This means that, for example, a personal credit agreement for £7,500 would not fall to be treated as a 'consumer credit agreement' if made on 18 May 1985, but would fall to be so treated if made on 20 May 1985.

### (b) Which consumer credit agreements are 'regulated'

A consumer credit agreement is a 'regulated agreement', and thus within the general system of control imposed by the Act, provided it is not within one of the following exceptions.

Agreements made before 1 April 1977 are not **regulated agreements** unless varied on or after that date (a varied agreement is taken to be made on the date of variation). Nor are **foreign agreements** or the **exempt agreements** described in section 4. The date 1 April 1977 is not applicable in all cases; the relevant date may be later. In determining whether a particular credit agreement is or is not a 'regulated agreement' it is necessary to bear three considerations in mind, namely the date of the agreement, the amount of the credit, and the relevant provision of the Act. The term 'regulated agreement' does not have the same meaning in each provision of the Act where it occurs. Differences mainly depend on when the relevant provision came into force, and what the financial limit was when the agreement was made or is deemed to have been made (namely £5,000 or £15,000).

## 4 Exempt consumer credit agreements

In order to understand which agreements are exempt from regulation under the Act we need first to tackle two further technical terms. A **consumer credit agreement** may either be a '**debtor-creditor-supplier agreement**' or a '**debtor-creditor agreement**'. If it is not a debtor-creditor-supplier agreement it must necessarily be a debtor-creditor agreement and we need, therefore, only consider the definition of the former expression.

### (a) The debtor-creditor-supplier agreement

In simple terms this is a **consumer credit agreement** which the **creditor** knows is to finance a particular transaction where either the creditor himself is also the supplier of the goods, services or property concerned or he has a business connection with the **supplier**. The creditor in such cases is sometimes described as a 'connected lender', though the term lender is scarcely apt to describe a dealer selling on credit or hire-purchase. The Act spells out three types of **debtor-creditor-supplier agreement**:

(1) The credit agreement is for **restricted-use credit** and finances (wholly or partly) a transaction between the **debtor** and the creditor (whether forming part of the credit agreement or not). Examples: hire-purchase, credit sale, conditional sale, two-party credit card, store budget account.

(2) The credit agreement is for restricted-use credit and finances (wholly or partly) a transaction between the debtor and a third party. Here the credit agreement must be made under pre-existing business arrangements between creditor and third party, or in contemplation of future such arrangements (as where a 3-party credit card agreement contemplates that further retailers will in future agree to honour the credit card). Examples: trading check or voucher, cash loan paid direct to supplier who introduced debtor to creditor.

(3) The credit agreement is for **unrestricted-use credit** and finances (wholly or partly) a transaction between the debtor and a third party. Here the credit agreement must be made by the creditor under pre-existing business arrangements between himself and the third party and in the knowledge that the credit is to be used to finance that transaction. Strangely, the Act does not include as a debtor-creditor-supplier agreement the parallel case where unrestricted-use credit is to be used to finance a transaction with the creditor

himself (for example where a trader combines money-lending and retail selling).

Before turning to the categories of **exempt agreement**, most of which are in terms making it necessary to distinguish between a debtor-creditor-supplier agreement and a debtor-creditor agreement, it may be helpful to consider the alternative way the distinction between the two types of agreement is presented in the official booklet *Regulated and Exempt Agreements*. The result is of course the same.

Start with question 1 and follow the instructions thereafter.

(1) *Is it agreed that the credit is to be used to finance a transaction between the debtor and the creditor?* If the answer is 'yes', it is a debtor-creditor-supplier agreement*. If 'no', go on to the second question.

(2) *Is it agreed that the credit is to be used to re-finance existing debts owed by the debtor, whether to the creditor or anyone else?* If 'yes', the agreement is a debtor-creditor agreement. If 'no', look at the diagram on page 13.

### (b) Categories of exemption

The categories of exempt consumer credit agreement are:

(1) Mortgage advances by building societies, local authorities, certain statutory corporations and specified insurance companies, friendly societies and charities. (For a list of the latter see Appendix 2, page 232). As from 28 April 1980 this has included advances of house insurance premiums and premiums on mortgage protection policies.

(2) Debtor-creditor-supplier agreements (whether secured or not) which finance land purchase and require not more than four payments (whether of interest or credit repayment) by the debtor.

(3) Certain **fixed-sum** debtor-creditor-supplier agreements which require not more than four credit repayments, by the debtor.

(4) **Running-account** debtor-creditor-supplier agreements where the credit provided in each period is repayable in one amount.

(5) Debtor-creditor agreements where the rate of the total charge for credit (see s 5 below) does not exceed the *higher*

---

* This is incorrect where the agreement is for **unrestricted-use credit.** Here if the answer is 'yes' it is a debtor-creditor agreement.

START HERE

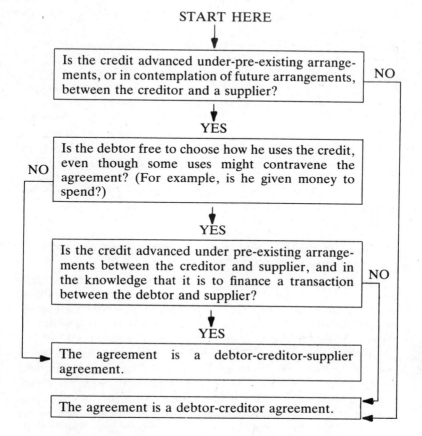

Is the credit advanced under-pre-existing arrangements, or in contemplation of future arrangements, between the creditor and a supplier? — **NO**

**YES**

Is the debtor free to choose how he uses the credit, even though some uses might contravene the agreement? (For example, is he given money to spend?) — **NO**

**YES**

Is the credit advanced under pre-existing arrangements between the creditor and supplier, and in the knowledge that it is to finance a transaction between the debtor and supplier? — **NO**

**YES**

The agreement is a debtor-creditor-supplier agreement.

The agreement is a debtor-creditor agreement.

of the following: 13 per cent per annum or 1 per cent above highest bank base rate.

(6) Trade agreements with a foreign connection, ie where the debtor is a trader who trades with a country outside the United Kingdom and the credit is provided in the course of that trade.

Further explanation is required of categories (3), (4) and (5).

*(c) Fixed-sum debtor-creditor-supplier agreements with not more than four credit repayments*

This limited exemption is designed to pick out the instalment buyer (who is taken to need protection) from the buyer who merely defers payment (whose agreement is exempt). The Crowther Committee identified the instalment buyer as one who pays by at least *three* instalments (excluding any deposit or down-payment). The legislation widens the exemption proposed by the Crowther Committee and only treats as an instalment buyer one who pays by *five* or more instalments. However, the exemption does not apply to goods sold on **hire-purchase** or **conditional sale**, nor where security is given by a pledge (other than of documents of title or bearer bonds). Neither does it apply to agreements financing the purchase of land, which fall under a different exemption (see category (2) above). The typical case where this exemption applies is ordinary trade credit extended where payment of the price of goods is to be made in one sum but is deferred to a time after the sale agreement is entered into, eg where goods are 'put aside' to be paid for later or are delivered in advance of payment.

### (d) Running-account debtor-creditor-supplier agreements with one credit repayment per period

This exempts from control the trader who has continuous dealings with his customer (eg the newsagent or grocer) and extends weekly or monthly credit. If the customer can, under the express or implied terms of his agreement with the trader, choose to pay for each period in two or more instalments the exemption will not apply. Nor will it apply if a specific period is not laid down in respect of which repayment must be made. Thus a newsagent who lets his accounts run on, and only demands settlement on a basis irregular as to time, will not be exempt. Agreements secured by a **pledge** (other than of documents of title or bearer bonds) are excluded from the exemption. Credit card agreements are within the exemption only where the customer *must* repay the whole credit advanced within the month in one sum after the end of the month. As with other trade credit, giving the customer an option to pay by instalments destroys the exemption. (Note however that, as with all the exemptions, what counts are the terms of the agreement—the possibility of default by the customer is disregarded.)

### (e) Debtor-creditor agreements with low charge for credit

The legislation does not extend protection to the consumer who takes a cash loan at a rate of interest not exceeding 13 per cent per annum (or 1 per cent above highest bank base rate if higher). (An exception is where the creditor knows the loan is to finance a transaction with a person with whom he has business arrangements when it becomes a debtor-creditor-supplier agreement.) This exemption is of particular relevance to staff loans, which are often at advantageous rates. Note however that other staff credit schemes, eg house mortgages with a particular building society or sales of the company's product on cheap credit, will not be within this exemption because the agreements will be debtor-creditor-supplier agreements. The base rate in question is that in operation on the date twenty-eight days before the credit agreement is made. If the rate changes on that date the later rate is to be taken. The exemption does not apply where the amount of principal repayable is index-linked.

### 5 The total charge for credit

The Act requires regulations to be made for determining the true cost to the debtor of the credit provided or to be provided under an actual or prospective consumer credit agreement. This true cost is described as '**the total charge for credit**'. The regulations, made in 1977 and re-issued in revised form in 1980, are highly complex. They bring in not only interest charges but various other items as well. They also lay down certain assumptions, necessary to calculate in advance the amount of the charge. These assumptions relate to the amount of **credit** which will be advanced, when it will be advanced, when it will be repaid, the amount of index-linked repayments, and the rate or amount of charges and when they will be paid. Finally the regulations make complicated provision for calculating the *rate* of the total charge for credit. The 'truth in lending' aim of the Act depends for its furtherance on enabling consumers to 'shop around' for credit. For this purpose they need to be able to compare rates and, so that sensible comparisons can be made, the rates need to be calculated on a uniform basis.

The amount and rate of the total charge for credit is relevant in connection with advertisements and quotations, and for determining whether a **debtor-creditor agreement** is exempt on the ground that the rate of the total charge for credit is below a certain figure (see above). In addition, the courts may refer to the total charge for credit when deciding whether a credit bargain is **extortionate**. A charge by a **credit-broker** may be disallowed if it falls within the total charge for credit—see pages 162 to 167.

The total charge for credit is also relevant for the following:

(i) *Prospective credit agreements*—to enable the consumer to know the credit rate *before* he commits himself to an agreement.

(ii) *Contract documents*—to enable the document embodying a concluded credit agreement to state the rate of the total charge.

(iii) *Interest on default*—to safeguard the debtor against having to pay an increased rate of interest on default, contrary to the Act.

(iv) *Rebate on early settlement*—to facilitate the calculation of the amount and rate of rebates to which the debtor is entitled on discharging his indebtedness in advance of the due date.

(v) *Pawn receipts* — to enable a pawn-receipt to state the rate of charge.

*(a) Items falling within the 'total charge for credit'*

First to be included in the total charge for credit is the most obvious item, interest on the amount of the principal advanced under the credit agreement. This is calculated by applying the various statutory assumptions already referred to. For example if the amount of the credit cannot be ascertained at the time the agreement is made, it is assumed to be £100, even though a much larger sum is probable.

In dealing with items of charge other than interest the regulations proceed by first bringing in various items but then knocking them out again if they are of certain types. The items brought in are charges of any description (other than interest under the **credit agreement**) payable by the debtor *or his relative* under:

(1) the credit agreement itself, or

(2) a transaction required by the credit agreement to be entered into, or

(3) a contract providing **security** in relation to the credit agreement, or

(4) any other contract to which the debtor or his relative is a party and which the creditor requires to be made or maintained as a condition of making the credit agreement.

It is immaterial that full consideration is given for the charge or that it is repayable. Examples of charges brought in are insurance premiums, maintenance payments, and charges for ancillary goods such as frozen food bought to stock a freezer acquired on credit.

The following charges are however excluded from the total charge for credit:

(1) Default charges.
(2) Charges which would be payable in a cash transaction.
(3) Charges which apply as well to other services or benefits supplied to the debtor, and are payable under an obligation incurred before the credit agreement was made.
(4) Charges for essential repairs.
(5) Freely-negotiated maintenance charges.
(6) Premiums under an insurance policy made before the debtor applied to enter into the credit agreement.
(7) Premiums under an insurance policy not *required* by the creditor.
(8) Premiums under motor vehicle insurance.
(9) Premiums under leasehold property insurance.
(10) Premiums under a protective life policy.
(11) Premiums under a freely-negotiated insurance policy (other than one where the policy money is to be used to repay the credit or pay a credit charge).
(12) Bank transmission charges.

*(b) Annual percentage rate (APR)*

The rate of the total charge for credit is defined as the 'annual percentage rate of charge' determined to one decimal place, ie truncated after the first numeral following the decimal point (so that 15.89% becomes 15.8% not 15.9%). The effective rate is therefore the annual percentage rate, known as the APR.

The regulations for calculating the APR are exceedingly complicated. The basic principle is supplied by what is called the 'present-value rule'. Broadly, this lays down that the APR is whatever rate per annum (compounding annually) will produce equality between the present value (at the date of the credit agreement) of the sums to be advanced to the debtor and the present value (at that date) of the repayments of principal and payments of charges to be made by the debtor. The formula for calculating the present value of a sum to be paid in the future is:

$$P = \dfrac{A}{(1 + r)t}{100}$$

where:

P  is the present value;
A  is the amount of the sum;
t  is the period of years beginning at the date of the credit
   agreement and ending on the date of payment of the sum;
r  is the APR.

Further formulae are supplied which make the present value rule simpler to apply in two common cases:

(1)      *Period rate transactions*, where a constant **period rate of charge** is charged (on advances outstanding) in respect of periods of equal length. Here the APR is equal to

$$100 \left[ \left(1 + \frac{x}{100}\right)^y - 1 \right]$$

where x is the period rate of charge expressed as a percentage and y is the number of periods in a year.

(2)      *Single-repayment transactions*, where **fixed-sum credit** is paid in one sum and only one payment (of principal and interest combined) is to be made by the debtor. Here the APR is equal to

$$100 \left[ \left(1 + \frac{c}{p}\right)^{\frac{1}{t}} - 1 \right]$$

where c is the total charge of credit and p is the amount of the credit to be advanced.

For practical purposes however it is usually necessary to calculate the APR by the use of tables.

*(c)  The Consumer Credit Tables*

These are published by HMSO in fifteen separate Parts. A consolidated complete version is also published (with an introduction) by Longman Professional as part of the present author's *Consumer Credit Control*. The Tables cover a wide range of three types of credit transaction most commonly met with, namely the two just mentioned for which special formulae are supplied and thirdly equal-instalment transactions, where a single advance of credit is made and the sum of the principal advanced and the total charge is payable by the debtor in equal instalments at equal intervals.

The Tables deal with single-repayment and equal-instalment transactions on two different bases: (i) *charge per pound lent* (Parts 1 to 10 of the Tables) and (ii) *flat rate charge* (Parts 11 to

14). Finally, period rate transactions are dealt with by themselves in Part 15.

The Tables have been designed to fit the current pattern of credit trading. There seems little doubt however that the full impact of the Act is beginning to modify that pattern. Effective rates of charge calculated on the same basis, ie the present value rule, have to be presented to the consumer in relation to all regulated agreements, whether money loans, **hire-purchase agreements**, credit card financing, pawnshop pledges or whatever. The term annual percentage rate of charge (or APR) is on the way to becoming a household word. Traders are finding it pointless to quote charges on a flat rate or other basis as well.

### (d) Representative total charge for credit

A trader is permitted to include in an advertisement a representative total charge for credit where charges for comparable transactions vary, or the characteristics of the ultimate customer are relevant. Here the trader selects a typical case from among those he engages in and gives details of the charges for that by way of example.

### (e) Approximate APR (using tolerances)

The regulations concerning advertisements, quotations and agreements ease the task of the trader by allowing certain tolerances in calculating the APR. One general tolerance, known as the *plus 1 per cent/minus 0.1 per cent* tolerance is available in all cases. This enables the true rate to be overstated by up to 1 per cent or understated by up to 0.1 per cent. Four other tolerances apply only in particular cases, and may not be used in addition to the general tolerance. These special tolerances are as follows:

(i) *Where one instalment differs from all the others* As long as the one different repayment of credit is within a specified range, its amount may be treated as varied so as to equal the amount of the other repayments, thus making them all the same for calculation purposes. The range is found by taking the total number of repayments. The tolerance may be used only where this number is equal to or greater than the number of pence by which the one odd instalment differs from all the others.

**Example 2** A loan of £50 is repayable (with the addition of a charge of £10) by thirteen monthly payments beginning after one month. The first twelve instalments are each of

£4.61, but the final instalment works out at £4.68. As the difference in pence (7) is not greater than the number of instalments (13) the final payment can be treated as £4.61 too. This gives an approximate APR of 37.5 per cent, which can be stated in an advertisement or quotation simply as the 'APR'.

*(ii) Where all intervals except the first are equal*     This allows for disparity caused by the fact that repayment dates may be fixed but the date on which an individual agreement is signed will of course vary with circumstances.

**Example 3** A firm offers credit-sale agreements under which the credit is repayable by twelve equal instalments on the first of each month, beginning with the month next but one after that in which the agreement is signed. An agreement is signed on 12 June, so the first instalment is due on 1 August.

The tolerance allows the APR to be worked out as if the forty-nine days between the signing and first instalment in Example 3 were a month, so that all intervals are the same. The amount by which the first interval exceeds the others must not be greater than one month or the length of each of the others, whichever is less. Nor is the tolerance available if the first interval is *shorter* than the others. On the facts in Example 3 therefore the tolerance could not be used if the first instalment were instead due on 1 July or 1 September.

**Example 4** A firm offers **hire-purchase agreements** involving credit of £80 and a charge of £16, payable in twelve instalments on the 15th of each month. Provided at least a month (but not more than two months) elapses before the first instalment is due, the first period can be treated as equal to one month. Using the Tables this gives an approximate APR of 41.3%, which can be quoted as the APR in advertisements or quotations.

*(iii) Where Tables do not exactly apply*     If the **charge per pound lent** or the **flat rate** or the **period rate of charge** is not exactly represented by an entry in the **Consumer Credit Tables**

this useful tolerance enables the APR to be found by reference to the *next greater* entry in the appropriate Table.

**Example 5** Credit of £100 is to be repaid by 12 monthly instalments of £9.75, a total of £117. The charge per pound lent is $\dfrac{£17}{£100}$ = £0.17. The relevant Table is contained in Part 4 of the Tables. Column 12 of the Table (containing the charge per pound lent for an agreement of 12 instalments) jumps from 0.16990 to 0.17035. It therefore does not contain the figure required here (0.17000). The tolerance enables 0.17035 to be taken, giving an approximate APR of 34.6%.

*(iv) Where period rate charged*    Where a **period rate of charge** is charged it will usually produce a payment amount including a fraction of a penny. If the trader rounds this fraction off (as for practical purposes he must) then apart from this tolerance he could not use the period rate formula or Tables. The tolerance allows him to ignore the rounding off in calculating the APR, though if a halfpenny is rounded off it must be done upwards not downwards.

**Example 6** An agreement for a loan of £225 provides for a period rate of interest of 1.9% per month, to be paid monthly. This produces an interest payment of £4.27½, which the creditor rounds up to £4.28. The rounding up does not prevent him using the Tables to calculate the APR (25.3%).

The four special tolerances described above may be used singly or in combination.

*(f) Statutory assumptions*

The legislation requires traders to state the total charge for credit or APR in circumstances where they cannot know all the facts needed for this. The total charge for credit may vary according to the date when credit is actually drawn. The APR may differ according to the length of the periods between instalment payments, and so on. It has therefore been necessary to lay down statutory assumptions to be made by the trader in calculating the

APR or total charge for credit. The assumptions relate to *dates* and *amounts*, and are to be applied only to the extent that the true facts are unknown and cannot be ascertained by applying the terms of the agreement. It is assumed throughout that the debtor will comply with the agreement, so that default terms are ignored.

*(g) Date when credit will be drawn*

Credit is provided when the credit agreement is made (this is usually when it is signed by the second party who signs). At that point the creditor becomes bound to make the loan, or provide the goods on hire-purchase, or whatever. But the relevant date for calculating the total charge for credit or APR is usually when the credit is actually drawn, namely when the cash is paid to the debtor or the hire-purchase **goods** are handed over, or whatever the necessary action is. This will sometimes be done on the date the agreement is made, but often it will be at a later date. In the case of **running-account credit** the credit is drawn from time to time and the dates of drawings are often impossible to determine in advance. To meet these difficulties three assumptions are laid down:

(1) If the terms of the agreement provide that the credit is to be drawn on or not later than a specified date, *assume it is drawn on that date.*

(2) If (1) does not apply, assume the credit is drawn on the *earliest* date on which the debtor is entitled to draw it.

(3) If (1) does not apply and the earliest date cannot be ascertained from the agreement, assume the credit is drawn *on the date the agreement is made.*

There is a special rule, modifying the above, for **running-account credit** and for certain types of **fixed-sum credit** (namely where the credit advanced is *not* repayable in specified amounts or at specified intervals). If a constant **period rate of charge** is imposed in respect of periods of equal (or nearly equal) length, credit provided *during* a period is deemed to be provided at the *end* of the period.

*(h) Date when credit will be repaid*

The credit drawn may be repaid in one sum or by instalments. In relation to any repayment the following assumptions apply. Any right of the creditor to demand early repayment is to be ignored.

(1) If the agreement requires the repayment to be made *not*

*later* than a specified date, assume it will be made *on that date*.

(2) If the agreement gives the debtor a choice of dates, assume the repayment will be made on the *earliest* date.

(3) If (1) and (2) do not apply, and a date can be calculated from the terms of the agreement by first making an assumption about the amount of credit (see below), take that date.

(4) If none of (1), (2) and (3) apply, assume the repayment will be made *one year* after the making of the agreement.

It will be seen that (1) and (2) are to some extent in conflict. The special rule mentioned above in relation to credit drawings applies here also. Where it would be otherwise assumed that a repayment would be *during* one of the equal periods it is to be assumed instead that it will be at the *end* of the period. This final complication will rarely need to be taken into account in practice because direct resort can be had to Part 15 of the Tables or the period rate formula (see page 18).

*(i) Date when a charge within the total charge for credit will be paid*

The assumptions as to when a charge falling within the **total charge for credit** will be paid are as follows:

(1) If the charge is to be paid *before* the credit is drawn, assume it will be paid on the date the credit is drawn.

(2) If the agreement provides a choice of dates, assume the charge will be paid on the *earliest* date.

(3) If there is only *one* charge of a certain description and it has to be paid *after* the agreement is made, assume it will be paid when the credit is drawn (unless this assumption is *unreasonable*, when you should assume it will be paid on the earliest reasonable date).

(4) If there are *two or more* charges of a certain description, apply (3) to the first and assume the last will be paid when the credit is repaid, with other charges being paid at equal intervals between.

The special rule applying to the date of credit drawing or repayment for running-account credit and certain types of fixed-sum credit (see above) also applies here, deferring the payment of a charge to the *end* of the period in question.

*(j) Amount of credit which will be drawn*

If the agreement is for **running-account credit** and there is a credit limit, assume that the credit drawn will be equal to the credit limit. In other cases assume the credit drawn will be £100.

*(k) Amount of a credit repayment*

Assume that each repayment of credit is the *minimum* for which the agreement provides. If the amount is index-linked, assume the index level will remain the same as at the making of the agreement.

*(l) Amount of a charge within the total charge for credit*

There are a number of assumptions regarding the amount of charges falling within the total charge for credit. These are as follows:

(1) Assume the amount of a charge is the *smallest* for which the agreement provides.

(2) If the agreement provides for variation of the rate or amount of a charge upon the *continuation* of any circumstance, assume that it will *not* continue.

(3) If the agreement provides for variation on the occurrence of any event (other than an event *certain* to occur on an *ascertainable* date), assume that it will *not* occur.

(4) If there will be at least one variation in the first year *and* the period for which credit is to be drawn is uncertain (so that the one-year assumption mentioned above applies), assume the rate or amount for that year will be the *highest* provided for by the agreement.

(5) If the amount or rate is *index-linked*, assume the index level will remain the same as at the making of the agreement.

(6) Disregard tax relief available to the debtor, except that there should be taken into account any insurance relief under s 19 of the Income and Corporation Taxes Act 1970 and Schedule 4 to the Finance Act 1976 without any deduction under s 21 of the 1970 Act.

(7) Assume that no assistance is given under the Home Purchase Assistance and Housing Corporation Guarantee Act 1978.

## 6 The Category A licence

If you carry on a **consumer credit business** (and are not within the £30 exception mentioned below) you have since 1 October 1977 needed a licence from the OFT. Unless (which is most unlikely) you are covered by a **group licence**, the licence you need is a Category A standard licence issued to your firm individually. By the end of 1985, 62,302 Category A licences had been issued. The only groups licensed by a group licence to carry on a consumer credit business are solicitors, chartered accountants and certified accountants. The details of the licensing system are explained in Chapter 8. A special authorisation in the licence is required if you wish to **canvass regulated agreements off trade premises**. For this an extra licence fee of £10 is payable. Canvassing restrictions are described in section 7 below.

The requirement to be licensed does not apply to a business carried on by an unincorporated sole trader or partnership in the course of which no **regulated** consumer credit agreements are made except agreements for **fixed-sum credit** not exceeding £30 or agreements for **running-account credit** where the credit limit does not exceed £30.

## 7 Canvassing of credit

The operative provisions of the Act restrict canvassing of **credit** in several ways. Doorstep canvassing of **individuals** needs a special licence, and in the case of the canvassing of money loans is prohibited altogether. Telephone canvassing is not restricted however. Nor is the sending of individually addressed letters, except to young people under eighteen. The use of circulars is regulated by the advertising controls (see section 8 below). The distribution of unsolicited credit cards, trading checks or other **credit-tokens** is forbidden (see section 10 below).

### (a) Definition of doorstep canvassing

In order to appreciate the exact nature of the restrictions, and the scope left for legitimately seeking business, it is important to grasp the intricacies of the definition. This is not in fact limited to doorstep canvassing as such, but extends to any oral (ie face-to-face) canvassing of individuals off 'trade premises'. So the first thing is to understand which premises are included in this phrase.

## (b) What are 'trade premises'

The Act does not object to soliciting for credit business on trade premises connected with the deal. Obviously this includes your own business premises if you carry on a **consumer credit business**, but the phrase goes wider than this. It includes the business premises of any trader whose transaction with the consumer would be financed by the credit agreement being canvassed.

> **Example 7** A retailer acts as agent of a moneylender, to whom he passes any customer who needs a cash loan to enable him to purchase the retailer's goods. The retailer's shop is 'trade premises' in relation to the canvassing of such loans.

The definition of trade premises goes further and includes any case where a credit canvasser carries on his own business or is employed (or is the agent of) a person who carries on a business. In such cases the place where the business is carried on counts as trade premises. The nature of the **business** is immaterial.

> **Example 8** A salesman who is employed by a second-hand car dealer has a commission arrangement with a hire-purchase company. Whenever the opening arises, he suggests to a potential purchaser of a car from his employer that he would be well advised to enter into a **hire-purchase agreement** with that hire-purchase company. The car dealer's premises are 'trade premises' in relation to the canvassing of the hire-purchase agreement. (Note that this does not fall within the previous example because the hire-purchase agreement does not finance a transaction between customer and car dealer. In law the customer's only transaction is with the hire-purchase company, to which the car dealer transfers ownership of the car.)

Finally, the definition of 'trade premises' also covers the business premises of the potential customer himself. This concession is designed to enable sole traders and partnerships to learn through canvassers of business opportunities which might be of advantage to them.

> **Example 9** An office equipment company employ canvassers who offer equipment on credit. A canvasser visits the office of a firm of solicitors to seek business. The firm is an individual

and therefore a consumer for purposes of the Act. Its office is 'trade premises' in relation to the canvassing of credit agreements.

A further point to note is that 'trade premises' includes not only the permanent address of a business but also any premises, such as an exhibition stand at a trade fair, where the business is carried on temporarily. It does not include trade premises unconnected with the deal, so that canvassing of customers in a pub or restaurant would count as being off trade premises.

To recapitulate, the restrictions on face-to-face canvassing relate solely to canvassing off 'trade premises', that is door-to-door canvassing of householders and any other face-to-face canvassing except that taking place on premises where a business is carried on (permanently or temporarily) by the credit company itself, by a supplier whose transaction with the consumer would be financed by the proposed regulated credit agreement, by the canvasser or his employer or principal, or by the consumer. This is not the whole story however, for not all forms of face-to-face canvassing off trade premises are caught by the Act.

### (c) The essential features of regulated canvassing

Apart from the fact that it must be off trade premises, canvassing will not be caught by the Act unless the following conditions are also satisfied.

(1) The canvassing must be of an individual. Obviously the person spoken to will be an individual, but the point of this condition is that if he is spoken to with a view to the entry of a limited company or other incorporated body into a credit agreement (eg because he is an employee of the company) this will not be caught by the Act.

(2) The canvassing must take place during a *visit* by the canvasser to the place in question. This means that the Act does not catch, for example, canvassing for a mail order company done by a housewife to neighbours invited to her own house. The visit need not be to private premises: canvassing of passers-by in the street is covered. On the other hand the person canvassed must already be present at the place visited. It is not regulated canvassing where discussions on trade premises are adjourned for lunch and the trader takes or accompanies the customer to a

restaurant, where he solicits him to enter a credit agreement.

(3) The visit must be carried out for the sole or main purpose of oral canvassing. Thus a bank manager who visits his golf club to play golf and enjoy social intercourse is not caught if he incidentally invites another member to use the bank's credit facilities. A visit solely for the purpose of delivering circulars is not covered even though the visitor changes his mind and does some spoken touting.

(4) The canvassing must be face-to-face, by the spoken word.

(5) The visit must not be in response to a request. The restrictions are aimed at unsolicited canvassing. If the canvasser is invited to call they do not apply—even though the visit was instigated by the canvasser. Circulars with tear-off strips which request a visit and can be returned by the consumer are therefore a means of avoiding the restrictions. The request must be made by (or with the authority of) the householder or other person in charge of the premises visited. It must be made on a previous occasion, so it is no use the canvasser asking the consumer to request a visit and then when he does so commencing the 'spiel'. He must go away and come back later. It must be sufficiently later to constitute a different 'occasion'. The request need not however relate to canvassing. An ordinary social invitation, eg to dinner, is enough to prevent subsequent canvassing falling within the Act. Nor need the request be in writing (but see below as to the special rule governing debtor-creditor agreements).

Note that the person solicited need not be the person whose entry into a contract is sought. It is regulated canvassing to persuade a housewife to ask her husband to enter a contract. Similarly with employees and their principals, and other like cases.

Having explained what types of face-to-face canvassing are caught by the Act, we next explain precisely how they are caught. Here once again we encounter the distinction, explained on pages 11 and 12, between debtor-creditor agreements and debtor-creditor-supplier agreements.

### (d) Prohibition of canvassing debtor-creditor agreements

It is a criminal offence to carry out off trade premises face-to-face canvassing of **debtor-creditor agreements** (that is, most types of cash loan). This has been the case since 1 October 1977. In the

Crown Court the offender is liable to imprisonment for up to one year and/or an unlimited fine. In a magistrates' court the maximum penalty is a fine of £2,000. In this respect only, the Act widens the definition of canvassing off trade premises described above. Normally a request made on a previous occasion prevents the canvassing from falling within the Act's restrictions. In relation to debtor-creditor agreements however the request is ineffective for this purpose unless it is *in writing* and *signed* by the person making it.

The Act contains an exception for the canvassing of bank overdrafts. It is not an offence to canvass an existing customer of a bank suggesting that he enters into a debtor-creditor agreement enabling him to overdraw on an existing or future current account. The canvassing must be done by an employee of the bank, not an independent agent. The current account must be of the type on which cheques can be drawn. An existing customer is defined as a person who already keeps an account with the bank, though this need not be a current account.

## (e) Restriction of canvassing debtor-creditor-supplier agreements

A **debtor-creditor-supplier agreement** may be canvassed either by the prospective creditor himself (or his employee or agent) or by a **credit-broker** (or his employee or agent). Either way, regulation by the Act is through the licensing system. As a consumer credit trader, you need, as explained above (page 25) a Category A licence. This covers all lawful activities done in the course of the business, with one exception. If in the course of the business you canvass (either directly or through agents) your debtor-creditor-supplier agreements off trade premises your Category A licence will *not* cover this unless it contains a specific canvassing authorisation, for which an extra £10 fee is demanded. It will not even cover it if your canvasser has his own Category C (credit broker's) licence containing a specific canvassing authorisation. You need your own canvassing authorisation too. The OFT must grant a canvassing authorisation if satisfied that the applicant is a fit person to engage in face-to-face canvassing (see page 199). The most obvious evidence that he is *not* a fit person is where he or his business associates have a record of intimidation or other harsh or oppressive conduct towards members of the public. The consequence of engaging in or using face-to-face canvassing off trade premises when your licence does not contain a specific canvassing authorisation is that you are guilty of unlicensed trading. As to the penalties for this see page 202.

You will observe that there is a vital difference between the canvassing off trade premises of debtor-creditor and debtor-creditor-supplier agreements. The one is nearly always illegal; the other is legal provided the simple licensing requirements are complied with. It is obviously in the credit trader's interest, where he wishes to engage in canvassing, to ensure that as many as possible of his agreements are debtor-creditor-supplier agreements and not debtor-creditor agreements. It may be quite easy to convert potential debtor-creditor agreements into debtor-creditor-supplier agreements.

> **Example 10** A moneylender holding a Category A licence with a canvassing authorisation wishes to engage in doorstep canvassing of his cash loans. He enters into business arrangements with a retailer dealing in a wide range of consumer durables and instructs his canvassers to offer cash loans to be used for the purpose of acquiring any goods they wish from the retailer. Consumers are told that provided they sign a statement to the effect that it is their *present* intention to use the money lent for that purpose they are perfectly free to change their minds later and use the money for any other purpose they choose.

Here the moneylending agreement is a debtor-creditor-supplier agreement within the last of the three categories described on page 11 above and canvassing of it is perfectly lawful. Yet if canvassed in the ordinary way as a straightforward cash loan it would have involved the commission of a criminal offence.

### (f) Prohibition on circulars to young persons

Since 1 July 1977 it has been a criminal offence to send circulars advertising credit to young persons under eighteen. (Similar restrictions apply to advertising goods for hire.) The penalties are the same as for canvassing debtor-creditor agreements off trade premises (see page 29). The provision only applies if the sending is done 'with a view to financial gain', but this would be the case with any business circular. The Act does not refer to circulars as such, but expresses the offence by using the wide phrase 'any document'. It thus covers, for example, a teenage magazine containing credit advertisements. Because of its width it is important to grasp the description of the contents of a document which brings it within the Act. It is prohibited if it invites the reader:

to borrow money, or

to obtain goods or services on **credit**, or

to apply for information or advice on borrowing money or otherwise obtaining credit.

A document which actually gives information or advice on obtaining credit does not offend provided it does not amount to an invitation to enter into a credit agreement. An 'invitation' will fall within the Act however even though it is merely implied.

### Sending of circulars

To constitute an offence the document must be 'sent' to the minor. Strangely, it is not illegal to hand it to him. This means that a canvasser could lawfully hand leaflets to sixth-formers leaving a school, though if he spoke to any of them he might be regarded as engaging in oral canvassing off trade premises. The sending need not be by post, though it seems that the document must be personally directed to the recipient. What if the sender is unaware of the recipient's age? Clearly any mass mailing incurs the risk that some of the names on the mailing list may be of under-age persons. The Act makes it a defence for the person charged to prove that he did not know *and had no reasonable cause to suspect* that the recipient was under eighteen but he cannot assert that he had no reasonable cause to suspect if he sent it to the minor at a school or other educational establishment for minors.

## 8 Advertisements for credit

In pursuit of the aim of 'truth in lending' the legislation imposes widespread controls on credit advertisements. In general these came into force on 6 October 1980.

### (a) Advertisements to which controls apply

*Advertisement medium* The controls are not confined to visual advertising. They apply whatever the medium, whether a newspaper, a poster, a radio, television or cinema commercial, a catalogue, a label on goods, or whatever. Every method of communication is covered, *except* one directed to a person individually (for example a telephone call or personal letter). The audience may be the public generally, a section of the public, or a private group such as the employees of a firm.

*Facilities advertised*    The term used to describe an advertisement subject to the controls is **advertisement for credit facilities**. To be within this definition the advertisement must indicate that the advertiser is willing to provide **credit**. All kinds of credit are covered, but the advertisement is caught only when published for the purposes of a **business** within one of the following categories:-

(1) The business of the person offering the credit (but only where he is carrying on a **consumer credit business,** or a business providing **individuals** with credit secured on land or buildings or afforded under **foreign agreements** being **consumer credit agreements** which would otherwise be **regulated agreements**).

(2) A business of **credit brokerage**.

(3) A business which, while not within the definition of credit brokerage, includes the effecting of introductions of individuals desiring credit to persons who provide credit secured on land or buildings.

An advertisement has been held not to fall within the definition of an 'advertisement for credit facilities' where the only information it gives about the provision of credit is the advertiser's name and/or trade logo. This applies even though the advertisement is attached to an article which might be bought with the credit. The ruling, of doubtful correctness, was made by the Divisional Court in *Jenkins v Lombard North Central* [1983] CCLR 15. The following example is based on this.

**Example 11** A car dealer displayed on a car in his showroom a sticker simply bearing the cash price together with the name and logo of a well-known finance company. The court held that this did not 'indicate' that credit was available, but merely suggested that it might be.

*Exempt advertisements*    An advertisement is not however treated as an 'advertisement for credit facilities' (even though it answers the description just given) if it is one of the following:

(1) An advertisement which indicates (1) that the credit taken *must* exceed £15,000 and (2) either that no **security** is required or that the security is to consist of property other than land and buildings.

(2) An advertisement which indicates that the credit is available only to a limited company or other incorporated body.

(3) An advertisement which relates to exempt agreements within categories (3), (4) and (6) on page 12 (or to agreements which would be such exempt agreements if the credit provided were not greater than £15,000).

*Parts of advertisements*    It is important to note that what would be regarded in fact as a single advertisement may for the purposes of the controls fall to be treated as two or more separate advertisements. For example what is factually one advertisement may relate partly to the provision of credit and partly to other matters extraneous to the legislation. The former will be treated as a credit advertisement in itself. Similarly a single advertisement may consist partly of controlled material and partly of exempt material. The latter will be treated as an exempt advertisement. The parts need not be physically severable. In so far as an inter-mixed advertisement relates to different matters it will be treated as a separate advertisement in relation to each.

*Split advertisements*    For the purpose of the controls it may be necessary to treat material which is factually separate as one advertisement (for example two stickers on a refrigerator, or a television display and voice over). The test is whether the combined message can be taken in by the recipient at one time.

## (b) Persons and penalties

Whatever the business for the purposes of which the advertisement is published, the Act treats the **advertiser** as being the person who is to provide the credit facilities advertised (the potential **creditor**). Even if the advertisement is inserted by a credit-broker without the knowledge or consent of the creditor, the latter is still treated as the 'advertiser'. If the controls are infringed, the advertiser is guilty of an offence. Conviction in a Crown Court carries a maximum penalty of imprisonment for one year and/or a fine of unlimited amount. In a magistrates' court the maximum penalty is a fine of £2,000.

In the case of an infringing advertisement, other persons are also liable to the same penalties. These are the publisher, an advertising agent who devised the advertisement, and (where the 'advertiser' did not himself arrange for publication) the person who actually procured its publication. The publisher is provided with a special defence where he had no reason to suspect that publication would constitute an infringement. For further details see Chapter 7.

*(c) Wider and narrower control*

There are two requirements that apply to every advertisement which falls within the definition given above of 'advertisement for credit facilities'. These are as follows:

(1) The advertisement must not convey information which in a material respect is false or misleading. (For this purpose information stating or implying an intention on the advertiser's part which in fact he has not got is taken as false.)

(2) If the advertisement offers **restricted-use credit** in relation to goods or services, those goods or services must also be available for cash.

Apart from being subject to these two requirements, some of the advertisements within the definition are free from control. These are ones covered by a further pair of exemptions, as follows:

(1) An advertisement which (1) indicates that the advertiser is willing to provide credit for the purposes of the business of any person (other than the business of the advertiser himself or a **credit-broker** acting in relation to the credit facility) and (2) does not indicate that the advertiser is also willing to provide credit *otherwise* than for the purposes of such a business (even though he may in fact be willing to do this).

(2) An advertisement which relates to exempt agreements within category (1) on page 12 (or to agreements which would be such exempt agreements if the credit provided were not greater than £15,000).

An 'advertisement for credit facilities' which is not within these two exemptions, and is therefore subject to the further detailed controls as to content and form, is referred to as a **regulated credit advertisement**.

We may summarise by saying:

(1) That an 'advertisement for credit facilities' is any credit advertisement published for certain business purposes other than one for credit over £15,000 without a land mortgage or for credit to an incorporated body or for certain exempt etc agreements.

(2) That every 'advertisement for credit facilities' must be free from false or misleading information and (if it relates to restricted-use credit) must be accompanied by availability of the goods or services for cash.

(3) That every such advertisement except one for business credit or for further types of exempt etc agreements is a 'regulated credit advertisement' and subject to further controls as to content and form.

We now proceed to describe these further controls, beginning with the controls as to *content*. After this we go on to describe the controls as to *form* (page 43).

### (d) Content of regulated credit advertisements

The controls over the content of a **regulated credit advertisement** have two objects, both concerned with 'truth in lending':

(1) To ensure that the potential customer is not given a partial or one-sided view of the credit offer. Either:

   (i) he must be given virtually no information other than that credit is available; or

   (ii) he must be given all relevant information; or

   (iii) if the information given is incomplete it must be balanced and contain essential items, and the customer must be told how to obtain the rest of it.

(2) Certain expressions, such as 'overdraft' or 'free credit' must not be used unless justified. This restriction has the effect of spelling out to some extent the 'false or misleading' test described above (page 34).

The first object is effected by lengthy and complex provisions, which we now describe. The provisions designed to achieve the second object will then be dealt with (page 42).

The provisions effecting the first object say that if an advertisement falls within the definition of 'regulated credit advertisement' its contents must comply with one or other of five alternative requirements. The advertiser can choose which one out of the five suits him best, but he must not go outside these categories. An advertisement giving virtually no information is called a *simple* advertisement. An advertisement giving all relevant information is a *full* advertisement, of which there are two categories. An advertisement giving incomplete information is either an *intermediate* advertisement or a *catalogue* advertisement for a calendar or seasonal period. These make up the five categories, and we now describe each in turn. Remember that your advertisement must comply with the requirements of one or other of them. A full advertisement may contain any additional credit information the advertiser chooses, but the other categories are restricted to what is specified in the legislation.

*(e) Simple credit advertisements*

A simple credit advertisement is an **advertisement for credit facilities** of a kind merely designed to keep the name of the credit business in the public eye. Examples are those displayed at sporting events, or printed on giveaway items such as biros or book matches.

There are two requirements for this category, as follows:

(1) The only indication in the advertisement that the advertiser is willing to provide credit must be a **simple indication of credit business**.

(2) The advertisement must not specify the cash price, or other price, of any goods, services, land or other things.

The definition of a 'simple indication of credit business' is as follows. It is an indication that the advertiser carries on one of the types of business relevant for the purposes of the controls (see page 31), being an indication which takes the form of:

(a) any name of his specified in his **standard licence** (or if he is not required to have a standard licence, any name under which he carries on business), and

(b) a statement either of an occupation of his or of the general nature of an occupation of his.

This is the official wording, but it is not altogether clear. It seems that it has the following meaning, bearing in mind that a simple advertisement is seen officially as a means of keeping the name of a business in the public eye. The name of the advertiser must appear. So must something about his 'occupation'. This is an odd word to describe the activities of what will usually be a limited company, but it must relate to the nature of the credit business. Examples are: 'moneylender', 'finance company', 'pawnbroker', 'bank', 'hire purchase company'. Examples of statements of the 'general nature' of an occupation are: 'car finance', 'agricultural loans', 'travel credit'.

> **Example 12** Ace Loans Ltd, holders of a Category A licence, present customers with desk diaries inscribed 'Ace Loans Ltd, Moneylenders'. This complies with the requirements of a simple credit advertisement.

Can more information be included? Three points arise. First, if the trader carries on two or more 'occupations' can they all be mentioned? It seems so. Secondly, can other information such as address and telephone number be included? Again, it seems so—provided the additional information does not in itself suggest that credit is available. Thirdly, can puffing descriptions be added to the words describing the occupation? Here the answer is no.

**Example 13** The following advertisement is inserted in a newspaper:

> KINDLY CREDITOR LTD
> Finance Chambers, 28 High St.
> Fast loans sympathetically
> handled. Hire purchase arranged.

This contravenes the requirements in two ways. The address indicates credit business by the words 'Finance Chambers', and the lending side of the business is described as fast and sympathetic. It should be altered to read as follows:

> KINDLY CREDITOR LTD
> 28 High St.
> Loans. Hire purchase arranged.

Note that provided the name 'Kindly Creditor Ltd' is specified in the Category A licence it is not objectionable even though it has a puffing element in suggesting kind treatment of debtors.

### (f) Full credit advertisements

The information which must be included in a full credit advertisement falls into two groups, basic information and additional information. (Special provisions, described below (page 40), apply to full advertisements containing an invitation to vary existing agreements.)

*Basic information*    The basic information, which is also required to be given in an intermediate advertisement (though not in quite the same terms), comprises: name and address of **creditor** or **credit-broker**, cash price of goods etc whose purchase is to be financed by the credit offered, annual percentage rate (APR), information where creditor requires insurance or security etc. These will now be explained in detail.

*Name and address of creditor*    Where the prospective creditor procures publication of the full advertisement, it must include his **name** and postal address unless it includes the name and address of a **dealer** or is displayed or (in the case of a sound advertisement) announced on the **premises** of the creditor or a dealer.

*Name and address of credit-broker*      Where a credit-broker procures publication, the advertisement must include his name and address and the fact that he is a credit-broker. Exceptions are that the name and address need not be given if the advertisement is displayed or announced on the credit-broker's premises and the fact that he is a credit-broker need not be stated where the prospective creditor is an incorporated body and the credit-broker is its **associate**.

*Cash price*      If the advertisement specifies particular goods etc which are to be acquired using the credit advertised it must give their **cash price**. This does not apply where the goods etc are described in *general* terms. So if a hi-fi dealer advertises a model A62 tape-deck on credit he must give the cash price, but not if he advertises credit terms for audio equipment generally. The requirement applies to **fixed-sum credit** to be provided under a **debtor-creditor-supplier agreement**, and extends to land and buildings and services as well as goods.

*Annual percentage rate of charge (APR)*      This must always be given in a full credit advertisement, unless there is no charge for credit (when there must be an indication that the **total amount payable by the debtor** does not exceed the **cash price**). Special rules apply to APR under budget accounts and bank overdrafts. In other cases the rule is that the advertisement must state the true **annual percentage rate of charge** or the **approximate rate** (using the permitted tolerances). If the advertiser gives typical or representative examples then the true or approximate rate of the **representative total charge for credit** must be given. In all cases it is sufficient to use the abbreviation 'APR' but if typical or representative cases are given this must be stated.

Example 14 A department store advertises its credit terms for goods with cash prices of between £40 and £500, payable by monthly instalments over periods of 12, 18 or 24 months (not being budget accounts). The APR differs slightly from one agreement to another, depending on the period for which credit is provided. The store can state in the advertisement the APR of an agreement representative of those into which it enters, eg 'credit of £100 repaid by 18 monthly instalments of £7.71 (APR 54.7%)'. There must be an indication that this APR is 'representative' (for example by saying 'typical APR 54.7%').

*APR (budget accounts)*   In the case of an advertisement for a **budget account agreement** the rules are the same as given above except that *two* APRs must be given, one on the **assumption that the account is fully used** and the other on the **assumption that the account is one-third used**.

*APR (bank overdrafts)*   Where the advertisement relates to a **debtor-creditor agreement** enabling the debtor to overdraw on a current account with a **recognised bank**, a trustee savings bank or the national savings bank run by the Post Office, the APR need not be given. Instead a rate can be given which is calculated in the same way except that it ignores everything but interest payments. Additional charges still have to be separately mentioned, but their omission from the quoted rate will lower it by comparison with competing credit offers.

*APR (other matters)*   Apart from quoting the APR itself (or other rate for bank overdrafts) the advertisement must comply with other requirements. If the rate or amount of any item included in the **total charge for credit** will or may be varied this must be stated. So must the fact that tax relief on premiums has been allowed for.

*Special requirements*   The advertisement must state the fact (if such is the case) that requirements are imposed concerning insurance, security or the opening of a deposit account. If, in the case of life insurance to pay off the credit, the creditor is or specifies the insurer, particulars must be given.

*Additional information*   Apart from the basic information described above, a full credit advertisement must also contain the following. If there is a requirement to make any **advance payment** this must be stated and particulars given. If the liability to make any payment (other than on default) is *uncertain* this must be stated. (For example it may not be known whether a legal or survey fee or maintenance contract will be required.) If the advertisement relates to **fixed-sum credit** (other than free credit or credit repayable at specified intervals or in specified amounts) the number of repayments and the total amount payable by the debtor must be stated (these may be based on **representative information**, but if so that fact must be stated). In all cases the requirements of the **credit agreement** as to amount and frequency of *repayments* of credit must be indicated (again, representative information may be used if this is indicated). If the offer is *restricted* to certain persons this must be stated (eg 'not available to persons under twenty-one'). Where an advantage is given to *cash purchasers* as compared to credit purchasers this must be set out.

*(g)  Full credit advertisements (invitation to vary agreements)*

This category applies to an advertisement which extends an invitation to **individuals** who are subject to existing **credit agreements** with the advertiser, the invitation being that they should agree to specified variations in those agreements. Here the advertisement must do two things in relation to the items given above as being required to be included in the ordinary category of full credit advertisements (disregarding irrelevant items):

(1) It must contain such of the information required by those items as will be *altered* if the invitation is accepted.

(2) It must indicate that the remaining items will remain unaltered (unless it repeats them in unaltered form).

The requirement is limited in this way because it is assumed that the debtor will know the terms of his existing agreement and only needs information about the proposed variations.

*(h)  Intermediate credit advertisements*

We have dealt with the simple advertisement, in which there must be a minimum of credit information. At the other extreme we have dealt with the full advertisement, specifying what credit information *must* be included (any other information being permissible in addition). Now we pass to the two final categories, where certain information is obligatory and additional optional credit information is strictly regulated. Both these insist on the potential customer being offered an opportunity to secure a quotation completing the information required for a full advertisement.

*Obligatory information*     What is required to be given by an intermediate credit advertisement is almost the same as the basic information required for the ordinary category of full credit advertisement. There are two differences, as follows:

(1) Subject to the special rules relating to budget accounts, information as to the APR is required only where the advertisement specifies **goods**, services, land or other things having a particular **cash price** (not less than £50) the acquisition of which from an **identified dealer** may be financed by the credit advertised.

(2) Except where it relates to things with a cash price less than £50, the advertisement must contain an indication that

individuals may obtain on request information in writing about the terms on which the advertiser is prepared to do business, and must contain either a postal address to which or the number of a telephone by means of which such requests for a quotation may be made. (As to quotations see pages 46 to 50.)

*Optional information*    Apart from the optional information about to be described, an intermediate advertisement must contain no other information indicating that the advertiser is willing to provide credit. The advertiser is free to include one or more of the following items if he wishes. As always, **representative information** may be given provided this is stated:

(1) A **simple indication of credit business.**
(2) A statement that specified credit facilities are available, explaining them.
(3) A statement that the credit is restricted to certain persons (eg 'not available to persons under twenty-one').
(4) A statement explaining advantages given to cash purchasers.
(5) The maximum amount of credit on offer.
(6) The minimum amount of credit on offer.
(7) Such of the APR information mentioned on pages 38 and 39 as is not *required* to be included.

Where such of the APR information mentioned on pages 38 and 39 as is relevant is included in the advertisement (whether by choice or because it is required to be included), and neither the maximum credit nor the minimum credit is given, the advertiser has an additional option. He can also include *one only* of the following:

(1) Particulars of **advance payments** required (or a statement that no advance payment is required).
(2) The period for which credit may be provided.
(3) The frequency of repayments (or an indication that credit is repayable in one sum).
(4) **The total amount payable by the debtor.**

*(i) Catalogue advertisements*

The last of the five categories into one or other of which a **regulated credit advertisement** must fall relates only to catalogues. A catalogue may cover a wide range of goods or services having credit terms that differ considerably. This category enables the dealer to give what is in effect a **simple credit advertisement** without being subject to the restriction on including cash prices which applies to such advertisements.

*Type of catalogue*          The advertisement may either be in the catalogue itself or in a separate leaflet issued with it. The catalogue must relate to goods or services which may be sold or supplied by a **dealer**. It must also specify the period for which it is in force (for example 'This catalogue is operative until 31 December 19. .').

*Information required*          The advertisement *must* contain the following information:

(1) The **name** and a postal address of the **creditor, credit-broker** or dealer by whom the catalogue is published.

(2) An indication that **individuals** may obtain on request a quotation giving the terms on which the advertiser is prepared to do business.

In addition, the advertisement may include a **simple indication of credit business**. It must not give any other indication that the advertiser is willing to provide credit.

### (j) Restricted credit advertising expressions

Apart from the controls described above, the contents of a regulated credit advertisement are governed by restrictions on the use of certain expressions, as follows:

*'Overdraft' etc.*          The advertisement must not use the word 'overdraft', or any similar expression, unless the arrangement offered is a genuine current account with cheque facilities.

*No charge for credit*          There must not be any suggestion that the credit transaction involves no greater charge than an equivalent cash transaction unless the **total amount payable by the debtor** does not exceed the **cash price**.

*No deposit*          The advertisement must not say 'no deposit', or use any similar term, unless certain conditions are satisfied. These are that the debtor is not required to pay any money as a condition precedent to the making of the credit agreement, and after it is made is not required to pay any money before being able to draw on the credit. For this purpose payments by the debtor are disregarded if they are part of the **total charge for credit** or are insurance premiums not falling within it.

An additional restriction applies only to full advertisements, since it relates to matter which is not in any case allowed to be included in any other type. A further difference from the restrictions mentioned above is that, whereas they spell out cases where an advertisement is positively misleading, in this case the requirement is merely to provide additional information. The advertisement must not suggest that the credit terms are less onerous than those of a competitor unless the competitor is named in the advertisement. Details of the competing offer must be given with no less particularity and prominence than is afforded to the advertiser's own offer, and in close proximity to the statement that the latter is less onerous. A similar rule applies to a statement suggesting that conditions precedent to the making of a credit agreement are less onerous than those imposed by competitors.

### (k) Form of regulated credit advertisements

Having described the restrictions on the *content* of a **regulated credit advertisement**, we pass to those concerning the way in which the content is arranged and presented. There are three criteria: clarity, prominence and grouping.

*Clarity*    The regulations say that information which is *required* to be included in an advertisement must be 'presented clearly'. This also applies to optional information allowed to be included in an intermediate advertisement. No definition of 'clearly' is given, nor any details about its application in particular cases. This is less informative than the previous legislation, which required information to be 'displayed clearly in the advertisement in such a way as not to give undue prominence to any part of it in comparison with any other part'. Prominence is now dealt with by a special provision relating only to the APR (see below). The requirement of clarity must be taken to refer to the need to word the information so that it is legible (or audible), can be easily understood, and is not such that people may mistake its meaning and effect.

*Prominence (of APR)*    Because the annual percentage rate of charge (APR) is officially regarded as an important guide to the consumer in 'shopping around' for the best credit offer and understanding its true cost to him, the regulations make special provision about the prominence with which it is to be shown. This applies whether or not it is *required* to be shown and regardless of whether it is the true rate, an approximate rate (using the tolerances permitted) or a representative rate. Whichever it is, it will normally be indicated simply by the letters APR, followed by a figure and percentage sign (though a word such as 'typical' must precede this where representative information is given).

The APR must be given *greater* prominence than a statement

relating to any other rate of charge (for example the annual flat rate or a monthly period rate). Since other rates may work out considerably lower, the advertiser may be tempted to quote them as well as the APR. This is likely to confuse the ordinary consumer, but cannot be faulted as lacking 'clearness' because it is impliedly permitted by this regulation. It is to reduce the possibility of confusion that greater prominence is required to be given to the APR. The difference need be no more than marginal however (for example using characters 5 mm high for the APR and 4 mm high for the alternative rate).

The APR must be given *no less prominence* than certain other items of information which may be included. These are as follows:

(1) A statement relating to any period (for example '3-year credit terms').

(2) A statement giving the amount of any **advance payment** (or stating that no advance payment is required).

(3) A statement giving the amount, number or frequency of any other payments or charges. (This does not apply to an indication of any cash price.)

Note that there is nothing to prevent the cash price, or any other information not specified above, from being given very much greater prominence than the APR. Note also that 'prominence' is not simply a question of the size of letters and figures. The colour of ink or design of typeface may be relevant. So too may the position of the information and the number of times it is given. In films, radio and TV, prominence may be affected by such things as vocal emphasis and volume.

*Grouping of information*    The regulations control the way relevant information is grouped in the advertisement. For this purpose information is 'relevant' if it is *required* to be included or (in the case of an advertisement other than a full advertisement of the ordinary type) is given voluntarily but would be required if the advertisement were an ordinary full advertisement. In the case of an intermediate advertisement, other optional material is also 'relevant'. The name, address and telephone number of the advertiser or any other person is not however 'relevant' for this purpose.

The general rule is that 'relevant' information must be presented *together as a whole*. Again there is no explanation of what exactly this means. It is clear however that the information must not be scattered about in different parts of the advertisement, or intermixed with other material. There are three exceptions to this general rule:

(1) Information likely to vary from time to time (for example cash prices or credit rates) can be given in a loose insert where the advertisement is published in any book, catalogue, leaflet or other document. Here the variable information must be set out 'together as a whole' in the loose insert while the remainder of the relevant information is set out 'together as a whole' in the main advertisement.

(2) To save repetition in a dealer's catalogue containing full advertisements in the ordinary category, it is permissible to present the relevant information in either of two ways. The cash price alone can be given against specific goods or services advertised, with the remainder of the relevant information being grouped together in one place in the catalogue. Alternatively there can be given against each item the following (with the remainder being grouped elsewhere):

> cash price,
> APR (unless there is no charge for credit),
> any advance payment required,
> total amount payable,
> frequency, number and amount of repayments.

(3) To save repetition in advertisements on dealers' premises (such as department stores), and cope with the fact that credit terms may vary in different departments or from item to item, it is permissible for a display advertisement to present part of the relevant information in one place while the rest is given on or near particular goods or at an enquiry point for services. This applies both to intermediate advertisements and to the ordinary category of full advertisements. There are strict limitations on what may be stated on or near the goods or at the enquiry point. The requirements are as follows:

(a) the cash price of the goods or services must be stated,

(b) any 'relevant information' not included in the display advertisement must be given,

(c) it is optional to give the maximum and/or minimum amount of credit on offer,

(d) if neither the maximum nor the minimum credit is given, *one* of the following may be stated: amount of any advance payment (or a statement that no advance payment is required), period or maximum period of credit, frequency of repayments, total amount payable,

(e) it must be stated that other relevant information is to be found in the display advertisement,

(f) no other credit information must be given.

It seems that the concessions in both (1) and (2) above can be utilised in the same catalogue. This would usually involve putting into a separate leaflet the information which is required by (2) to be put against specific items.

### 9  Quotations of credit terms

The legislation gives consumers the right, as from 6 October 1980, to obtain written quotations setting out the terms on which a trader is prepared to offer **credit**. These supplement the incomplete information given in an intermediate advertisement, which must indicate that a quotation is available (see page 40). The right exists quite apart from any advertising there may have been. The trader is required to supply a quotation only if he receives an 'obligatory credit quotation request'. If however he chooses to supply a quotation in response to a non-obligatory request he must observe the same standards. Breach of these requirements constitutes an offence. Conviction of the credit trader in the Crown Court carries a maximum penalty of imprisonment for one year and/or a fine of unlimited amount. In a magistrates' court the maximum penalty is a fine of £2,000.

#### (a)  Which requests are obligatory

A request for a quotation is obligatory only if:

(1) it is made by a qualifying **individual**,

(2) it is made by a specified method,

(3) it is made to a **credit-trader** or **credit-broker** (or his representative) and,

(4) it asks for information in writing about the terms on which the credit-trader is prepared to do business with the individual, being business indicated in the request consisting of entry into certain types of credit agreement.

These requirements are now examined in more detail.

*The qualifying individual*    Any individual qualifies provided he is not a minor and is not resident outside the United Kingdom.

*The specified method*    A request will not be obligatory unless it is made in writing, or is made orally on the trader's premises. A telephone request is however in order if made in response to an advertisement. No request is obligatory if made on the trader's premises in a case where a full advertisement is conspicuously displayed.

*The relevant agreements* The request will not be obligatory unless it relates either to a **regulated agreement** or to a **personal credit agreement** which is secured on land or buildings. However, if the cash price of the goods or services in question does not exceed £50 the quotation request is not obligatory. Nor is it obligatory if a **full credit quotation** in respect of the agreement in question was given by the trader to the individual within the preceding 28 days. This is to prevent repeated requests which are unjustified.

## (b) The trader's response

The trader who receives an obligatory credit quotation request has two basic options. Either he must give a full credit quotation (the requirements for which are set out below, and are much the same as for a **full credit advertisement**) or if he does not want the business (perhaps because of the enquirer's low credit rating or because he does not do business of that kind) he must notify the enquirer accordingly. If he only does business through a third party (eg a mortgage broker) he must say so.

Suppose the trader, while not wishing to decline the business, has insufficient information on which to base a full quotation? Here he has two options. Either he may give an *estimated credit quotation* (see below) or he may ask for the missing information.

## (c) Full credit quotations

A full credit quotation must be in writing, and may be framed as an offer capable by acceptance of ripening into a contract. If however the trader does not wish to commit himself to this he is free to express the quotation accordingly.

> **Example 15** XYZ Loans Ltd do not wish their quotations to be capable of immediate acceptance as binding contracts since it is company policy to verify credit status in every case. On their quotation forms they therefore have printed the words 'This quotation is for information only and does not constitute a binding offer'.

The quotation must indicate the *minimum* period during which the information is to apply, so that the recipient knows how long he has to make up his mind. This can be expressed in any appropriate way, for example by saying 'This quotation is operative for fourteen days from the date hereof'. The information required by the regulations to be given must be presented *clearly* and *together as a whole*. There are certain rules as to the prominence to be given to the APR. Since these are exactly the same as for full advertisements they are not repeated here (see page 43). The information required to be given is as follows.

*Name and address*    The **name** and a postal address of the person giving the quotation. Where he is a credit-broker the name of the credit-trader by whom the credit is to be provided must also be given (but his address need not be).

*Cash price*    If the quotation specifies particular goods etc which are to be acquired using the credit it must give their **cash price**. This does not apply where the goods etc are described in *general* terms. The requirement applies to **fixed-sum credit** to be provided under a **debtor-creditor-supplier agreement**, and extends to land and buildings and services as well as goods.

*Annual percentage rate of charge (APR)*    This must always be given, unless there is no charge for credit (when there must be an indiction that the **total amount payable by the debtor** does not exceed the cash price). Special rules apply to APR under budget accounts and bank overdrafts. In other cases the rule is that the quotation must state the true **annual percentage rate of charge** or the **approximate rate** (using the permitted tolerances). If the trader gives typical or representative examples then the true or approximate rate of the **representative total charge for credit** must be given. In all cases it is sufficient to use the abbreviation 'APR' but if typical or representative cases are given this must be stated.

*APR (budget accounts)*    In the case of a quotation for a **budget account agreement** the rules are the same as given above except that *two* APRs must be given, one on the **assumption that the account is fully used** and the other on the **assumption that the account is one-third used.**

*APR (bank overdrafts)*    Where the quotation relates to a **debtor-creditor agreement** enabling the debtor to overdraw on a current account with a **recognised bank**, a trustee savings bank or the national savings bank run by the Post Office, the APR need not be given. Instead a rate can be given which is calculated in the same way except that it ignores everything but interest payments. Additional charges still have to be separately mentioned, but their omission from the quoted rate will lower it by comparison with competing credit offers.

*APR (other matters)*    Apart from quoting the APR itself (or other rate for bank overdrafts) the quotation must comply with other requirements. If the rate or amount of any item included in the **total charge for credit** will or may be varied this must be stated. So must the fact that tax relief on premiums has been allowed for.

*Special requirements*    The quotation must state the fact (if such is the case) that requirements are imposed concerning insurance, security or the opening of a deposit account.

*Additional information*    Apart from the basic information described above, the quotation must also contain the following. If there is a requirement to make any **advance payment** this must be stated and particulars given. If the liability to make any payment (other than on default) is *uncertain* this must be stated. (For example it may not be known whether a legal or survey fee or maintenance contract will be required.) If the quotation relates to **fixed-sum credit** (other than free credit or credit repayable at specified intervals or in specified amounts) the number of repayments and the total amount payable by the debtor must be stated (these may be based on **representative information**, but if so that fact must be stated). In all cases the requirements of the credit agreements as to amount and frequency of *repayments* of credit must be indicated (again, representative information may be used if this is indicated). Where an advantage is given to *cash purchasers* as compared to credit purchasers this must be set out.

So far the information required has been the same as for full advertisements (except that the quotation need not state the fact that the offer is restricted to certain persons). Now we come to additional items not required in advertisements. If fixed-sum credit is to be supplied under a debtor-creditor agreement or a **credit-token agreement** the quotation must indicate the amount of credit on offer. Similarly if **running-account credit** is offered there must be information about the credit limit. Information must be given about certain charges not within the total charge for credit. These are repair charges, insurance premiums or bank charges within paragraphs (4), (5), (8), (9), (11) and (12) of the exemptions listed on page 17. If the quotation includes particulars of goods etc which the debtor is not *required* to acquire the latter fact must be stated.

### (d) Estimated credit quotations

If the trader lacks some of the information needed for a full quotation he may, as explained above, give an 'estimated credit quotation' instead. This contains just as much detail, except that some of it is based on assumptions which may not be correct in fact. They are comparable in principle to **representative information**, and must be reasonable in all the circumstances of the case. The quotation must indicate the assumptions made, and include a statement indicating that if any of them are incorrect the enquirer may make a request for another quotation based on additional information supplied by him.

### (e) Optional quotation requests

Where a request for a credit quotation does not comply with the requirements for an obligatory credit quotation request it may nevertheless have some legal effect. If it complies with the less strict requirements for an optional credit quotation request then, while the trader is not bound to respond to it, the legislation requires him, if he does decide to furnish a quotation, to do so in the same way as for an obligatory request. In other words there are three types of quotation request, as follows:

(1) Obligatory—the trader *must* respond as outlined above.

(2) Optional—the trader need not respond, but if he chooses to provide a quotation it must be a **full credit quotation** or (where he lacks sufficient information) an **estimated credit quotation**.

(3) Unregulated—the trader's response is not controlled by the legislation at all.

The requirements for an optional request are wider than for an obligatory request in the following ways:

(1) Requests from minors or foreign residents are not excluded.

(2) The request does not need to be made by any particular method.

(3) There is no exclusion of the case where a previous quotation was given within the preceding 28 days.

In other respects the criteria are the same. The enquirer must be an individual, the trader must be a credit-trader or credit-broker, and the agreement in relation to which a quotation is requested must be a **regulated agreement** or else a **personal credit agreement** secured on land or buildings.

## 10 Steps prior to entry into credit agreement

This section deals with miscellaneous matters that may arise before your customer has entered into a credit agreement with you:

(1) his making with you of a contract to enter a future credit agreement;

(2) the suspension of linked transactions until the principal agreement is made;

(3) withdrawal by the customer from a prospective **credit agreement**; and

(4) your duties in relation to credit reference agencies consulted about the status of a prospective debtor.

### (a) Contracts to enter future credit agreements

The Act places restrictions on the effectiveness of contracts entered into by consumers purporting to bind them to enter into future credit agreements. This was done because it was thought desirable to limit the ability of credit grantors to induce consumers to commit themselves to enter into possibly onerous future commitments. The only exception allowed concerns the case where the customer is himself carrying on a business, and requires goods on credit for use in that business.

Unless it is within this business exception (described in detail below), an agreement made on or after 19 May 1985 is therefore void if, and to the extent that, it purports to bind a person to enter as the **debtor** into a prospective **regulated agreement**.

*The business exception*    The business exception is somewhat complicated. To be within it, an agreement to enter into a future credit agreement must comply with the following conditions:

(1) It must be in writing;

(2) It must be an agreement to enter into a **restricted-use credit agreement** for **fixed-sum credit** to finance the purchase of **goods**;

(3) The goods must be required by the debtor for the purposes of a **business** carried on by him. Here it is sufficient if the debtor holds himself out as requiring the goods for such purposes;

(4) The earlier agreement must contain or refer to such information relating to the prospective credit agreement, presented clearly and together as a whole, as is required to be included in a **full credit quotation** (as to this see page 47).

In addition, there is a further requirement, expressed in the alternative. To be within the business exception, the earlier agreement must comply with one or other of the following conditions. *Either* it must not have been preceded by **antecedent negotiations** which included oral representations made when in the presence of the debtor by an individual acting as, or on behalf of, the negotiator, *or* (if it *was* preceded by such negotiations) it must be signed by the debtor at trade premises, that is **premises** at which any of the following is carrying on any business (whether on a permanent or temporary basis)—

(1) the creditor, or

(2) any party to a **linked transaction** to the prospective credit agreement (other than the debtor or a relative of his), or

(3) the negotiator in any antecedent negotiations.

*(b) Suspension of linked transactions until principal agreement made*

With certain exceptions, a **linked transaction** entered into before the making of the agreement to which it is linked has no effect until such time (if any) as the principal agreement is made. This is one aspect of the protection given by the Act in relation to linked transactions (as to the reasons for this protection see page 79). It applies only to linked transactions entered into on or after 19 May 1985.

The exceptions from this protection consist of the following linked transactions: collateral insurance policies, guarantees against defects in **goods**, and bank current or deposit account agreements.

*(c) Withdrawal from prospective credit agreement*

Part V of the Act contains two provisions concerned with withdrawal from prospective credit agreements. The first confers special protection on consumers contemplating entry into land mortgages, while the second deals with various aspects of the right to withdraw from any prospective regulated credit agreement. Each applies as from 19 May 1985.

*Duty to give notice of right to withdraw from prospective land mortgage.*     The Act seeks to ensure that the prospective debtor under certain agreements to be secured on land receives notice of his right to withdraw from the agreement. Failure to comply means that the agreement, if made, will be treated as improperly executed (for the significance of this see page 60).

The duty to give this notice arises where a prospective **regulated agreement** (other than an **excepted agreement**) is to be secured on land, except that it does not apply where the prospective agreement is:

(1) a **restricted-use credit agreement** to finance the purchase of the mortgaged land; or

(2) an agreement for a bridging loan in connection with the purchase of the mortgaged land *or other land*.

Where the duty applies, the creditor, before sending the **unexecuted agreement** to the debtor for his signature, must give him a copy of it. This must include a box containing only a notice indicating the right to withdraw, and how and when it is exercisable.

*(d) Withdrawal from prospective credit agreements generally*

The Act lays down three rules relating to withdrawal from any prospective **regulated** credit agreement. These:

(1) make clear that a withdrawal notice need not be in any particular form;

(2) specify persons who are deemed to be agents for the receipt of withdrawal notices, and

(3) lay down the effect of a withdrawal notice. Each applies as from 19 May 1985.

*Giving of withdrawal notice*    The giving to a party of a written or oral notice which, however informally expressed, indicates the intention of the other party to withdraw from a prospective regulated credit agreement operates as a withdrawal from it. This provision does not apply to an **excepted agreement**. Since however the provision is declaratory of the common law the same result applies here too.

*Creditor's agents for receipt of withdrawal notice.*    Each of the following is deemed to be the agent of the **creditor** for the purpose of receiving a notice to withdraw from a prospective regulated credit agreement (other than an **excepted agreement**):

(1) a **credit-broker** or **supplier** who is the negotiator in antecedent negotiations;

(2) any **person** who, in the course of a business carried on by him, acts on behalf of the **debtor** in any negotiations for the agreement.

*Effect of withdrawal*    Unless the credit agreement is an **excepted agreement**, then, whether or not it would if made have been a **cancellable agreement**, the withdrawal of the debtor operates to apply the cancellation provisions of the Act (for the effect of these see page 75). The cancellation provisions apply not only to the credit agreement itself, but to any **linked transaction**, and to any other thing done in anticipation of the making of the credit agreement.

*(e)  Duties in relation to credit reference agencies consulted*

If you run a consumer credit business, the Act places on you a duty to give certain persons the name and address of any **credit reference agency** you may have consulted about the credit rating of a prospective customer. This duty only applies where the agreement in question is a **regulated agreement**. In one instance the duty arises irrespective of there being any request made to you for this information. Otherwise it only arises on request. We begin with the former case, which only arises where you decide not to enter into the regulated agreement.

Duty to inform credit-broker

This duty is imposed where the consumer has been introduced to you by a credit-broker (eg a retailer who wishes to help his customer obtain credit so he can buy the retailer's goods). If, after consulting the credit reference agency, you decide not to proceed with the making of the credit agreement you will doubtless either tell the consumer of this directly or else tell the credit-broker. If you do the former you are not obliged to give the name and address of the agency unless the consumer asks for it under the procedure described below. If on the other hand you only tell the credit-broker, you must also give him the name and address of the agency at the same time (or earlier). If you fail to do this you are not liable to any criminal penalty, but it may prejudice your licence (see pages 206 and 207). (Rather strangely, this duty does not apply if you do not hold a licence under the Act.)

Duty to inform consumer

Whether or not you have informed the consumer of your decision about proceeding with the agreement, he has a right to obtain from you the name and address of any **credit reference agency** you have consulted about him. This applies even where the proposed agreement is actually made. The consumer must comply with the procedure laid down. He must make the request in writing, and give you his own name and address so that you know where to send the information. His request must reach you before the end of the prescribed period. This runs from the time you are first in touch with the consumer over the agreement. If the agreement is made, the period expires twenty-eight days after the date on which it is made. If the agreement is not made, the period expires twenty-eight days after the negotiations for it end. They are taken to end on the date you give notice to the customer (or credit-broker) that you do not intend to proceed with the making of the agreement. If you do not give such notice, the negotiations end at such time as it would be reasonable for the customer to conclude from your silence that you have abandoned the matter.

If you receive a request which complies with these requirements, your duty is to give the consumer notice in writing of the name and address of any relevant credit reference agency. (An agency is relevant if you applied to it for information about the financial standing of the consumer during the period beginning when you were first in touch with him over the agreement and ending when, as explained above, the negotiations ended.) The notice must be given within seven **working days** after receiving the request. This duty applies whether or not you are a licensee. Breach of it is punishable (in a magistrates' court only) by a fine of up to £1,000.

## Agents and employees

If you employ agents, or have numerous branches, you should take steps to ensure that head office is kept informed about approaches by them to credit reference agencies. An enquiry made by an agent in the course of his authorised activities is treated as made by his principal.

## 11 Form and content of credit agreements

### (a) Introductory

A central feature of agreement control relates to the form and content of regulated agreements. These provisions (contained in Part V of the Act) are basic to the concept of truth in lending, being aimed at ensuring that the consumer is given all the information he needs about the commitment he is undertaking, with adequate opportunity to withdraw if he has second thoughts.

The controls revolve round the concept of *proper execution* of agreements. If you as credit-grantor fail to observe any statutory requirement, your agreement is treated as improperly executed. This has the routine consequence that you are unable to enforce it against the customer without a court order (known as an enforcement order).

This section therefore begins by explaining when a regulated credit agreement is improperly executed. Then we go on to consider the rules about the content, form and signing of credit agreements. This is followed by a description of the duties imposed on creditors with regard to the supply of copies of agreements. Finally we look at what the exact consequences of improper execution are:

A further type of consumer protection given by agreement control, namely cancellation rights, is explained in a later section (see section 15, beginning on page 75).

### (b) When agreement is 'improperly executed'

Unless the requirements described below in this section are complied with in relation to a **regulated** credit agreement, other than an **excepted agreement**, the agreement is treated as improperly executed.

This rule is subject to the following alleviation. If, on an application made to the Director General of Fair Trading by a person carrying on a **consumer credit business**, it appears to the Director General impractical for the applicant to comply with any requirement concerning the *form* of the agreement in a particular case, he may direct that the requirement be waived or varied in relation to such agreements, and subject to such conditions (if any), as he may specify. He can do this only where he is satisfied that to do so would not prejudice the interests of debtors. Applications must be made on Form CCD 30/83, and be accompanied by supporting information on Form CCD 31/83. The application fee is £95.

For the detailed *consequences* of improper execution see the end of this section (page 60).

### (c) Contents of agreement document

The Act and regulations lay down detailed rules about the form of the agreement. It must be expressed in a *document* complying with the following requirements. (If the agreement is a **modifying agreement** the requirements given below are adapted accordingly, the principle being that the debtor must be informed of changes from the original agreement.)

*Terms of the agreement*     The terms of any agreement may

either be express or implied. When express, they may be set out in the agreement document or in some other document. The rules we are considering require the agreement document itself to contain certain basic terms (the 'prescribed terms'), namely the amount of the credit supplied (or credit limit in the case of **running account credit**), the rate of interest, and the number, amount, frequency, and timing of **repayments**. Where further express terms are set out in some other document, this must be identified in the agreement document.

*Information for debtor*    The Act requires various further items of information to be set out in the agreement document. These consist of an informative heading, names and addresses of parties, description and cash price of goods etc acquired by the credit, amount of any advance payment, and description of any **security** provided.

*Statement of protection and remedies*    The agreement document must also contain the prescribed form of statement describing the debtor's statutory protection and remedies. These forms, set out in Sched 2 to the Consumer Credit (Agreements) Regulations 1983, are too detailed and numerous to be reproduced here.

*Signature box*    The agreement document must contain a 'signature box' in the appropriate form set out in Sched 5 to the Consumer Credit (Agreements) Regulations 1983. Again the forms are too detailed and numerous to be given, but their central purpose is to ensure that in the place where he signs the document the debtor is reminded of the nature of the transaction he is committing himself to. Thus the 'signature box' for hire-purchase agreements includes the words—

This is a **Hire-Purchase Agreement** regulated by the Consumer Credit Act 1974. Sign it only if you want to be legally bound by its terms.

After the space allocated to the debtor's signature, the form goes on—

The goods will not become your property until you have made all the payments. You must not sell them before then.

*Lettering and layout of document*    The lettering of the provisions required to be included in the agreement document must, apart from any signature, be easily legible, and of a colour which is readily distinguishable from the colour of the paper. The provisions must be shown together as a whole. The **APR** must be given no less prominence than information about the cash price, or any other rate.

### (d) Signing of agreement document

Having ensured that the form and content of the agreement is correct, you must then consider the manner of signature. The agreement document must be signed by both parties. When presented or sent to the **debtor** for signature, the document must be in such a state that all its terms are readily legible.

The Act contemplates that the agreement document will either be presented for signature personally, that is face to face, or will be sent to the debtor by post. It does not contemplate that the debtor will himself fill in details and then present the document for signature to the trader.

Where an application form is employed it is thus necessary for the creditor, using the particulars filled in on the form by the customer, to draw up an agreement document for signature by him. It is an element in the Act's scheme of consumer protection that a debtor should always have an opportunity, when deciding whether or not to sign a regulated agreement, of being able to read it through and have before his eyes *all* its express terms. The unexecuted agreement is thus finally put forward by the creditor, even though some of its terms may have been suggested by the consumer in filling in an application form.

The agreement document must be signed by the debtor in the space indicated for the purpose (the 'signature box' described above).

A date must also be inserted in the signature box. This will be the date of signing by the debtor, except that where the agreement is not a **cancellable agreement** the date on which the **unexecuted agreement** becomes an **executed agreement** may be inserted instead.

The agreement document must be signed by or on behalf of the **creditor** outside the signature box in which the debtor signs. A date must also be inserted outside the signature box. This will be the date of signing by or on behalf of the creditor, except that, as in the case of the debtor, where the agreement is not a cancellable agreement the date on which the unexecuted agreement becomes an executed agreement may be inserted instead.

The signature of a witness may be placed near the debtor's or creditor's signature, provided it is not in the signature box.

In the case of a land mortgage where the duty arises to give a copy incorporating notice of withdrawal rights (see page 52 above), that duty must of course have been complied with. In addition, the agreement document must have been sent, for his signature, to the debtor *by post* not less than seven days after the copy was given to him.

The giving of the copy starts a 'consideration period', which goes on until either the debtor returns the agreement document signed by him or seven days elapses following the date on which the document was sent to the debtor for signature. The agreement will be improperly executed unless during this consideration period the creditor refrains from approaching the debtor (whether in person, by telephone or letter, or in any other way) except in response to a specific request made by the debtor after the beginning of the consideration period. Furthermore no notice of withdrawal by the debtor must have been received by the creditor before the sending of the agreement document.

### (e) Supply of copies of credit agreements

The statutory duty imposed on the creditor to supply the debtor with a copy of a credit agreement differs according to whether signature by the debtor of the agreement document does or does not convert it into an 'executed agreement', that is a document which fully complies with the Act and regulations and is signed by *both* parties. If for example the document is sent by post to the debtor for signature, this question will depend on whether or not it had already been signed on behalf of the creditor.

There are two principles. The first is that, at the time the agreement document is presented or sent to the debtor for his signature, he must at the same time receive for retention a copy of what he is being invited to sign. Furthermore if the document refers to other documents, copies of these also must be provided.

This first principle does not apply where the document is presented face to face, and on that occasion becomes an executed agreement. Here the case is fully covered by the second principle.

The second principle is that, except where the agreement document was sent to him and on signature by him became an executed agreement (in which case the first principle is deemed sufficient), the debtor must always receive a copy of the executed agreement, so that he can retain a document which completely embodies the contract he has committed himself to. If the agreement document is presented for signature face to face, and on that occasion becomes an executed agreement, the debtor must then and there be given his copy of the executed agreement. Otherwise it must be given to him within seven days after the second signature is added. In the case of a **cancellable agreement** it must be sent by post, so that the debtor is not pressurised by personal contact.

The regulations allow certain omissions. For example a copy of an unexecuted agreement may omit the name and address of the debtor. No copy need include information relating to the debtor or a **surety** which is for the use of the creditor only and is not statutorily required to be included in the agreement document.

Equally there are various exceptions to the requirement to supply copies of documents referred to in the agreement document. If this were not so, every debtor would need to be supplied with a copy of the Consumer Credit Act for example.

### (f) Consequences of improper execution

As stated above (page 56), where the requirements outlined in this section are not complied with the result is that the agreement falls to be treated as 'improperly executed'. We now look at what this entails.

Where a credit agreement is to be treated as not properly executed it is enforceable against the debtor only where the county court makes an order (an 'enforcement order') to that effect. This means that if you fail to observe the rules you will be unable to enforce your agreement (including retaking goods or land) until the court has had an opportunity to consider the matter and decide what would be the fair result.

Here the court does not have a free hand. Section 127 of the Act places fetters on its ability to grant an enforcement order. There must have been a document at least containing the 'prescribed terms' (see page 57 above), and it must have been signed by both parties, even though not in the correct manner.

The court has power to strike out a term of the agreement omitted from the signed document. It may also reduce or discharge any sum payable by the debtor in order to compensate him for prejudice suffered as a result of the contravention.

Where an application for an enforcement order is dismissed (except on technical grounds only) the **section 106 rules** apply to any **security** provided in relation either to the credit agreement or any actual or prospective **linked transaction**.

## 12 Secured credit agreements

### (a) Meaning of 'security'

The Act defines a '**security**' as a mortgage, charge, **pledge**, bond, debenture, **indemnity, guarantee**, bill, note or other right which is provided in relation to a **consumer credit agreement** or **linked transaction**, either by the **debtor** or at his express or implied request, in order to secure the carrying out of his obligations under the agreement. In practice this definition applies only where the agreement is a **regulated agreement**.

### (b) Restrictions on use or effectiveness of security

It is the policy of the Act that its protective provisions are not to be evaded by taking a security. It contains a general provision to this effect (s 113), which limits the effectiveness of such a security to the degree to which the creditor's remedies are available apart from the security, ie are not cut down by the protective provisions. This means that where the secured agreement or linked transaction is enforceable only on an order of the County Court or the Director General of Fair Trading, enforcement of the security is similarly restricted. A security to which these restrictions apply cannot be used to benefit the creditor indirectly (eg by being vested in an associated company) to an extent not permissible directly.

*Prospective agreements*   Where a security is provided in relation to a prospective credit agreement, the security is ineffective unless and until the agreement is actually made.

**Example 16** L, a loan company, is approached by D for a loan. L tells D that he will need to find a guarantor. D produces S, who signs a document guaranteeing any future loan by L to D and also indemnifying L against the possibility that D will not enter into the loan agreement. D has second thoughts, whereupon L threatens to enforce the indemnity if D refuses to sign. S can release himself by giving L written notice requiring the section 106 rules to apply.

*Section 106 rules*   In many cases the Act reinforces the general protective provisions by applying 'the section 106 rules'. These rules treat the security as never having effect. They require the creditor to return any property lodged with him for the purpose of the security, and to cancel any security registration. If the security has been realised the money arising must be repaid to the **surety**.

*Negotiable instruments*     Special protective provisions are laid down as respects negotiable instruments such as cheques and other bills of exchange, and promissory notes. The broad purpose is to protect consumers from traders who otherwise, having discounted or passed a negotiable instrument to a holder in due course (who would take free of any duty under the Act), might fail altogether to provide the goods or services financed by the credit agreement, or might fail to comply with the statutory conditions. The Act first prohibits the taking of negotiable instruments other than bank notes and cheques *in payment* of any sum due under a **regulated agreement**. It then goes on to prohibit the taking of a negotiable instrument of *any* kind *as security* for sums due under a regulated agreement. A cheque taken in payment must not be negotiated by the creditor with anyone other than a banker.

*Land mortgages*     Where any security is charged on land, it is unenforceable (so far as provided in relation to a **regulated agreement**) except on an order of the County Court.

*Savings*     The Act contains certain savings which disapply the security provisions described above. The provisions do not affect the rights of a proprietor of a registered charge (within the meaning of the Land Registration Act 1925) who does not carry on a business of **debt-collecting** and who acquired the charge as a transferee of it for valuable consideration and without notice of any infringement of the Consumer Credit Act. Nor do they affect rights under the Law of Property Act 1925, s 104 (which enables a mortgagee to convey free of incumbrances).

### (c) *Proper execution of securities*

The Act imposes certain documentation requirements in relation to securities. Any security which is provided in relation to a **consumer credit agreement** being a **regulated agreement** must, if it is *not* provided by the debtor, be expressed in writing. Further rules apply to any **regulated security instrument**, defined as a document in which is expressed in writing a security being either a **guarantee** (other than a mortgage, charge, or **pledge**), or an **indemnity**. Such an instrument must conform to the detailed requirements mentioned in the next paragraph. If any of the documentation requirements are not complied with, a security is enforceable on an order of the County Court only. If the court refuses an order, except on technical grounds, the **section 106 rules** apply.

The detailed provisions applying to a regulated security instrument are as follows. The instrument must embody *all* the terms of the security, other than implied terms. It must be headed 'Guarantee [*or* Indemnity] subject to the Consumer Credit Act 1974', and must contain the names and addresses of the creditor, the debtor, and the surety. It must describe the subject-matter of the **security**, and must include the statutory statement of the rights of the **surety** and the statutory form of signature box. Special requirements are laid down to ensure legibility. The surety must be given copies of the security instrument and the regulated agreement.

### (d) Duties of creditor as to provision of information

The Act places the following information requirements on creditors in relation to securities. If any of these are not complied with, the security is enforceable on an order of the County Court only. If the court refuses an order, except on technical grounds, the **section 106 rules** apply.

The creditor under any consumer credit agreement, being a regulated agreement which is not fully paid up, must on receipt of a written request from a surety and payment of a 50p fee send the following to the surety:

(1) A copy of the credit agreement, and of any document referred to in it.

(2) A copy of the **regulated security instrument** (if any).

(3) If the agreement is for **fixed-sum credit**, a statement showing the total sum paid under the agreement by the debtor, the sums which have become payable but remain unpaid, and the sums which are to become payable in future.

(4) If the agreement is for **running-account credit**, a statement showing the state of the account, the amount (if any) currently payable by the debtor, and any amounts which (if the debtor does not draw further on the account) will later become payable.

The creditor under any consumer credit agreement, being a regulated agreement which is not fully paid up and in relation to which a **regulated security instrument** is executed *after* the making of the agreement, must on receipt of a written request from the debtor and payment of a 50p fee send the debtor a copy of the security instrument.

When a debtor is given a **default notice**, or an **enforcement notice**, or a **termination notice**, the creditor must give a copy of the notice to any surety.

### (e) Pawnbroking

The security provisions of the Act include special requirements regulating the activities of pawnbrokers.

*Record-keeping*    A person who takes any article in **pawn** under a **consumer credit agreement** which is a **regulated agreement** has a general duty to keep such books or other records as are sufficient to show and explain at any time all dealings by him with the article, including its taking in pawn, and its redemption or sale. Entries must contain specified information, and must include sufficient cross-references. They must be retained by the pawnbroker until a date five years after the pawning of the article or three years after it is redeemed or sold (whichever is later). No penalty is laid down for breach of the record-keeping duties, but they may be taken into account in considering whether to renew, suspend, or revoke the pawnbroker's category A licence.

*Minors*    A person who takes any article in pawn from a person whom he knows to be under eighteen, or who appears to be and is under that age, commits an offence. The penalty on indictment is a maximum of two years' imprisonment and/or an unlimited fine. On summary conviction the maximum is a fine not exceeding £2,000.

*Supply of copies etc*    In the case of pawnbrokers, criminal penalties are imposed where certain duties applicable to credit agreements generally are infringed. The duties in question are the duty to supply a copy of the unexecuted agreement, the duty to supply a copy of the executed agreement, and the duty to give notice of cancellation rights. The maximum penalty on summary conviction is a fine of £1,000.

*Pawn-receipts*    It is an offence not to give a pawn-receipt when receiving an article in pawn. This may be a separate document or combined with the credit agreement, and must conform to the statutory requirements. The penalty on summary conviction is a fine not exceeding £1,000.

*Redemption of pawns*    The Act lays down elaborate protective provisions regarding the redemption of articles pawned. The 'redemption period' is the longest of the following:

(1) six months after the article was pawned;

(2) any period fixed by the parties for the duration either of

the credit or the redemption period. (This means that a pawnbroker cannot require a redemption period of less than six months.)

Whatever the agreement may say, the article is redeemable at any time during the redemption period. Even when the period has expired, the article remains redeemable until it is realised by the pawnbroker or its ownership passes to him. Charges must not be increased just because the redemption period has expired. Unreasonable refusal to allow redemption is an offence for which the maximum penalty on summary conviction is a fine of £1,000.

Where the redemption period is six months, and the credit does not exceed £25, ownership of the pawned article automatically passes to the pawnbroker if it is not redeemed by the end of that period. In other cases the pawnbroker has a statutory power to sell the article, passing any surplus proceeds to its owner.

## 13 Statutory agency and connected-lender liability

One of the important ways in which the Act affects a **consumer credit business** is in making the **credit-trader** responsible for the acts and statements of other **business** people whom he has not in fact authorised to make commitments on his behalf. This potential liability clearly has disquieting aspects. It is also somewhat complicated.

There are two basic cases. The first (which can only arise in relation to **goods**) is where the **credit** is to finance a transaction between the **creditor** himself and the **debtor** (eg a **hire-purchase agreement**, which the Act treats as credit) and the goods are sold to the creditor for this purpose by a dealer. Here the creditor (the hire-purchase company) may be held responsible for *misrepresentations* by the dealer.

The other basic case (which may arise in relation to goods, services or land with or without buildings) is where the credit is to finance a transaction in the goods, services or land between a third party and the debtor, the creditor being a 'connected lender' (ie one having ongoing business arrangements with the third party). Here the creditor may be held responsible for *misrepresentations* or *breaches of contract* by the third party.

We now proceed to examine these two basic cases in detail, the detail being unfortunately rather complicated. To ease the complication we deal with the first case in two parts, one concerned with hire-purchase and the other with further instances where a dealer sells goods to a credit grantor. Similarly, the treatment of the second basic case is subdivided so as to show separately the liability of a connected lender for misrepresentations by the supplier where the credit is restricted-use credit and where it is unrestricted-use credit, and then to show the liability of a connected lender for breaches of contract by the supplier.

*(a) Liability of hire-purchase company for misrepresentations by dealer*

This liability was first introduced by the Hire-Purchase Act 1964. It was designed to deal with abuses found to be prevalent in the following circumstances. The customer goes to a dealer in consumer durables (such as cars or television sets). He desires to obtain goods on credit but the dealer is not in a financial position to give the credit himself. He has an ongoing relationship with a finance house. After the consumer has selected the goods and agreed the amount of the price and deposit (allowing for any goods given in part exchange) the dealer in effect passes him on to the finance house. However, the dealer himself stocks the hire-purchase forms issued by the finance house, which exclude all liability for warranties and other representations made by the dealer. The customer fills in the forms and pays the deposit to the dealer, who sells the goods to the finance house. The finance house enters into the hire-purchase agreement with the customer and allows the dealer a commission. The finance house pays the dealer his commission and the cash price for the goods (less the deposit, which is in fact retained by the dealer though treated in law as paid by the customer to the finance house as part of the hire-purchase price). The dealer is not party to the hire-purchase contract and is not the agent of the finance house. Neither the dealer nor the finance house is liable for any misrepresentation about the goods made by the dealer to the customer unless it is held to be fraudulent—in which case the dealer only is responsible.

This lack of liability for innocent misrepresentation was considered to be unfair to the consumer, so the 1964 Act provided that the dealer was to be treated as the finance company's agent, regardless of anything to the contrary in the hire-purchase contract. The 1974 Act repeats this. The exact position under the 1974 Act, which has operated since 16 May 1977, is as follows:

(1) The liability of the finance company covers any kind of representation made by the dealer to the customer about the goods (even a representation made before the question

of hire-purchase arose). It includes not merely words spoken by the dealer or his staff, but material in the form of posters, signs, newspaper advertisements, etc. It covers both innocent and fraudulent misrepresentations.

(2) The liability arises only where the **hire-purchase agreement** is a **regulated agreement.**

(3) The liability arises only where the dealer is a **credit-broker** and the goods are to be sold by the credit-broker to the finance company. The credit-broker need not be acting as such at the time.

**Example 17** Mr A goes into the car showroom of B Ltd, who hold a Category C licence as credit-brokers. He chooses a car on the windscreen of which is written '10,000 miles only'. Unknown to B Ltd, the car has in fact done over 50,000 miles. Mr A makes his own arrangements to buy the car on hire-purchase from D Ltd, with whom he has had several previous hire-purchase transactions. For this purpose, B Ltd sell the car to D Ltd, who were previously unknown to them. The hire-purchase contract between Mr A and D Ltd contains a term exonerating D Ltd from liability for misrepresentations by B Ltd. D Ltd are liable to Mr A for the innocent misrepresentation about the mileage, notwithstanding the exonerating term. The Act treats B Ltd as the agents of D Ltd in relation to such misrepresentations, and no contractual term can disapply this.

This example is of course unusual. In the vast majority of cases the dealer has ongoing business arrangements with the finance company and does introduce the customer to them. Either way, it is prudent for the finance company to insist on including (whether in the contract by which the goods are sold to it or in a general contract defining their business relationship) an indemnity under which the dealer is required to reimburse the finance company for loss sustained by it through compensating the consumer for the dealer's misrepresentations. The Act does not affect any liability the dealer may have on his own account, eg for fraudulent misrepresentation. Here the customer has the choice of which party to sue.

An important additional point should be noted. The creditor's liability for misrepresentations by the dealer does not only arise where the customer and the finance company go through with the hire-purchase deal. The liability may cause loss to the prospective creditor even though the proposed hire-purchase agreement is not in fact entered into.

> **Example 18** A customer signs hire-purchase forms for a car. Before the hire-purchase company agree the transaction the dealer's salesman allows the customer to drive away the car, since he has signed the forms and paid the deposit. Not satisfied with his credit rating, the hire-purchase company refuse to complete the transaction. Meanwhile the customer has an accident with the car due to brake failure. He suffers personal injury in the accident. The salesman had assured the customer that the brakes were in good order. The court finds that this assurance was given negligently and awards the customer damages *against the hire-purchase company*.

In this example the damages were given for the tort (non-contractual civil wrong) of *negligence*. Another tort for which such liability may arise is *deceit*, where misrepresentations are made fraudulently. Note however that a prospective creditor will not be liable in tort where the hire-purchase agreement is not ultimately made unless there was a course of dealing under which the prospective creditor normally accepted business introduced by the credit-broker. In a case such as Example 17 D Ltd would not be liable in tort for misstatements by B Ltd if D Ltd refused to enter into the hire-purchase agreement. Nor in such a case would D Ltd be under any other form of liability.

*(b) Other cases of creditor's liability for misrepresentation where goods sold to creditor by credit-broker*

The liability just described is not limited to hire-purchase cases. It applies in exactly the same way in relation to any other debtor-creditor-supplier agreement of the first type described on page 11. In practice this means that the liability arises in three cases: hire-purchase, conditional sale and credit sale. In other words, in addition to the hire-purchase cases just described, the transaction for the purposes of which the goods are sold by the credit-broker to the prospective creditor may be a conditional sale or credit sale by the creditor to the customer. The Act defines a conditional sale as a sale under which the purchase price is payable by instalments but the ownership is not to pass to the purchaser until certain conditions (usually as to completion of the payment of instalments) are satisfied. Where the ownership passes to the purchaser right away but the price is payable by instalments the transaction is a credit sale. (Conditional sale differs from hire-purchase only in that hire-purchase is taken not to be a 'contract of sale' within the technical meaning laid down by the statutes relating to sale of goods.)

Having completed our consideration of the first of the two basic cases mentioned above (the case where the credit is to finance a transaction in goods between creditor and debtor and the goods are sold to the creditor for this purpose by a credit-broker), we turn to the second basic case. Here, it will be remembered, we may be concerned not only with goods but also with services or land. The credit is to finance a transaction in the goods, services or land between the supplier and the debtor, the creditor being a 'connected lender'. We begin with the creditor's liability for *misrepresentations* by the supplier, continuing after that with his liability for *breaches of contract*.

### (c) Liability of connected lender for misrepresentations by supplier (restricted-use credit)

The Act imposes this liability by two distinct but overlapping provisions: s 56 (which bases the liability on a notional agency) and s 75 (which imposes joint and several liability). The complaining party may rely on either or both of these sections, though the scope of s 75 is somewhat narrower since it excludes non-commercial agreements and very small and very large transactions. Both sections however are concerned with the same type of **restricted-use credit**, namely **debtor-creditor-supplier agreements** of the second type mentioned on page 11. The principal cases are 3-party credit cards (excluding those exempt from regulation because credit is repayable in full at the end of each month or other accounting period—see page 14), trading checks or vouchers, and cash loans paid direct to the supplier by a connected lender (that is one having ongoing business arrangements with the supplier, in pursuance of which the advance is made).

The s 56 liability arises in relation to transactions where the first representations were made by the supplier to the customer after 16 May 1977. In making the representations the supplier is treated as being the agent of the creditor, who is therefore responsible for them. The s 75 liability arises in relation to credit agreements made after 30 June 1977; but the following are excluded from it:

agreements not made in the course of a business (eg a loan between personal friends); and
agreements financing the sale etc of a single item to which the supplier has attached a cash price not exceeding £100 (including VAT) or exceeding £30,000 (including VAT). [These figures were raised from £30 and £10,000 respectively on 20 May 1985.]

Since credit cards etc issued under a **credit-token** agreement made before 1 July 1977 are excluded there are now, in effect, two classes of credit card holders: those within s 75 protection and those outside it.

Under s 75 the customer, even where he has infringed a term of the credit agreement (as by exceeding his limit on a credit card), is given the like claim against the creditor for the misrepresentation as he has against the supplier. He can proceed against either or both, but cannot of course recover twice over.

An important difference between s 56 and s 75 is that the latter applies only to concluded agreements whereas the former applies also where the proposed credit agreement is not in fact made. It does this in a similar way to that explained above in relation to proposed hire-purchase agreements (pages 67 and 68).

We look now at examples showing how s 56 and s 75 respectively operate in the case of restricted-use credit.

> **Example 19** Mrs X, using a credit card issued by Y Ltd under a **regulated agreement**, buys from Z Ltd for £200 a brooch on the strength of a representation that it is of 22-carat gold. In fact it is only 18-carat. Under s 56 Mrs X could sue Y Ltd for rescission of the contract and return of the price, or (in certain cases) for damages for misrepresentation, on the ground that Z Ltd were deemed to be acting as their agents in representing the brooch to be 22-carat. However, if the representation is a term of the contract Mrs X also has, under ordinary rules of contract law, a right to sue Z Ltd for breach of warranty. This means that under s 75 she has a like claim against Y Ltd. She has three distinct causes of action, two against Y Ltd and one against Z Ltd.

Here we see that Y Ltd, in issuing the credit card to Mrs X, have laid themselves open to claims of this kind in respect of any shop which agrees to honour their cards, whether it so agrees before or after the issue of that particular card. If Z Ltd prove unreliable and Y Ltd receive a number of claims in respect of their transactions, Y Ltd can only protect themselves from further claims by terminating Z Ltd's authority to process their credit cards.

**Example 20** Mr K wishes to buy a table for £200 from L Ltd, but lacks finance. In accordance with ongoing arrangements they have with M Ltd, a firm of moneylenders, L Ltd introduce the customer to M Ltd. They agree to the loan but insist on paying the money direct to L Ltd. L Ltd have represented to Mr K that the table is genuine Chippendale. In fact it is a modern reproduction.

The loan is a debtor-creditor-supplier agreement of the second type mentioned on page 11. Under s 56, M Ltd are liable as principals for the misrepresentation by L Ltd. If he decides to rescind the contract of purchase, Mr K can in effect cancel his obligation to repay the loan (though strictly his claim would be by way of set-off). Alternatively, and with the same result, Mr K could proceed against M Ltd under s 75.

In this example M Ltd are only liable for the misrepresentation by L Ltd because they have acted in accordance with existing business arrangements between the two firms. Such arrangements need not be of a formal nature; it will suffice to establish liability if there is shown to be a practice of accepting business in this way. M Ltd could protect themselves against future claims by sending a clearly-worded letter to L Ltd stating that they were ending the relationship and would accept no further business introduced by them.

*(d) Liability of connected lender for misrepresentations by supplier (unrestricted-use credit)*

Sections 56 and 75 operate in the same way as just described where the credit, instead of being restricted-use credit, falls into the last of the three categories of debtor-creditor-supplier agreement described on page 11 and is for **unrestricted-use credit**. A loan will be for unrestricted-use credit if it is paid direct to the borrower, so that he is free *in fact* to use it as he wishes (whatever his duty *in law* may be). If in Example 20 M Ltd had paid the loan money to Mr K the case would have fallen into this category. Here is another example.

**Example 21** Mr P, an employee in a camera shop, is a personal friend of Miss Q. In the pub one night she tells him she wants to buy a camera for £25 but has no money. He takes five £5 notes from his pocket and says 'Pay me back when you can'. Next day Miss Q comes into the shop. Mr P shows her a camera, telling her (untruly) that it has a telescopic lens. She buys it using the £5 notes. Angry at the deception, she wishes to claim from Mr P personally. In fact Mr P had made a genuine mistake over the lens.

Miss Q can only claim against the owners of the shop. There are no pre-existing arrangements between the owners and Mr P in furtherance of which the loan was made. If there had been however, the following position would arise. Under s 56 Miss Q could sue Mr P because his employer would, under ordinary agency principles, be responsible for his innocent misrepresentation and s 56 would make the employer the agent of Mr P in his capacity as lender. Under s 75 Miss Q could not sue Mr P, first because the loan was not made by him in the course of a consumer credit business and second because the cash price of the camera was less than £100.

*(e) Liability of connected lender for supplier's breach of contract*

The overlap between ss 56 and 75 does not extend to breaches of contract. Here connected-lender liability rests solely on s 75. If a representation to which s 56 applies is made a term of the contract, its falsity may involve breach of contract but this will not in itself fall within s 56.

**Example 22** Mr S uses a credit card issued by T Ltd to buy goods from U. U had told S that he bought the goods from another customer, but in fact U had stolen the goods. In making this representation, U was (under s 56) the statutory agent of T. Accordingly s 56 gives S remedies for misrepresentation, on the lines explained above, against T. He also has (under s 75) joint and several claims against T and U in respect of the misrepresentation (ie he can proceed against both or either of them).

The general law relating to sale of goods states that there is an implied condition (ie fundamental term of the contract) on the part of the seller that he has a right to sell the goods. This condition was broken in the present case and accordingly S has a claim for breach of contract against U. Section 75 gives him a like claim against T. The remedies for breach of contract and misrepresentation are slightly different, so in this respect s 75 does not overlap with s 56.

The importance of s 75 lies however in the fact that it covers (as s 56 does not) the many types of breach of contract which do not depend on prior misrepresentation. Whatever remedy the buyer has against the **supplier**, s 75 gives him a like remedy against the creditor (connected lender). As in the case of all these provisions, the buyer cannot recover more than once however. There is no limit on the amount of the claim, the Government having rejected the argument that it should be restricted to the amount of the credit. Matters giving the supplier a counterclaim or set-off will avail the creditor only where they arise out of the transaction in question. Where a remedy depends on a factual situation affecting the supplier only it may in the nature of things be available only against the supplier (eg a claim for an order of specific delivery of an antique purchased from the supplier with a connected loan could not be made against the creditor since he is not in possession of the article). The customer can effectively take against the creditor any incidental steps required to pursue his remedy, eg service of a notice of rescission or a notice stating that he is treating the contract with the supplier as repudiated. If the customer obtains judgment against one party but the judgment is unsatisfied he can still proceed against the other. If the creditor is sued he is entitled to have the supplier made a party to the proceedings.

### (f) Creditor's statutory indemnity (section 75 only)

The Act is inconsistent in giving the connected lender an indemnity against the supplier for claims under s 75 but not for claims under s 56. (This inconsistency may make it important to be clear under which section the customer is claiming.) The statutory indemnity covers all loss suffered by the creditor in satisfying his liability under s 75, including costs reasonably incurred by the creditor in defending proceedings brought by the customer. Normally, costs would be taken to be reasonable if allowed on taxation, but not otherwise. The terms of the statutory indemnity only apply in so far as the parties have not overridden them by their own indemnity agreement.

*(g)  Limits of section 56 agency*

We have described the statutory agency arising under s 56 as rendering the creditor liable only for *misrepresentations* by the credit-broker or supplier. This is the main area, but in certain cases the creditor's liability may go wider. The agency arises in relation to any negotiations or other dealings between the customer and the creditor-broker or supplier over the transaction which is to be financed (wholly or partly) by the credit agreement. The word 'dealing' seems wide enough to cover the receipt of a deposit for example, so that the customer who had paid a deposit to a dealer in a case where the transaction did not go through could claim it back from the creditor (or prospective creditor where the credit agreement was separate and did not go through either).

It is arguable that 'dealing' is even wide enough to cover the making of a contract.

> **Example 23**  A dealer, R Ltd, is in the practice of passing customers to a finance house, S Ltd. R Ltd has a stock of hire-purchase forms issued by S Ltd, but the practice is to pass completed forms to S Ltd for approval. On one occasion a salesman new to the employ of R Ltd purports to accept a hire-purchase proposal by a customer without waiting to see if S Ltd are willing to approve. Is there a binding contract between the customer and S Ltd?

If what the salesman did in this example is treated as a 'dealing' relating to the proposed hire-purchase agreement, then he (or rather his employer R Ltd) is to be treated as the statutory agent of S Ltd. His 'acceptance' would therefore bind S Ltd and the hire-purchase contract would be treated as made. While the matter is not free from doubt, it is thought that a court would not hold this to be the case. The agency provisions of s 56 are in terms of 'antecedent negotiations'. To make a contract is surely to go beyond antecedent negotiations, or at least to bring them to an end. It involves the parties in potential liability for breach of contract. The fact that s 75 imposes vicarious liability on creditors for breaches of contract suggests that such liability is not also imposed by s 56 (an argument weakened however by the fact that misrepresentation is dealt with in an overlapping fashion by both sections).

## 14 Liability for negotiator's acts or omissions

In the days of untrammelled freedom of contract it was a frequent practice on the part of finance companies and other credit grantors to evade liability for representations, whether by their own employees or those of dealers passing business to them. This was done by a disclaimer in the hire-purchase or other agreement. Sometimes the practice went to the lengths of inserting a term purporting to make the employee the agent of the customer.

These practices are rendered ineffective by the Act. An agreement (whenever made) is void to the extent that it purports, in relation to an actual or prospective **regulated agreement**, to provide that a salesman is to be treated as the agent of the customer or to provide in any other way for relieving a salesman or his employer from liability. This applies not only to negotiations conducted by or on behalf of the credit grantor, but also to those by a credit-broker or supplier who is to be treated, under the provisions discussed in section 13, as the statutory agent of the credit grantor.

## 15 Cancellation of credit agreement by debtor

An important feature of the protection conferred by the Consumer Credit Act on **debtors** is the right to cancel certain agreements during a brief 'cooling-off period'. Basically, these are **credit agreements** where there was oral or 'face-to-face' solicitation and the agreement was not signed on trade premises. Where cancellation rights exist, a duty is imposed on you as creditor to give the debtor who has just entered into the cancellable agreement notice of these rights. He may exercise them by serving a notice of cancellation on you, or on another person (such as a credit-broker) whom the Act deems to be your agent for this purpose. The Act spells out the consequences that arise when the debtor serves a notice of cancellation.

We now proceed to look at the cancellation provisions in detail. First, which agreements are cancellable? The provisions dealing with this question are highly complex. We begin with the concept of 'antecedent negotiations'.

### (a) Antecedent negotiations

The activities leading up to the making of a credit agreement are called by the Act 'negotiations'. Since of course they precede the agreement, they are referred to as *antecedent* negotiations. It would be simple to describe this concept if it were not artificially extended so as to increase protection. First, it is not confined to ordinary negotiations. Second, it brings in discussions with persons other than the creditor and his staff.

*Meaning of 'negotiations'*    In addition to negotiations in the ordinary sense, the Act treats as 'negotiations' any representations made to the customer by the person who acts, or is deemed to act, on behalf of the prospective creditor (called the 'negotiator'). These may include representations made by an **advertisement**. The Act adds that the term 'negotiations' also includes any other dealings between customer and 'negotiator'. The concept is thus very wide. Negotiations begin when the negotiator and customer first enter into communication. Entry into communication may begin when the potential customer sees or hears an advertisement, or in any other manner. During the period while 'negotiations' continue, successive individuals may act as negotiator. There are four basic cases. Not all situations within these are relevant to cancellation, since the Act's concept of 'antecedent negotiations' has other applications too.

(1) *Negotiations conducted by the creditor or his staff* The most obvious case is where the preliminaries are conducted by the creditor or a member of his staff. If the credit agreement when made will be a **regulated agreement**, these count as 'antecedent negotiations'.

(2) *Negotiations conducted by a credit-broker* Any 'negotiations' with the prospective **debtor** are antecedent negotiations where they are conducted by a **credit-broker** in relation to **goods** sold or proposed to be sold by the credit-broker to the creditor before forming the subject of a **debtor-creditor-supplier agreement**. This will be an agreement to finance (wholly or partly) a transaction relating to the goods between the debtor and the creditor (whether the transaction forms part of the debtor-creditor-supplier agreement or not). The typical case is where goods, for example a motor vehicle, are selected in a shop or showroom and then sold to a finance company to form the subject of a **hire-purchase agreement**. The finance company is then treated as the 'creditor', but the customer's discussions in the shop or showroom are made to form part of the 'antecedent negotiations'. (For the consequences of this in relation to liability see section 13 above.)

(3) *Negotiations conducted by a connected supplier (restricted-use credit)* Any 'negotiations' with the prospective debtor are antecedent negotiations where they are conducted by the **supplier** in relation to a transaction financed (wholly or partly), or proposed to be financed, by a debtor-creditor-supplier agreement of the second type mentioned on page 11. Even if the debtor-creditor-supplier agreement was made previously, the negotiations are still treated as 'antecedent'.

**Example 24** Discussions take place between a shopkeeper and a customer about goods the customer then buys using a credit-card issued by the Universal Credit-card Company under a **regulated agreement**. The discussions constitute 'antecedent negotiations' of this type, the shopkeeper being the 'supplier' and 'negotiator' and the Universal Credit-card Company being the 'creditor'.
Obviously what these negotiations are truly 'antecedent' to is in fact the making of the purchase. The significance of this piece of artificiality by the Act is explained in section 13 above (see page 70).

(4) *Negotiations conducted by a connected supplier (unrestricted-use credit)* Any 'negotiations' with the prospective debtor are antecedent negotiations where they are conducted by the **supplier** in relation to a transaction financed (wholly or partly), or proposed to be financed, by a debtor-creditor-supplier agreement of the third type mentioned on page 11. Here again, the negotiations are truly related to the making of the financed transaction rather than the credit agreement. (As to the reason for this artificiality see section 13 above (page 69).

## (b) What agreements are cancellable

Having explained the meaning of 'antecedent negotiations', the key to cancellability, we go on to explain which credit agreements fall within the Act's category of 'cancellable agreements'.
*Agreements incapable of being cancellable* The Act makes certain types of agreement incapable of cancellation. In the first place, no **excepted agreement** can be a 'cancellable agreement'. The other exclusion relates to certain agreements relating to **land**, namely—

(1) any agreement where land is made the **security** for the performance of the obligations imposed on the debtor by the agreement;

(2) any agreement for **restricted-use credit** to finance (wholly or partly) the purchase of land;

(3) any agreement for a bridging loan in connection with the purchase of land.

*The twin test for cancellability*     If not within the descriptions just mentioned, a credit agreement which is a **regulated agreement** will be cancellable if the following criteria both apply. First, the **antecedent negotiations** must include oral, that is spoken, representations made when in the presence of the customer (telephone conversations and radio broadcasts do not count) by an **individual** acting as, or on behalf of, the **negotiator**. The second is that the **unexecuted agreement** must be signed elsewhere than on **trade premises.**

In addition, a **modifying agreement**, not being a non-commercial agreement, is a 'cancellable agreement' if the agreement it modifies was cancellable and the modifying agreement is made within the **cooling-off period** applicable to that earlier agreement.

### (c)  Duty to give notice of cancellation rights

The requirements regarding the provision of copies of credit agreements have been explained above (pages 59 and 60). In the case of a cancellable agreement, the required copy must include notice of the debtor's cancellation rights. The form of the notice is laid down by the Consumer Credit (Cancellation Notices and Copies of Documents) Regulations 1983. Where a copy is required to be sent by post, a cancellation form must also be included. (The wording of this is set out in form 16 in Part IV of the Schedule to the Regulations.) In certain cases the notice of cancellation rights is required to be sent to the debtor separately by post.

### (d)  Service of notice of cancellation

A notice of cancellation of a **cancellable agreement** must be in writing, but does not need to take any particular form. It may be expressed in any way the debtor chooses, so long as it indicates his intention to withdraw from the agreement. It must however be served within the 'cooling-off period', which starts when the debtor signs the **unexecuted agreement** and finishes at the end of the fifth day following the day on which the debtor receives by post the notice of his cancellation rights.

A notice of cancellation is effective if served on the **creditor** or his agent, or on any person designated by the creditor in the notice informing the debtor of his cancellation rights, or on a **credit-broker** or **supplier** who was the **negotiator** in the **antecedent negotiations**, or on any person (such as a mortgage broker) who in the course of his business acted *on behalf of the debtor* in any negotiations for the credit agreement.

Whether or not it is actually received, a notice of cancellation sent by post to one of these persons is deemed by the Act to be received by him at the time of posting. This means that the debtor is sure of being able to make his cancellation effective immediately.

## (e) Effect of notice of cancellation

*Usual effect*     Except in certain special cases, mentioned below, the effect of a valid notice of cancellation is of course to cancel the credit agreement. It also however cancels any **linked transaction** (other than an **excepted linked transaction**). The result generally is that the agreement or linked transaction is to be treated thereafter as if it had never been entered into. Furthermore the cancellation operates to withdraw any offer by the **debtor** or his **relative** to enter into a linked transaction (other than an excepted linked transaction). It also applies the **section 106 rules** to any security provided in relation to a cancelled agreement or transaction. Any interested party may apply to the County Court for a declaration that cancellation has been effected.

The protection given by the Act to linked transactions was in response to the observation by the Crowther Committee that—

Where goods are bought on credit, it is common to have ancillary contracts [in the Act called linked transactions] such as guarantees or indemnities, insurance and maintenance, and the like. Protection given to the main transaction may be substantially undermined if not carried through to such ancillary contracts, which are sometimes used as a vehicle for imposing further and excessive charges.

*Special cases*     Where either:

(1) the credit financed the doing of work, or the supply of goods, to meet an emergency; or
(2) goods supplied under the credit have become incorporated in any land or thing,

the effect of the notice of cancellation is modified so as to retain the obligation of the debtor to pay for the doing of the work or the supply of the goods.

*(f) Incidental consequences of cancellation*

The Act sets out certain specific consequences of its requirement that on cancellation an agreement or transaction is to be treated as never having been entered into.

*Recovery of money*    On cancellation, broadly speaking any sum paid under the cancelled agreement or linked transaction by the debtor or his relative is repayable (exceptions are mentioned below). In the case of a fee, commission or other sum paid to a **credit-broker** all but £3 is repayable.

*Liability for future payments*    If the debtor has already received credit under the agreement (for example if he has run up an overdraft with the creditor), he remains liable to repay this. He must also pay the agreed interest, unless he repays in full within a month after serving the notice of cancellation or (where repayment is by instalments) before the date on which the first instalment is due. It follows that the recovery provisions mentioned in the preceding paragraph do not apply to such sums which, if they had not been paid by the debtor, would have remained payable.

*Return of goods*    Where the credit agreement financed the acquisition of goods (for example on hire-purchase or credit sale), and these have been handed over to the debtor before cancellation, he is under a duty to return them. Exceptions apply in the case of perishables, or goods which by their nature are consumed by use, or goods supplied to meet an emergency, or goods which have become incorporated in any land or thing. Until they are returned, the debtor must take reasonable care of returnable goods.

*Part-exchange goods*    Where goods were taken by the creditor in part exchange, then on cancellation the debtor is entitled to receive them back unless the creditor chooses to pay a monetary allowance in lieu of this.

## 16 Duties as to giving of information

The Act places on both parties to a credit agreement various duties in relation to the giving of information.

*(a) Information to be provided at request of debtor*

The debtor under a **regulated agreement**, other than a **paid-up agreement** or a non-commercial agreement, is entitled to request certain information from the creditor. The request is effective only if the Act's conditions are complied with. It must be in writing, and accompanied by a fee of 50p. It must not be made within one month after compliance by the creditor with a similar request from that debtor relating to the agreement in question. Failure to comply with the duty renders the agreement unenforceable by the creditor while the default continues. If it continues for a month the creditor commits an offence punishable on summary conviction with a fine not exceeding £1,000.

Within twelve **working days** after receiving an effective request, the creditor must send the debtor a **prescribed copy** of the **executed agreement** (if any), and of any other document referred to in it (other than an **excepted document**), together with a signed statement (which is binding on the creditor). The form of statement differs according to whether the agreement is for **fixed-sum credit** or **running-account credit**.

*Fixed-sum credit*    If the agreement is for fixed-sum credit, the statement must contain, according to the information available to the creditor, the following information:

(1) the total sum so far paid under the agreement by the debtor;

(2) the total sum which has become payable under the agreement by the debtor but remains unpaid, showing the various amounts comprised in that total sum and the date when each became due; and

(3) the total sum which is to become payable under the agreement by the debtor in future, showing the various amounts comprised in that total sum and the date, or mode of determining the date, when each will become due.

*Running-account credit*    If the agreement is for running-account credit, the statement must contain, according to the information available to the creditor, the following information:

(1) the state of the account;

(2) the amount, if any, currently payable under the agreement by the debtor to the creditor;

(3) the amounts and due dates of any payments which, if the debtor does not draw further on the account, will later become payable under the agreement by the debtor to the creditor.

#### (b) Periodic information to running-account debtor

In relation to a **regulated agreement** for **running-account credit**, the Act also imposes on the creditor an information duty which does not depend on the making of a request by the debtor, but operates automatically. This duty does not apply if the agreement is a **paid-up agreement**, a non-commercial agreement, or a **small agreement**. There is no specific sanction for a failure to comply with the duty, but it would fall to be taken into account in considering whether to renew, suspend or revoke the creditor's licence.

The duty is somewhat complicated. To understand its nature we first need to consider two relevant periods, the accounting period and the service period.

*Accounting period*     The first accounting period under the agreement is a period starting on or before the first movement in the account (that is the first payment in or out) and ending not more than twelve months later. Each subsequent accounting period is a period starting at the end of the previous accounting period and ending not more than twelve months later. Subject to anything said in the agreement, the creditor can fix the precise periods provided they correspond to these criteria.

*Service period*     The service period varies according to whether, in sending the statement in question to the debtor, the creditor demands any payment. There are three possible cases:

(1) where the statement for an accounting period includes a demand for payment, the service period is one month beginning at the end of that accounting period;

(2) where the statement for an accounting period does not include a demand for payment, and does not indicate that there is a nil balance on the account at the end of that accounting period, the service period is six months beginning at the end of the accounting period;

(3) where the statement for an accounting period does not include a demand for payment, and *does* indicate that there is a nil balance on the account at the end of that accounting period, the service period is twelve months beginning at the 'relevant time' (as explained below).

The 'relevant time' for the purposes of para (3) above depends on whether there has been any debit or credit balance on the account at any time during the accounting period. If there has been such a balance, the 'relevant time' is the date on which there is first a debit or a credit balance following the end of the accounting period. Otherwise the 'relevant time' is the end of the accounting period.

*Nature of duty*     The creditor must, within each service period, give the debtor a prescribed statement relating to the relevant accounting period. The form of statement is set out in the Schedule to the Consumer Credit (Running-Account Credit Information) Regulations 1983. It covers balances at the beginning and end of the accounting period, dates and amounts of payments in and out, and interest charges.

### (c) Information as to whereabouts of goods

Where a **regulated agreement**, other than a non-commercial agreement, requires the debtor to keep **goods** to which the agreement relates in his possession or control (for example where they are held on hire-purchase) the Act gives the creditor the right to information concerning them. Within seven **working days** after he has received a request in writing to that effect from the creditor, the debtor must tell the creditor where the goods are. The information need not be given in writing: a telephone call will do.

If the debtor fails to comply with this requirement, and the default continues for fourteen days, he commits an offence for which he is liable on summary conviction to a fine not exceeding £400.

## 17 Credit cards, trading checks and other credit-tokens

The recent growth in the use of cards, checks and other tokens as a means of obtaining cash, **goods** or services on **credit** required special provisions in the Act. The easier it is to acquire credit by such means, the more fraud and other abuses abound. This fact called for specially-designed protective measures.

The Act coined the term '**credit-token**' to describe this easily portable means of obtaining ready credit. A credit-token is defined as a card, check, voucher, coupon, stamp, form, booklet or other document or thing issued to an **individual** by a person carrying on a **consumer credit business**. The Act distinguishes two-party and three-party credit-tokens. The first type is simply a means by which, on producing it, the holder can readily obtain credit from the credit-token issuer. This type is really no more than a means of easy identification of a person who has already entered into a credit contract with the issuer.

The three-party credit-token is more complicated. The issuer undertakes that where, on production of the credit-token by the holder to a third party, the third party supplies the holder with cash, goods or services, the issuer will reimburse the third party (whether or not deducting any discount or commission) in return for payment to the issuer (in instalments, or in one sum at the end of the month or other trading period) by the holder of the credit-token. In practice discount or commission is invariably deducted. If the holder is allowed to repay by instalments (as with Barclaycard or Access) he is getting substantial credit facilities. If on the other hand he is required to repay in full at the end of each period, the credit is merely nominal and the agreement is exempt from regulation by the Act (see page 14). In either case the Act says the credit is to be treated as drawn on whenever the third party supplies cash, goods or services to the holder.

The Act refers to 'production' of the card or other token. This may be for inspection and recording by the person providing the cash, goods or services. To a growing extent, however, the 'production' is to a machine which delivers cash, goods (such as petrol) or services (such as car parking) and automatically records particulars of the transaction for billing. The following types of credit-token are in common use:

(1) *Credit cards:* These are either of the two-party or three-party variety, as described above;

(2) *Trading checks*: These are issued by a check trader to his customers in return for a down-payment and a promise to pay a certain sum weekly until the face-value of the check (plus interest) is paid off. Meanwhile the holder, as soon as he likes, can use the check to obtain, from stores which have agreed to honour checks issued by that trader, goods to the full face-value;

(3) *Trading vouchers*: Similar to trading checks but usually for larger amounts, repayable over longer periods, and made out for purchase of a specified article at a specified shop;

(4) *Cash cards*: These may take the form either of a punched metal card for operating a cash dispenser or of a plastic card (incorporating a magnetic strip) for operating an automatic teller. Since it can be used even where there are no funds in the account, a cash card is a two-party credit-token unless issued on the express condition that it is not to be used to overdraw.

A question sometimes raised by retailers (eg furniture stores) is whether an invitation to take further credit issued to a customer who has proved himself creditworthy counts as a credit-token. It is a common practice for some stores to issue an object called a 'golden key to credit', or some such name, on production of which the customer is promised easy credit facilities. Is this a credit-token within the meaning of the Act? The answer depends on the facts. Such an object may be equivalent to the two-party credit card described above. On the other hand it may be little more than an advertising gimmick. The question turns on whether or not the arrangement amounts to an undertaking by the issuer (whether binding or not) to provide the consumer with financial accommodation. It is immaterial that the undertaking is conditional, or is not intended to be taken at its face value.

A further question concerns cheque cards. These are issued by clearing banks under schemes whereby the bank undertakes to honour cheques up to a specified amount where the payee has taken the cheque in reliance on the cheque card and in conformity with specified conditions. It is immaterial whether there are funds in the account sufficient to meet the cheque—it will be honoured even if there are not. The Act does not treat a cheque card as a form of credit-token since although it enables the customer to overdraw and thus effectively obtain credit it does not conform to the three-party credit-token definition. In making payment, the cheque card issuer is not reimbursing the third party but simply honouring the cheque.

The Act contemplates that whenever a credit-token is issued there will be an agreement (express or implied) between the issuer and the holder governing its use. Where the holder is an **individual** this will be a **consumer credit agreement** within the technical meaning laid down by the Act (see page 9). If this is a **regulated agreement** (ie neither an **exempt agreement** nor a **foreign agreement**) it will be what the Act calls a 'credit-token agreement'.

## (a) Prohibition of unsolicited credit-tokens

It is a criminal offence to issue a credit-token to any individual unless he has asked for it. This prohibition arose from the outcry caused when the Access card was launched by mass mailing. In the Crown Court an offender is liable to imprisonment for up to two years and/or a fine of any amount. In a magistrates' court the maximum penalty is a fine of £2,000. Except where the credit-token agreement is a debtor-creditor-supplier agreement which is a **bona fide small agreement** (ie for credit not exceeding £50) the request for a credit-token must be in writing signed by the person making it if it is to be effective in saving the issuer from the risk of conviction.

So as not to interfere with the ordinary working of a credit-token agreement, the Act provides an exception for a credit-token issued without prior request for use under an existing agreement (whether the first to be issued under the agreement, or one issued in replacement of a credit-token which has expired). It is not objectionable, in other words, to carry out an agreement the consumer has already entered into.

### (b)  Acceptance of credit-token

The debtor is not liable under a credit-token agreement for use made of the credit-token by any person unless either the debtor had previously *accepted* the credit-token or that use constitutes acceptance of it by him.

The acts that constitute 'acceptance' of a credit-token are any of the following:

(1) the signing of the credit-token by the debtor or a person authorised by him to use it (such as a member of his family); or

(2) the signing of a receipt for the credit-token by the debtor or such an authorised person; or

(3) first use of the credit-token by the debtor or such a person.

The onus is on the creditor to prove that acceptance has occurred. (As to liability for misuse of a credit-token see page 105 below.)

### (c)  Replacement credit-tokens

Whenever a credit-token (other than the first) is given to the debtor by the creditor, the creditor must also give the debtor a **prescribed copy** of the **executed agreement** (if any), together with a prescribed copy of any other document referred to in the executed agreement (other than an **excepted document**). Failure renders the agreement unenforceable while it continues. If it continues for one month the creditor commits an offence and is liable on summary conviction to a fine not exceeding £1,000.

## 18  Reopening extortionate credit bargains

A remarkable feature of the Consumer Credit Act is the sweeping power it gives the court to reopen a credit transaction (whether hire-purchase, cash loan or any other type of financial accommodation) on the ground that it is extortionate. It is important to note that, while the transaction must be with an **individual**, the £15,000 limit does not apply and no agreements are exempt. Credit transactions (other than **foreign agreements**) of any size, however large, may be reopened. Clearly this presents you with serious risks if you carry on a credit business, particularly since the Act places the onus of disproving extortion on you. All the customer has to do is assert that the transaction is extortionate. He will succeed unless you can satisfy the court that it is not.

### (a) What transactions are affected

We begin by explaining precisely what transactions are subject to these powers of the court. As always with this Act, the matter is complicated.

There are two types of case. The first, which is likely to be the most usual, is relatively straightforward. It is where the only relevant transaction is what the Act calls a 'personal credit agreement'. This is defined as any agreement between an **individual** (the debtor) and another person (the creditor) by which the **creditor** provides the **debtor** with **credit** of any amount. Note that where, as frequently happens, there are different contracts for the transaction financed and for the provision of credit it is only the latter that is subject to the court's powers.

**Example 25** Mr A, an antique dealer who is also a moneylender, persuades Mrs B to buy a carpet at the grossly inflated price of £1,000. By a separate contract he lends her £750 to help her pay for the carpet. Only the second contract is within the court's power to reopen extortionate credit transactions. In considering whether the terms of the loan are **extortionate** the court must in general disregard the fact that the price of the carpet is excessive. It would be otherwise if the carpet were sold on credit sale. Here there would be only one contract, all the terms of which would be relevant in considering the question of extortion. (See however the further discussion of this Example on pages 90 and 91.)

The second type of case is where the court is allowed to look at other transactions in addition to the **personal credit agreement** itself. We saw above (page 16) that, in determining for the purposes of the Act the amount and rate of the total charge for credit, certain additional items apart from interest may be brought in. These include payments made by the debtor or his relative under contracts required to be entered into as a condition of getting the credit. Whenever a payment of this kind arises, the transaction under which it is to be made (called by the Act a **linked transaction**) is open to the court's consideration.

> **Example 26** Before he will allow Mrs D to enter into a hire-purchase contract for the acquisition of a freezer, the salesman insists that her husband enter into a contract for the purchase of frozen food to stock it. The Act requires all payments which are to be made by Mr D under his contract to be included in the **total charge for credit** under Mrs D's hire-purchase agreement. Accordingly Mr D's contract must be considered by the court in deciding whether Mrs D has suffered extortion.

The Act uses the term 'credit bargain' as a collective description for the personal credit agreement together with any other transaction or transactions which the court must look at to see whether the creditor has been extortionate.

### (b) What 'extortionate' means

The Act contains elaborate provisions defining what it means by 'extortionate'. The term is a more up-to-date version of the expression 'harsh and unconscionable' used in the Moneylenders Acts (now repealed).

The definition of 'extortionate' lays down two alternatives. The credit bargain is to be treated as extortionate if it requires the debtor or a relative of his to make payments which are *grossly exorbitant* or if it otherwise grossly contravenes what the Act calls *ordinary principles of fair dealing*. This twofold classification makes it clear that it is not only the payments that are relevant, though clearly these will be of prime importance.

### Grossly exorbitant payments

The court must look at all the payments which the debtor or his relative have to make, whether under the personal credit agreement itself or any other transaction falling within the 'credit bargain'. This includes payments which only arise on a certain contingency, eg default. The court then has to consider whether any of these payments is grossly exorbitant in itself or, if that is not the case, whether the combined effect of the payments can fairly be accorded this description. The Oxford dictionary defines 'exorbitant' as 'exceeding ordinary or proper bounds'. In relation to pay, rates etc, it gives the meaning 'grossly excessive'. In using the term *grossly* exorbitant the Act indicates that the credit charges must be unusually stringent in order to entitle the debtor to relief. It does not reproduce the old Moneylenders Act provision under which interest in excess of a stated rate (48 per cent) was presumed excessive.

In considering whether payments to be made by the debtor are excessive it is relevant to consider the costs incurred by the creditor, and also any other receipts accruing to him. Some credit grantors suffer very high operating costs. Pawnbrokers, for example, incur heavy clerical expenses and storage charges for loans which are usually of small amount. A case where other receipts are to be taken into account is that of **credit-token** issuers. For example, check traders make their profit out of the discount they charge to retailers. In considering whether a check trader's charge to a customer is extortionate this other source of income must obviously be taken into account.

The length of the credit period is also a relevant consideration. The costs of entering into and concluding the transaction are the same whether it endures for a week or a year. The rate of interest must cover these, and the annual rate will be high if the loan is only for a week or two.

Another important aspect is that of **security**. In a nineteenth-century case a judge asked ironically: 'Suppose you were asked to lend a mutton chop to a ravenous dog, upon what terms would you lend it?' The Crowther Committee pointed out that money-lenders' loans are usually unsecured not because the moneylender is averse from taking security, but because those who come to him often have little property on which security could be taken. The moneylender is at the end of the credit line. He will consider any application, and his clients usually could not secure accommodation elsewhere. Legitimately, therefore, the rate of interest is high.

It is important to realise that the relevant payments are not limited to those which in ordinary commercial terms are charges for the credit provided. As we have seen, the credit bargain may include a transaction, such as the sale of frozen food to stock a freezer sold on credit, where the payments are made in return for value provided. How far should the court take account of this value?

> **Example 27** A television set with a cash price of £300 is sold on conditional sale. The ordinary credit charges, spread over a period of three years, total £150. During this period the customer is also required to insure the set for premiums totalling £80 and agree to quarterly maintenance visits at a cost of £10 per visit. The 'total charge for credit' (as defined by the Act) is therefore £350.

It seems that in this case the court should not proceed as if the entire £350 were made up of interest charges (which then might well be 'grossly exorbitant'). It should on the contrary make allowance for the fact that the customer receives the benefit of insurance cover and maintenance work. This leads to an important point. The court may often have to consider not merely whether the true charge for credit is disproportionate to the value of the service for which it is charged (ie the provision of credit) but also whether a charge for linked goods or services is disproportionate to their commercial value taken in themselves. So the court must not merely assess the true value of credit (as under the old Moneylenders Acts) but also the value of linked goods and services. From this it is a short step to saying that the court must evaluate goods or services forming the subject-matter of the personal credit agreement itself, such as the carpet disposed of on credit sale mentioned in Example 25 on page 87.

Grossly contravening ordinary principles of fair dealing

In considering this alternative head of extortion the court is primarily concerned with matters other than money payments. The test is vague, but the repeated use of 'grossly' indicates that as with financial aspects the unfair element must be pronounced. Unreasonable rights to forfeit security or demand the return of goods are examples of non-financial terms that may be held to offend.

In one respect this head goes wider than the financial head. Not only is it concerned with the actual terms of the personal credit agreement and any linked transaction falling within the 'credit bargain' but it brings in the circumstances in which the agreement was made as well. If in the loan transaction described in Example

25 Mrs B had been a feeble old lady whom Mr A had browbeaten into agreeing to buy a carpet at a grossly inflated price, that circumstance might have been considered relevant in deciding whether the loan contract amounted to unfair dealing. The point is not free from difficulty because on one view a loan fair in itself granted to finance an unfair sale by the lender should not be treated as tainted by the unfairness of the sale. One cannot be sure which line the courts will take on this point until cases come before them for decision. (Compare the case, discussed on pages 97 to 99, where the extortionate element in a credit bargain is loaded on to a linked transaction.)

While this second head of the definition of extortion is mainly concerned with non-financial aspects, payments are not ruled out altogether in applying it. It is quite possible that, while the payments to be made under a credit bargain are not 'grossly exorbitant' within the meaning of the first head of the definition, they are on the high side and if taken along with non-financial terms and the surrounding circumstances would render the transaction as a whole a gross departure from what ordinary fair-minded traders would think proper.

> **Example 28** A ring worth £200 is pawned for £50. The rate of interest is high, but not quite high enough to be classed as grossly exorbitant in itself. However, the pledge agreement provides for the ring to be forfeited to the pawnbroker if not redeemed within three months. The court might hold that the forfeiture term, taken together with the high interest rate, meant that the pledge agreement grossly contravened ordinary principles of fair dealing and was therefore 'extortionate'.

A forfeiture term of this kind in a pawnbroking agreement is in fact ineffective (see pages 64 to 65). Notwithstanding this, the court might hold its inclusion in the pledge agreement to constitute unfair dealing. Indeed to include in an agreement a term which the Act renders ineffective might be held unfair in itself, since it suggests an intention to evade the Act.

### (c) Evidence of extortion

The Act specifies certain types of evidence which the court must admit as relevant if put forward. The weight to be attached to the evidence is however a matter for the court, and evidence on other aspects is by no means excluded. The points specifically mentioned by the Act include the rather obvious one of the level of interest rates prevailing at the time the agreement was made. It is clear that to charge a certain rate for a particular agreement at a time when rates generally are low might be extortionate while it would not be extortionate at another time when rates were much higher. In relation to the debtor, the Act goes on to single out evidence on personal factors such as his age, experience, business capacity and state of health. It also mentions the degree to which, at the time of making the credit bargain, he was under financial pressure, and the nature of that pressure. His relationship to the creditor is regarded as relevant too. So is the question whether he was advised by a solicitor.

As regards the transaction itself, the Act specifies that evidence is to be admissible on the degree of risk it involves to the creditor, having regard to the value of any security provided. If an unrealistically high cash price was affixed to **goods** or services with the object of apparently reducing the credit charge that might be evidence of extortion. Finally, the Act specifies as relevant any evidence on whether, where a linked transaction was insisted on by the creditor, it was reasonably required for the protection of the debtor or creditor (eg an insurance policy) or was in the interest of the debtor (eg the purchase of goods for use with equipment bought on credit).

The Act specifies these various factors in a neutral way. In other words they could tend in either direction. The debtor's age, for example, may point in the direction of extortion if it is low or high but away from extortion if he is in the prime of life. What is interesting about the listing of these factors is that it shows the test of extortion to be subjective. An agreement freely entered into by a debtor who is an experienced and competent middle-aged businessman in good health and free from financial pressure might be held not to be extortionate, while the opposite ruling would be given about the same terms when agreed to by an ailing elderly lady in acute financial straits.

The point about the references to financial pressure and the relationship of the debtor to the creditor is that these factors may indicate that the debtor was not entirely free when he made the decision to enter into the transaction. It was said in an old case that 'necessitous men are not, truly speaking, free men'. The law seeks to prevent people in desperate need of money from being taken advantage of. Under the old law this led to relief being given in cases such as the following:

the drawer of a bill of exchange which he cannot meet borrows from a moneylender to avoid disgrace;

an impecunious tenant whose lease is about to expire, fearing eviction, buys the freehold on harsh mortgage terms;

a stockbroker borrows to avoid being 'hammered' on the Stock Exchange;

a debtor threatened with bankruptcy and consequent loss of his employment borrows to avoid this.

Similarly, the debtor's freedom may be restricted if he has a relationship with the moneylender which puts the latter in a stronger position. Examples are a parent and his child, a husband and his wife, a solicitor and his client and a doctor and his patient.

The test of extortion is to be applied in the light of conditions prevailing at the time the credit bargain was made. This includes the knowledge then available to the creditor and the way the risks and prospects appeared to him at that time. Hindsight has no place here. It follows that there is no question of an agreement not extortionate at the time it was made being subsequently treated as extortionate because of events occurring later. The opposite is also true: an extortionate agreement cannot cease to be such. (Both these statements assume of course that the agreement is not subsequently modified by a further contract.)

While the Act gives considerable help in deciding whether a particular credit bargain is extortionate, much is left to the discretion of the court. This means that if your customer alleges extortion you may have difficulty in deciding what view a court is likely to take. A useful rule of thumb was provided by Lord Chancellor Thurlow in the eighteenth-century case of *Gwynne* v *Heaton*. It is still apt today. If the bargain is such as to cause a man of common sense to make an exclamation at the inequality of it, the court will interfere. Otherwise not.

## (d) First cases under Act

During the first ten years the provisions were in force, many attempts were made by debtors to have their credit bargains declared 'extortionate'. They had little success. Out of nine cases on the topic included in the Consumer Credit Law Reports (published as part of the present author's four-volume work *Consumer Credit Control*), only one (*Barcabe Ltd* v *Edwards* [1983] CCLR 11) includes a finding that the bargain in question was grossly exorbitant, or otherwise grossly contravened the principles of fair dealing.

*(e) Who can get relief*

The only persons who can be given relief against an extortionate credit bargain are the debtor himself and any **surety**. Even where a relative of the debtor is a party to a **linked transaction** comprised in the credit bargain, the relative cannot get relief himself. This applies although the transaction with the relative is the only extortionate part of the credit bargain (but see pages 97 to 99 in relation to cases where the extortionate element is loaded on to a linked transaction).

*(f) Against whom relief can be ordered*

The only person against whom an order for relief can be made is the creditor. Where another person (eg an associated company of the creditor) is a party to a linked transaction comprised in the credit bargain, no relief can be ordered against that other person. However, the Act specifically provides that where another person has unfairly enjoyed an advantage under such a linked transaction, the creditor may be ordered to make restitution. This applies even where there is no connection between the two parties and the creditor has received no benefit from the linked transaction. Such a case is unlikely to arise in practice. The only reason why a creditor would think it necessary to insist on entry into another transaction with an unconnected supplier is where this is required to safeguard the value of property treated as security (eg goods subject to a hire-purchase agreement). The legislation provides however that freely-negotiated maintenance or insurance agreements are not to be treated as falling within the credit bargain.

*(g) Proceedings in which relief can be sought*

The debtor or surety seeking relief against extortion can either make a special application to the court for that purpose or raise the matter in other proceedings (eg where he is being sued by the creditor). A special application must be made to the county court if the personal credit agreement is a **regulated agreement** for credit of any amount or an **exempt agreement** for credit not exceeding £5,000. In other cases the special application must be made to the High Court. (In Scotland any application may be made either to the sheriff court or the Court of Session.)

Where the debtor or surety does not make a special application he can raise the question of extortion in the course of any proceedings brought to enforce the personal credit agreement, any security related to it, or any linked transaction. Furthermore he can raise it in any other legal proceedings where the amount paid or payable under the personal credit agreement is relevant. This would include bankruptcy proceedings. If, following the making of a receiving order, the debtor's trustee in bankruptcy considers that the creditor's debt proved in the bankruptcy is extortionate the trustee may ask for the debt to be reopened by the court.

The court can never reopen an agreement on its own initiative; it has to be done on an application by the debtor or surety (or someone, such as a personal representative, who stands in his shoes). The court may however suggest to a debtor or surety, particularly where he is not legally represented, that it would be opportune to ask for the agreement to be reopened.

## (h) Conditions for obtaining relief

Four conditions must be satisfied if the debtor or surety is to obtain relief: the credit bargain must be extortionate; the court must consider it just to give relief; the remedy must not be barred by lapse of time; and the relief must not involve reopening a previous court order.

As we have seen, once the debtor or surety raises the allegation of extortion the onus is on the creditor to satisfy the court that the credit bargain is not extortionate. What this means is that if at the end of the case the court is uncertain it must decide against the creditor. This reverses the normal rule that if the balance of probabilities is even the plaintiff loses.

Even if the court finds that the credit bargain is extortionate, it will not give relief unless it is just to do so. The creditor might be in such financial straits himself that an order against him would be oppressive or futile. Or he may have already made restitution in some other way, eg by granting favourable terms in another transaction. Or the debtor may have been dishonest in the information he gave to obtain the credit, or dilatory in pursuing his remedy. In *Ketley* v *Scott* [1980] CCLR 37, Foster J held that, even if the credit bargain in question had been extortionate, it would not have been just to grant relief because the defendant had acted deceitfully.

Relief will be positively barred by lapse of time if the period laid down by the Limitation Act is exceeded. Usually this period is six years. The period starts to run on the date a claim for the relief in question could first have been made.

*(i)  Nature of relief for debtor*

The object of the court, having found that the credit bargain is extortionate, must be to make what order is necessary 'for the purpose of relieving the debtor from payment of any sum in excess of that fairly due and reasonable'. This is somewhat narrow, in view of the fact that, as we have seen, the definition of extortion brings in factors other than monetary payments and also requires attention to be given to agreements (if any) to which the debtor's relative rather than the debtor himself is a party. However, the Act is clear. Whatever may be considered in deciding whether extortion is present, only relief of the debtor himself from payment of money is relevant in deciding what form relief should take. This presents certain problems, as will appear.

Various types of order may be made. To establish the exact financial position where this is not clear, the court may order accounts to be drawn up. It may set aside (that is, pronounce void) any obligation imposed on the debtor by the credit bargain *or any related agreement.* The latter phrase brings in contracts not forming part of the credit bargain, and thus goes very wide. The court may require the creditor to repay the whole or part of any sum paid under the credit bargain or any related agreement by the debtor (but not by his relative). This applies even where the sum was paid under a linked transaction to a person having no connection with the creditor. Finally, the court may alter the terms of the personal credit agreement (but not any linked transaction).

It is stressed that these powers, all or any of which may be exercised in a particular case, are solely for the purpose of relieving the debtor from payments in excess of what is fairly due and reasonable. This is not intended however to limit relief to sums currently owing under the agreement. Where a sum has already been paid by the debtor the question is what amount was 'fairly due and reasonable' at the time of payment.

**Example 29** M Ltd lend Mr B £10,000 on the basis that he will repay £15,000 in twelve months' time. He does so, but later claims repayment of part of this sum on the ground that the agreement was extortionate. The court finds that a fair and reasonable repayment would have been £12,000, but this does not necessarily mean that the agreement was extortionate. That question is to be decided by asking whether the charge of £5,000 over twelve months is 'grossly exorbitant'. If, but only if, the court finds that it is, the court will order repayment of the excess over what was fairly due and reasonable, ie a repayment of £3,000.

Note that even though a non-monetary term may be 'extortionate' the court cannot give relief for it. Thus the court's power to vary the personal credit agreement would not authorise it to strike out the forfeiture term in Example 28. The power is reserved for alteration of monetary terms, so far as concerns their future operation.

**Example 30** A loan agreement provides for interest at 90 per cent per annum. The agreement is determinable by one month's notice on either side. After interest of £300 has been paid, the court finds that the agreement is extortionate and that a fair and reasonable rate of interest would be 30 per cent. It makes an order that the creditor repay £200 and that for the remainder of its currency the terms of the agreement be altered by substituting 30 per cent for 90 per cent. To safeguard the debtor from financial embarrassment the court might wish to alter the termination provision by requiring the creditor to give, say, six months' notice of termination instead of one but it appears that its powers do not extend that far.

## (j) Loading the linked transaction

Problems may arise where the extortionate elements in a credit bargain are loaded on to one or more **linked transactions**, leaving the personal credit agreement itself free of unfair features. We take first the simplest case, where there is one linked transaction only and it is made with the debtor himself (rather than his relative).

**Example 31** As a condition of making an agreement with Mr A for a loan of £1,000 at 20 per cent per annum, C Ltd require him to buy certain furniture for cash at a price of £500. The whole transaction is embodied in a single contract. The court finds that, while the rate of interest on the loan is fair, the furniture is worth only £200. For this reason it holds the credit bargain to be extortionate.

What order can the court make? First we need to note that the contract is what the Act calls a **multiple agreement**. Although in fact it is one contract, the Act requires it to be treated as two. First, there is a personal credit agreement for the loan of £1,000 to Mr A at 20 per cent interest. Second, there is a cash sale of furniture for £500. The latter is a linked transaction forming part of the credit bargain. If the court is considering the matter while the contract is still executory (not yet performed), its powers are limited to two remedies. It can set aside the whole or part of any obligation imposed on Mr A and/or alter the terms of the personal credit agreement. Since the terms of the personal credit agreement are fair, the court will limit itself to setting aside part of the obligation to pay for the furniture. If the court holds that the amount fairly due and reasonable for the furniture is £200 it will set aside the obligation to pay the remaining £300. If on the other hand the full price of £500 has already been paid the court will order the return of £300.

The case could be dealt with similarly where there were two or more linked transactions entered into by the debtor. We see that loading the extortionate element on to linked transactions does not avail the creditor if they are entered into by the debtor himself. Nor will it help if associated companies are brought into the picture. Suppose that in Example 31 the furniture was to be bought not from the creditor, C Ltd, but from C Ltd's associated company, D Ltd (thus keeping the profit in the group). Although D Ltd cannot be made a party to the court proceedings, and no order can be made against it, the Act enables the same result to be achieved by the making of an order against C Ltd, the creditor. As we have seen, the Act expressly states that a repayment (or similar) order may be made notwithstanding that its effect is to place a burden on the creditor in respect of an advantage unfairly enjoyed by another person who is a party to a linked transaction.

So far so good. The position becomes more obscure however where the linked transaction is made not with the debtor but his *relative*. Suppose that in Example 31 the contract required the over-priced furniture to be bought not by the debtor, Mr A, but by his wife, Mrs A. The Act confers no power to make an order in favour of Mrs A. The only purpose of an order must be to relieve *the debtor* from payment of any sum in excess of that fairly due and reasonable. The debtor here is Mr A. His liability is confined to payment of loan interest at 20 per cent, which is reasonable. Or is it? Here we come to the nub of a question which may prove to be of considerable practical importance in the working of the Act. For if moneylenders and other creditors can evade the risk of having extortionate agreements reopened by insisting on linked transactions with relatives and loading the extortionate element on to them, a serious inroad will have been made in the protection intended by the Act. The answer cannot be known for sure until authoritative rulings have been given by the courts. Meanwhile, the following is put forward.

There is a strong argument for saying that, in considering whether the terms of the debtor's agreement are fair, the terms of the linked transaction which he has been required to persuade his relative to enter into must also be considered. In Example 31 loan interest of 20 per cent might well be fair if no other agreement were involved. But that is not the position. The creditor has insisted on the making of an additional agreement as well. It accords with the true intention of the Act to hold that, in considering what sum is fairly due and reasonable from the debtor, the court should allow for the fact that his wife is being over-charged by £300 and deduct that sum, or something approaching it. This could be done by adjusting the loan interest payable or even by reducing the capital sum due on repayment of the loan. There seems no reason why, if the court thinks it necessary, it should not also include in its order a term amending the personal credit agreement by inserting a requirement that the debtor pay over the amount in question to the relative who has actually suffered the loss. In that way justice would be fully secured.

## (k) Relief for sureties

In addition to providing the relief for debtors just outlined, the Act also provides parallel relief for guarantors and other sureties. It would be little use giving power to reopen extortionate agreements if grasping creditors could protect themselves against this by taking security for the full amount required by the agreement to be paid.

The Act contains a general provision preventing a security from being enforced so as to benefit the creditor more than would be the case if the security were not provided and the obligations of the debtor were carried out only to the extent to which they would be enforced by the court, having regard to the safeguards in the Act. This general provision only applies to **regulated agreements**, but as we have seen the power to reopen extortionate agreements applies to any credit transaction with an individual, regardless of whether it is embodied in a regulated agreement. The protection for sureties of extortionate agreements goes equally wide, and follows exactly the same lines.

We take first the case where the debtor himself applies for relief against extortion and is successful. If the security has not previously been enforced, it will have effect in future only in respect of the reduced obligations of the debtor. The surety need not therefore join in the court proceedings to gain protection. If however the security has previously been enforced, so that the surety requires direct relief, he will need to join in the proceedings. Alternatively, the debtor may have taken no action. If the surety wishes to assert that the credit bargain for which he has provided security is extortionate, and to reduce his obligation accordingly, he can himself apply to the court. He can do so in exactly the same way as the debtor could, and the court can make similar orders in his favour. In addition, the court has power to direct the return to the surety of any property provided for the purposes of the security (such as an article pledged).

Note that surety relief is available to any person who has given security in relation to the credit bargain, whether to secure the carrying out by the debtor of his obligations under the credit agreement itself or to secure the carrying out by the debtor or his relative of obligations under a linked transaction.

### 19  Varying a credit agreement

The Act contains special provisions to deal with problems that may arise when the terms of a **credit agreement** are altered after the agreement has been entered into. It deals differently with the case where the alteration is effected under a provision included in the agreement and the case where it is effected by the making of a further agreement.

*(a) Variation of regulated agreement under power contained in agreement*

Agreements frequently include a power, exercisable by one party or both, to vary one of the terms of the agreement. For example a loan agreement may entitle the **creditor** to alter the rate of interest, or a **hire agreement** for a fixed period may give the hirer the right to extend the period. In relation to credit businesses, the only specific provision in the Act deals with the case where the creditor has a right of variation. No comparable provision is made for rights of variation by the debtor. The Act prevents a variation by the creditor from taking effect until the lapse of seven days after a notice in writing describing it has been given to the debtor.

**Example 32** A regulated loan agreement made by L Ltd and Mr B contains the following terms:
'15. The rate of interest under this agreement shall be 20 per cent.
16. L Ltd may at any time determine to alter the rate of interest current under this agreement.'
On 30 April L Ltd determine to increase the rate to 25 per cent with immediate effect. They do not inform Mr B until 15 June, when a written notice is served on him specifying the increase and stating that it operates from 1 May. In fact, because of the Act, the increase does not operate until seven days have elapsed following service of the notice, ie it operates as from 23 June.

There is doubt about whether the seven-day rule goes wider than is stated above and covers every case where a rate of interest or other term is capable of change. Many agreements link the rate of interest to a general index such as Bank of England base rate or a creditor bank's base rate. In the former case it seems clear that when the rate payable changes this is not because of any alteration of a term of the agreement. On the contrary, the rate changes because a term of the agreement is operating in accordance with its original wording. Where however the creditor changes the rate, even though he does so generally and not by reference to that particular agreement, the position is less clear. The official view seems to be that such a change does come within the seven-day rule. Indeed, largely for this reason an alternative notice procedure is provided for current-account overdrafts. Instead of serving individual notices on borrowers, it suffices if notice of a variation of the rate of interest is published in at least three daily newspapers and posted up in the bank's premises. The notice is effective immediately, and the creditor need not wait seven days.

Although the seven-day notice rule (with the variant just mentioned) is the only specific provision in the Act dealing with alteration of a regulated agreement under a power contained in the agreement, it is possible, under the general provisions of the

Act, for the use of such a power to alter the category into which an agreement falls.

> **Example 33** A bank makes an overdraft agreement with Mr D under which the credit limit is £20,000. The agreement contains a power enabling the bank to reduce the limit to any figure it wishes on giving one month's notice. On 30 September the bank gives Mr D notice that as from 1 November the limit will be £5,000. The original agreement is not a **consumer credit agreement** (and therefore not a **regulated agreement**) because the credit limit exceeds £15,000. As from 1 November, however, the agreement becomes a regulated consumer credit agreement.

## (b)  Effect of a modifying agreement

We now pass to the second of the two types of case mentioned at the beginning of this section. A *new agreement* is made by which the earlier agreement is modified or added to. The Act calls this a **modifying agreement**, and lays down special rules governing its effect.

The main rule is that for the purposes of the Act the modifying agreement is to be treated as revoking the earlier agreement and substituting provisions reproducing the combined effect of the two agreements. This is best understood in a schematic way. Suppose the original agreement (made on 1 February) contained five terms, which we will call terms A, B, C, D and E. Later (on 1 August), a new agreement is made by the same parties. It varies the earlier agreement by substituting a new term (let us call it term X) for term D. Furthermore it supplements the earlier agreement by adding two more terms (call them terms Y and Z). The result of the rule laid down by the Act is that the old agreement disappears on 1 August. The parties are deemed to have made on that date a new agreement consisting of terms A, B, C, E, X, Y and Z. Obligations outstanding on 31 July in relation to the old agreement are from 1 August to be treated as outstanding instead in relation to the notional new agreement (unless of course they have been terminated by the modifying agreement).

One consequence of this rule may be to turn an agreement which is not a regulated agreement (because it was made before the commencement date of 1 April 1977) into a regulated agreement (because the modifying agreement is made after that date). As with the first type of case, alteration of the terms may also move the old agreement into a different category for the purposes of the Act.

**Example 34** On 1 January M Ltd enter into a moneylending agreement with Mr D at a rate of interest of 60 per cent. Later Mr D alleges that this rate is extortionate, whereupon M Ltd enter into a further agreement with him by which the rate of interest is reduced as from 1 July to 40 per cent. Later still, claiming that the reduced rate is still extortionate, Mr D applies for relief to the court. The court finds that while 60 per cent was extortionate 40 per cent is not. The court makes an order giving relief in respect of the period from 1 January to 30 June. It can give no relief in respect of what is to be treated as an entirely separate credit agreement beginning on 1 July.

There are many other possible ways in which a later modification may move an agreement from one category to another. This is obvious, since the Act will bite on the later agreement according to its revised terms, regardless of what its original terms were. This is subject to one exception however. If the earlier agreement is a **regulated agreement** and the revised agreement is for **fixed-sum credit**, then the revised agreement is treated as regulated also even though it does not satisfy the normal requirements of a regulated agreement.

**Example 35** On 1 January 1988 a finance house F makes a three-year hire-purchase agreement with a sole trader, Mr T, for equipment priced at £14,000 with a down-payment of £1,000. The credit (amounting to £13,000) is within the £15,000 limit so the agreement is a regulated agreement. On 1 January 1990, when £1,000 of the original cash price is still outstanding, F and T agree on an 'add-to' arrangement under which further equipment is provided on the basis that an additional £14,500 (plus interest) becomes payable in instalments by T. The Act treats the old agreement as revoked and assumes a new agreement to have been made on 1 January 1990 for credit totalling £15,500. Although this exceeds the £15,000 limit, the new agreement is a regulated agreement simply because the old one was.

The Act imposes this rule because it is considered that the

protection afforded to the customer by making his agreement a regulated agreement should not be withdrawn just when he is entering into deeper commitments and may need it even more. The rule does not apply to the other type of **credit agreement**, the **running-account** agreement. Here it is not the amount of credit taken, but the amount available (the credit limit) which governs whether or not it is within the £15,000 limit. The position is a fluctuating one, since there will normally be credits to the account, as well as drawings on it. The Act is therefore content to let the question of regulation depend solely on the current credit limit.

## 20 Restrictions on enforcement of agreement by creditor

The Act places certain restrictions on your right as creditor to enforce the contractual terms of a credit agreement. These are in addition to the Act's restrictions in relation to termination of the agreement, which are dealt with separately (see section 21 of this chapter, beginning on page 108).

### (a) Notice requirement

In certain cases, seven days' written notice is required before action under the agreement can be taken by the creditor. If this notice is not duly given, the action will be unlawful. (The provisions about to be explained do not apply in case of default, which is dealt with separately later in this section.)

*Cases where requirement applies*    The notice requirement applies to any **regulated agreement** (other than a **non-commercial agreement** in relation to which no **security** was provided), but only where the agreement specifies a period for its duration and that period is not yet ended. The requirement applies whether or not any party is entitled to terminate the agreement before the end of the specified period.

*Acts to which requirement applies*    The notice requirement applies where the creditor intends to do any of the following, except by reason of a breach of the agreement:

(1) demand earlier payment of any sum; or
(2) recover possession of any **goods** or **land**; or
(3) treat any right conferred on the debtor by the agreement as terminated, restricted or deferred.

However, the requirement does not prevent the creditor from treating the right to draw on any credit (for example a bank overdraft) as restricted or deferred, and taking such steps as may be necessary to make the restriction or deferment effective.

*What the notice must say*    To be effective, the written notice must say that it is served under s 76(1) of the Consumer Credit Act 1974, and must contain prescribed information and advice as set out in Sched 1 to the Consumer Credit (Enforcement, Default and Termination Notices) Regulations 1983.

*Misuse of credit facilities otherwise than by debtor*    The Act restricts the ability of creditors to insist on the insertion of a contractual term (whether in the credit agreement or otherwise) which would render the debtor liable for misuse of the credit facility by other persons.

*General restriction*    In the case of a **regulated agreement** which is a **consumer credit agreement** other than a **non-commercial agreement**, the creditor cannot effectively impose on the debtor liability for loss arising from use of the credit facility by another person who is not acting (or to be treated in law as acting) as the debtor's agent. The restriction does not apply to loss arising from misuse of a cheque.

*Exception for credit-tokens*    In the case of a **credit-token agreement** the restriction just set out is slightly relaxed, provided the agreement contains, prominently and so as to be easily legible, the name, address, and telephone number of a **person** stated to be the person to whom notice is to be given under s 84(3) of the Consumer Credit Act 1974.

The relaxation enables the agreement to make the debtor liable, but only to the extent of £50 (or the **credit limit** if lower), for loss to the creditor arising from use of the credit-token while it is in the possession of a thief or other unauthorised person.

A further relaxation enables the agreement to make the debtor *fully* liable for misuse of the credit-token by a person who acquired possession of it with the debtor's consent. However, this only applies in respect of the period before notice that the credit-token is liable to misuse is received by the person whose name, address, and telephone number is given, as stated above, in the agreement. (The agreement may state that notice given by telephone lapses unless confirmed in writing within seven days.)

*(b) Default by debtor*

The giving of a default notice in writing is usually necessary before action can be taken by the creditor in the case of default by the debtor. If this notice is not duly given, the action will be unlawful. (The provisions about to be explained do not apply to *termination* of an agreement on grounds of default, which is dealt with separately in section 21 of this chapter, beginning on page 111.)

*Cases where requirement applies*	The default notice requirement applies to any **regulated agreement** (other than a **noncommercial agreement** in relation to which no **security** was provided).

*Acts to which requirement applies*	The default notice requirement applies where the creditor intends to do any of the following (a 'restricted act') by reason of a breach of the agreement:

(1) demand earlier payment of any sum; or

(2) recover possession of any **goods** or **land**; or

(3) treat any right conferred on the debtor by the agreement as terminated, restricted or deferred; or

(4) enforce any **security** (not including doing any act whereby a floating charge becomes fixed).

However, the requirement does not prevent the creditor from treating the right to draw on any credit (for example a bank overdraft) as restricted or deferred, and taking such steps as may be necessary to make the restriction or deferment effective.

*What the default notice must say*	To be effective, the written default notice must say that it is served under s 87(1) of the Consumer Credit Act 1974, and must contain prescribed information and advice as set out in Sched 2 to the Consumer Credit (Enforcement, Default and Termination Notices) Regulations 1983 as amended.

*Where breach capable of remedy*	Where, in the case of a breach capable of remedy, the default notice specified what action was required to remedy it, and the date before which that action was to be taken, a restricted act must not be done by the creditor before that date. (If the necessary remedial action was taken in time, the default is treated as not having occurred.) Where no such date was specified in the default notice, the restricted act must not be done by the creditor until seven days have elapsed from the giving of the default notice.

*Where breach not capable of remedy*	Where, in the case of a breach not capable of remedy, the default notice specified the sum required to be paid as compensation for the breach, and the date before which it was to be paid, a restricted act must not be done by the creditor before that date. (If the required sum was paid in time, the default is treated as not having occurred.) Where no such date was specified in the default notice, the restricted act must not be done by the creditor until seven days have elapsed from the giving of the default notice.

*Default provisions in credit agreement*     The Act makes special provision as regards any term in the credit agreement which specifically relates to default (for example a penalty clause). Failure to comply with such a default provision is not in itself to be treated by the default notice as a breach of the agreement, but once the time restrictions relating to the default notice have expired the creditor is free to enforce the default provision as well as doing any restricted act.

*Recovery of goods by creditor*     The Act gives protection to goods held under a regulated agreement which is either a **hire-purchase agreement** or a **conditional sale agreement**, provided the debtor has paid at least one-third of the amount of the total price (including in that amount any sum payable on the exercise of an option to purchase). Such protected goods can be recovered by the creditor only on an order of the County Court. Even where less than one-third of the total price has been paid, the creditor is precluded from entering on any premises to retake the goods without a County Court order (unless of course the occupier consents).

*Increase of interest on default*     Where any sum due under a regulated agreement is owing by the debtor, the creditor is precluded from charging increased interest on that sum because of the default, even though the agreement provides for this.

## (c) Death of debtor

The Act places certain restrictions on what the creditor may do because of the death of the debtor under a regulated agreement. (The provisions about to be explained do not apply to *termination* of an agreement on the debtor's death, which is dealt with separately in section 21 of this chapter, beginning on page 112.)

*Acts to which restrictions apply*     The restrictions apply where the creditor wishes to do any of the following (a 'restricted act') by reason of the debtor's death:

(1) demand earlier payment of any sum; or
(2) recover possession of any goods or land; or
(3) treat any right conferred on the debtor by the agreement as terminated, restricted or deferred; or
(4) enforce any **security** (not including doing any act whereby a floating charge becomes fixed).

However, the restrictions do not prevent the creditor from treating the right to draw on any credit (for example a bank overdraft) as restricted or deferred, and taking such steps as may be necessary to make the restriction or deferment effective. Nor do they affect any provisions concerning the payment of sums due under the agreement out of the proceeds of a policy of assurance on the debtor's life.

*The restrictions* The restrictions depend on whether the credit agreement is fully secured. If it is, then the creditor is not entitled to do any restricted act by reason of the death. (An act is treated as being done by reason of the death if it is done under a power conferred by the agreement which is either

(a) exercisable on the debtor's death, or
(b) exercisable at will and exercised at any time after the debtor's death.)

If the credit agreement is *not* fully secured, then a County Court order is required before a restricted act can be done by reason of the death. To obtain such an order the creditor must prove that he has been unable to satisfy himself that the deceased debtor's obligations are likely to be discharged.

## 21 Termination of credit agreements

The Act contains various provisions regarding the termination of **consumer credit agreements** which are **regulated agreements**.

### (a) Early settlement by debtor

Despite any term to the contrary in the agreement, the debtor is entitled at any time to discharge his indebtedness under the agreement without waiting for the agreed date (if any). When doing so, he may be entitled to a rebate of credit charges to allow for the fact that the creditor will be out of his money for a shorter period than contemplated. This rebate is normally calculated according to the so-called 'rule of 78', details of which are given in the Consumer Credit (Rebate on Early Settlement) Regulations 1983.

In order to exercise this right of early settlement, the debtor must send written notice of his intention to the creditor and pay him all amounts payable under the agreement (whether due or not), less any rebate allowable. The notice may embody the exercise of any option to purchase, and deal with any other matter arising in relation to the termination of the agreement.

*Settlement information*     To help the debtor exercise his right of early settlement, the creditor is under a duty, if sent a request in writing, to give the debtor the information he needs. This must be supplied within twelve **working days** after the request is received. Failure to observe this requirement renders the agreement unenforceable by the creditor while the default continues. If it continues for one month, the creditor commits an offence and is liable on summary conviction to a fine not exceeding £400.

The information is to be given by reference to a 'settlement date'. This may be named by the debtor in his request, but he must not name a date earlier than the one that will apply if he does not choose to name a date, that is the date of the next instalment due after twenty-eight days elapse from the receipt of the request by the creditor.

The information must be given in writing, and must include the amount needed to discharge the indebtedness, the amount of any rebate allowable, and the settlement date by reference to which the rebate is calculated. The full details are given in the Schedule to the Consumer Credit (Settlement Information) Regulations 1983.

*Linked transactions*     Where the debtor takes advantage of the provisions permitting early settlement, he, and any relative of his, are at the same time released from any liability (other than a debt which has already become payable) under a **linked transaction**, not being an **excepted linked transaction** or one itself providing credit.

### (b)  Termination of agreement by debtor

Early settlement accelerates the carrying out of the credit agreement, bringing it to a natural conclusion sooner. At the other extreme is a calling-off of the agreement, in effect altogether preventing its being fulfilled. The debtor has the right to do this only in relation to a **hire-purchase agreement** or a **conditional sale agreement**. (Cf rights of cancellation, described in section 15 of this chapter, page 75 above.)

This right of termination is exercised by giving notice in writing to any person entitled or authorised to receive payments under the agreement. There is no restriction on the exercise of this right in the case of hire-purchase agreements, but the nature of conditional sale agreements led to certain restrictions being imposed in their case. Where they relate to land, the right cannot be exercised once title has passed to the debtor. Where they relate to goods and the property in the goods has passed to the debtor, the right cannot be exercised if the debtor has transferred the property to some other person.

*Liabilities of debtor*    If he terminates a hire-purchase or conditional sale agreement, the debtor naturally has obligations. He must, if the agreement so provides, pay the creditor the 'outstanding amount', which is calculated in a certain way (see below). If in any court action the court is satisfied that a smaller sum would meet the creditor's loss, it may order that the smaller sum shall be payable instead. Where the debtor wrongfully retains the goods after terminating, the court may order him to hand them over without receiving any allowance for what he has paid.

*The 'outstanding amount'*    To arrive at the 'outstanding amount' it is first necessary to work out the 'payable sum'. This is normally one-half the total price. If the total price includes any installation charge, the whole of this is included along with one-half of the remainder of the total price. If the debtor has contravened an obligation to take reasonable care of goods or land to which the agreement relates, the 'payable sum' is increased by the amount required to compensate for this.

From the 'payable sum' there is deducted what the debtor has already paid under the agreement, together with any overdue instalments. The remainder represents the amount payable by the debtor on termination, or 'oustanding amount'.

## (c) Termination by creditor (ordinary cases)

Seven days' written notice is usually required before an agreement can be effectively terminated by the creditor. However, this restriction does not prevent the creditor from treating the right to draw on any credit (for example a bank overdraft) as restricted or deferred, and taking such steps as may be necessary to make the restriction or deferment effective. (The provisions about to be explained do not apply in case of default, which is dealt with separately later in this section.)

*Cases where requirement applies*    The notice requirement applies to any **regulated agreement** (other than a **non-commercial agreement** in relation to which no security was provided), but only where the agreement specifies a period for its duration and that period is not yet ended. The requirement applies whether or not any party is entitled to terminate the agreement before the end of the specified period.

*What the notice must say*        To be effective, the written notice must say that it is served under s 98(1) of the Consumer Credit Act 1974, and must contain prescribed information and advice as set out in Sched 3 to the Consumer Credit (Enforcement, Default and Termination Notices) Regulations 1983.

### (d)  Termination by creditor (default cases)

The giving of a default notice in writing is usually necessary before an agreement can be terminated on the ground of default by the debtor. However, this requirement does not prevent the creditor from treating the right to draw on any credit (for example a bank overdraft) as restricted or deferred, and taking such steps as may be necessary to make the restriction or deferment effective.

*Cases where requirement applies*        The default notice requirement applies to any **regulated agreement** (other than a **noncommercial agreement** in relation to which no **security** was provided).

*What the default notice must say*        To be effective, the written default notice must say that it is served under s 87(1) of the Consumer Credit Act 1974, and must contain prescribed information and advice as set out in Sched 2 to the Consumer Credit (Enforcement, Default and Termination Notices) Regulations 1983 as amended.

*Where breach capable of remedy*        Where, in the case of a breach capable of remedy, the default notice specified what action was required to remedy it, and the date before which that action was to be taken, the agreement must not be terminated by the creditor before that date. (If the necessary remedial action was taken in time, the default is treated as not having occurred.) Where no such date was specified in the default notice, the agreement must not be terminated by the creditor until seven days have elapsed from the giving of the default notice.

*Where breach not capable of remedy*        Where, in the case of a breach not capable of remedy, the default notice specified the sum required to be paid as compensation for the breach, and the date before which it was to be paid, the agreement must not be terminated by the creditor before that date. (If the required sum was paid in time, the default is treated as not having occurred.) Where no such date was specified in the default notice, the agreement must not be terminated by the creditor until seven days have elapsed from the giving of the default notice.

*Default provisions in credit agreement*     The Act makes special provision as regards any term in the credit agreement which specifically relates to default (for example a penalty clause). Failure to comply with such a default provision is not in itself to be treated by the default notice as a breach of the agreement, but once the time restrictions relating to the default notice have expired the creditor is free to enforce the default provision as well as treating the agreement as terminated.

## (e) Termination by creditor (death of debtor)

The Act places certain restrictions on what the creditor may do because of the death of the debtor under a regulated agreement. Among these is one relating to the termination of the agreement by reason of the death.

*Cases where restriction applies*     The restriction applies to any **regulated agreement** (other than a **non-commercial agreement** in relation to which no **security** was provided), but only where the agreement specifies a period for its duration and that period is not yet ended. The restriction applies whether or not any party is entitled to terminate the agreement before the end of the specified period.

*The restriction*     The nature of the restriction depends on whether the credit agreement is fully secured. If it is, then the creditor is not entitled to terminate the agreement by reason of the death. (An act is treated as being done by reason of the death if it is done under a power conferred by the agreement which is either:

    (a) exercisable on the debtor's death; or
    (b) exercisable at will and exercised at any time after the debtor's death.)

If the credit agreement is *not* fully secured, then a County Court order is required before the agreement can be terminated by the creditor by reason of the death. To obtain such an order the creditor must prove that he has been unable to satisfy himself that the deceased debtor's obligations are likely to be discharged.

## (f) Termination notices

The Act gives debtors the right to obtain from the creditor written confirmation that a credit agreement (other than a non-commercial agreement) has come to an end.

To exercise this right, the debtor must give the creditor a notice in writing stating that:

(1) he was the debtor under a regulated agreement described in the notice, and the other party was the creditor under the agreement; and

(2) he has discharged his indebtedness to the creditor under the agreement; and

(3) the agreement has ceased to have any operation,

and requiring the creditor to give him a signed notice confirming that those statements are correct.

Within twelve **working days** after receiving the notice, the creditor must either comply with it or serve a counter-notice. This must either say that the creditor disputes the correctness of the debtor's notice (stating what is wrong with it) or say that the debtor is not indebted to him under the agreement. If the creditor complies with the debtor's notice or states that the debtor is not indebted to him under the agreement, this is binding on the creditor unless a court gives relief on the ground that a mistake has been made.

If a creditor defaults in his duty under this provision for one month, he commits an offence and is liable on summary conviction to a fine not exceeding £400.

# Chapter 2

# The Consumer Hire Business

## 1 What a 'consumer hire business' is

The Consumer Credit Act brings consumer protection into the field of rental and hire for the first time. The reason for this new departure was stated by the Crowther Committee in terms which likened the long-term rental of a customer durable such as a television set to the giving of credit. Where an object such as a television set is rented for a substantial part, perhaps the whole, of its useful life then, said the Committee, 'whatever the transaction may be in law, its economic content is such as to place it on a direct par with the hire-purchase of the same article, where credit is clearly involved'. As we have seen, the Act actually brings hire-purchase within its definition of **credit**. It does not deal with ordinary hire in this way. Instead, it creates a separate category of business called a '**consumer hire business**'. This it regulates in much the same way as a **consumer credit business**.

The definition

The statutory definition of 'consumer hire business' states that the term includes any **business** so far as it comprises or relates to the hiring of **goods** under regulated **consumer hire agreements**. The precise spelling out of the definition of such agreements is a matter of some complexity however (see section 3 below). What is clear is that we are here concerned solely with goods. The act does not regulate 'hire' of land or services. The term 'goods' includes any movable object, however large or small.

## 2 How the Act affects your business

If your business is or includes a **consumer hire business** the following controls operate:

You must have a licence issued by the OFT.

You are restricted in the way you canvass for business.

You must comply with the requirements governing advertisements and quotations.

You must give information about enquiries made by you as to the financial standing of prospective hirers.

You cannot avoid liability for statements by your negotiators.

You must give the prescribed notice when varying an agreement.

You must supply customers with relevant basic information before they commit themselves to an agreement.

Withdrawal from a prospective hire agreement will cancel any **linked transaction**.

Your agreements, and any security taken, must comply with the documentation requirements.

Most agreements are cancellable by the customer if the **antecedent negotiations** included face-to-face representations made off trade premises.

Restrictions are placed on your ability to enforce contractual terms.

Your customers will usually have the right to terminate an agreement.

All these provisions, and others of less importance, are explained in the present chapter.


## 3 What hire agreements are regulated by the Act

Agreements which are subject to the general system of control imposed by the Act are called '**regulated agreements**'. They may be either consumer credit agreements or consumer hire agreements. The former are described in Chapter 1 (page 9). Note that a word of mouth arrangement is an 'agreement' even if not reduced to writing.

### (a) The 'consumer hire agreement'

This is defined as an agreement, between an **individual** (called the hirer) and any other person (called the owner), for the hiring of **goods** where two specific conditions are satisfied. **Hire purchase** (which is treated as credit) and furnished letting agreements are excluded.

The first of the two conditions is that the agreement must be worded in such a way that it is *capable of subsisting for more than three months.* Only long-term hire is regarded as equivalent to **credit** and therefore in need of regulation. Ordinary car hire, for example, is not meant to be caught; contract hire is. The question turns on the wording of the agreement. If nothing is said about its duration, then it will be treated as capable of subsisting for more than three months. Equally, if it is stated to be for a fixed period of say three months but either party (or both) can extend the period, it will be treated as capable of exceeding three months. The lesson is that, in order to avoid regulation, agreements should specify a duration of three months or less except where this is commercially inconvenient. If it is later decided to extend the term this should be done by an entirely separate fresh agreement, since an agreement which varies *or supplements* an earlier agreement may be treated as extending it.

The other condition is that, to be a consumer hire agreement the contract must not *require* the hirer to make payments exceeding £15,000. For this purpose all payments are included, whether of the nature of hire or not. Thus a deposit or security payment will count towards the £15,000 limit. Payments are not counted however unless they become payable under the ordinary working out of the agreement, so that special payments arising only on default are excluded. So is the fact that the agreement might terminate (before the £15,000 limit had been reached) on some extraordinary occurrence specified in it, such as riot or civil commotion, or the bankruptcy of the hirer. If payments under the agreement will not exceed £15,000, but the agreement is capable of extension, the question turns on which party has the right to extend it. If it is the hirer alone the condition is satisfied. He is not *required* to make payments which depend on his choosing to exercise an option. If the option lies with the owner, the result is the opposite. The agreement does require the hirer to make payments exceeding £15,000 if it is in the owner's power to extend its operation with that result.

Note that attempts to evade the Act may misfire if they are too blatant.

**Example 36** A rental agreement with an individual H is for three years at £1,500 a quarter (payable on the usual quarter days). However, the agreement provides that if H pays his quarterly rental more than fourteen days before it is due it will be reduced to £600. He can easily limit his total outlay to £7,200 although in a sense he is 'required' to pay a total of £18,000. Accordingly the agreement is a consumer hire agreement.

Where the total outlay depends on uncertain factors, there may be difficulty in deciding whether the hirer is required to pay more than £15,000. If his payments may or may not exceed that figure then he is not so required. The right to return of a payment after it has been made is ignored.

**Example 37** A rental agreement with an individual H is for three years at £6,000 a year. At the end of that time the goods are to be sold. H is to be given a refund equal to the proceeds of sale. These are likely to amount to about £4,500. This is not a consumer hire agreement. H's outlay is £18,000. Although this might be reduced to £13,500 later there is no certainty of this. In any case it is the sums initially to be paid out that count, regardless of any later reimbursement.

The £15,000 limit was raised from £5,000 on 20 May 1985. The increase is not retrospective. This means that, for example, a hire agreement for £7,500 would not fall to be treated as a 'consumer hire agreement' if made on 18 May 1985, but would fall to be so treated if made on 20 May 1985.

*(b) Which consumer hire agreements are 'regulated'*

A consumer hire agreement is a 'regulated agreement', and thus within the general system of control imposed by the Act, provided it is not within one of the following exceptions.

Agreements made before 1 April 1977 are not regulated agreements unless varied on or after that date (a varied agreement is taken to be made on the date of variation). Nor are **foreign agreements** and **exempt agreements** within the term 'regulated agreement'. There is no equivalent in the hire field to the elaborate exemptions given to credit agreements. Hire exemptions are limited to agreements for renting electricity, gas or water meters from statutory undertakers.

The date 1 April 1977 is not applicable in all cases; the relevant date may be later. In determining whether a particular hire agreement is or is not a **'regulated agreement'** it is necessary to bear three considerations in mind, namely the date of the agreement, the amount of the hire payments, and the relevant provision of the Act. The fact is that the term 'regulated agreement' does not have the same meaning in each provision of the Act where it occurs. Differences mainly depend on when the relevant provision came into force, and what the financial limit was when the agreement was made or is deemed to have been made (namely £5,000 or £15,000).

## 4 The Category B licence

If you carry on a **consumer hire business** you have since 1 October 1977 needed a licence from the OFT. The licence in question is called a Category B standard licence. By the end of 1985, 34,572 Category B licences had been issued. The details of the licensing system are explained in Chapter 8. A special authorisation is required if you wish to canvass regulated hire agreements off trade premises. For this an extra licence fee of £10 is payable. Canvassing restrictions are described in section 5 below.

## 5 Canvassing

### (a) General restriction

Doorstep canvassing of consumer hire agreements needs a special licence, though telephone canvassing is not restricted. Nor is the sending of individually-addressed letters, except to young people under eighteen.

The Act does not in fact use the term 'doorstep canvassing', but refers to canvassing off trade premises, which goes wider. It treats as trade premises any premises where a **business** is carried on by the proprietor of the consumer hire business, or by the canvasser or his employer or principal, or by the consumer. The premises may be permanent business premises or merely temporary, such as an exhibition stand at a trade fair. (For a fuller explanation of the meaning of 'trade premises' see pages 26 and 27.)

Not all forms of face-to-face canvassing of **consumer hire agreements** off trade premises are caught by the Act. The five conditions which must be satisfied before canvassing of **credit agreements** is caught by the Act (see pages 27 and 28) apply in exactly the same way to hire agreements and so will not be repeated here. As with credit agreements, the person solicited need not be the person whose entry into a contract is sought, but may be his wife, employee etc.

The regulation of canvassing is through the licensing system. As explained above, you need, as a consumer hire trader, a Category B standard licence. If in the course of the business you canvass (either directly or through agents) your consumer hire agreements off trade premises in a way which satisfies the five conditions, your Category B licence will *not* cover this unless it contains a specific canvassing authorisation. It will not even cover it if your canvasser has his own Category C (credit or hire brokerage) licence containing a specific canvassing authorisation. You need your own canvassing authorisation too.

The OFT must grant a canvassing authorisation if satisfied that the applicant is a fit person to engage in face-to-face canvassing (see page 199). The most obvious evidence that he is *not* a fit person is where he or his business associates have a record of intimidation or other harsh or oppressive conduct towards members of the public. The consequence of engaging in or using face-to-face canvassing off trade premises when your licence does not contain a specific canvassing authorisation is that you are guilty of unlicensed trading. (As to the penalties for this see page 202.)

### (b) Prohibition on circulars to young persons

It is a criminal offence to send circulars advertising hire facilities to young persons under eighteen. Conviction in a Crown Court carries a maximum penalty of imprisonment for one year and/or a fine of unlimited amount. In a magistrates' court the maximum penalty is a fine of £2,000. The provision only applies if the sending is done 'with a view to financial gain', but this would be the case with any business circular. The Act does not refer to circulars as such, but defines the offence by using the wide phrase 'any document'. It thus covers magazines containing hire advertisements. To constitute an offence the document must invite the recipient to obtain goods on hire or apply for information or advice on hiring goods. It is not an offence actually to give the information provided there is no 'invitation' (whether express or implied).

For further details of the offence see the final paragraph of section 7 of Chapter 1 (page 31), which applies to hire circulars in the same way as to credit circulars.

## 6 Advertisements

In pursuit of the aim of 'truth in lending' the legislation imposes widespread controls on advertisements for hire facilities where they are comparable to consumer credit. These came into force on 6 October 1980.

### (a) Advertisements to which controls apply

*Advertisement medium*     The controls are not confined to visual advertising. They apply whatever the medium, whether a newspaper, a poster, a radio, television or cinema commercial, a catalogue, a label on goods, or whatever. Every method of communication is covered, *except* one directed to a person individually (for example a telephone call or personal letter). The audience may be the public generally, a section of the public, or a private group such as the employees of a firm.

*Facilities advertised*     The term used to describe an advertisement subject to the controls is **advertisement for hire facilities**. All kinds of hiring of **goods** are covered (other than hire-purchase, which is classed as credit), but the advertisement is caught only when published for the purposes of a **business** within either of the following categories:

(1) The business of the person offering the hire facility (but only where he is carrying on a **consumer hire business**, or a business providing individuals with hire goods under **foreign agreements** being **consumer hire agreements** which would otherwise be **regulated agreements**).

(2) A business of **credit brokerage**.

*Exempt advertisements*     An advertisement is not however treated as an 'advertisement for hire facilities' (even though it answers the description just given) if it is an advertisement which indicates that the advertiser is *not* willing to enter into a consumer hire agreement. Illogically, the legislation does not contain a hire exemption corresponding to the exemption for any advertisement which indicates that **credit** advertised is available only to a limited company or other incorporated body.

*Parts of advertisements*     It is important to note that what would be regarded in fact as a single advertisement may for the purposes of the controls fall to be treated as two or more separate advertisements. For example, what is factually one advertisement may relate partly to the hire of goods and partly to other matters extraneous to the legislation. The former will be treated as a hire advertisement in itself. Similarly a single advertisement may consist partly of controlled material and partly of exempt material. The latter will be treated as an exempt advertisement. The parts need not be physically severable. In so far as an intermixed advertisement relates to different matters it will be treated as a separate advertisement in relation to each.

*Split advertisements*　For the purpose of the controls it may be necessary to treat material which is factually separate as one advertisement (for example two stickers on a video recorder, or a television display and voice over). The test is whether the combined message can be taken in by the recipient at one time.

### (b) Persons and penalties

Whatever the business for the purposes of which the advertisement is published, the Act treats the advertiser as being the person who is to provide the hire facilities advertised (the potential **owner**). Even if the advertisement is inserted by a **credit-broker** without the knowledge or consent of the owner, the latter is still treated as the 'advertiser'. If the controls are infringed, the advertiser is guilty of an offence. Conviction in a Crown Court carries a maximum penalty of imprisonment for one year and/or a fine of unlimited amount. In a magistrates' court the maximum penalty is a fine of £2,000.

In the case of an infringing advertisement, other persons are also liable to the same penalties. These are the publisher, an advertising agent who devised the advertisement, and (where the 'advertiser' did not himself arrange for publication) the person who actually procured its publication. The publisher is provided with a special defence where he had no reason to suspect that publication would constitute an infringement.

### (c) Wider and narrower control

There is one requirement that applies to every advertisement which falls within the definition given above of 'advertisement for hire facilities'. The advertisement must not convey information which in a material respect is false or misleading. (For this purpose information stating or implying an intention on the advertiser's part which in fact he has not got is taken as false.)

Apart from being subject to this requirement, one type of advertisement within the definition is free from control. This is an advertisement which:

(1) indicates that the advertiser is willing to provide goods on

hire for the purposes of the **business** of any person (other than the business of the advertiser himself or a credit-broker acting in relation to the hire facility); and

(2) does not indicate that the advertiser is also willing to provide goods on hire *otherwise* than for the purposes of such a business (even though he may in fact be willing to do this).

An 'advertisement for hire facilities' which is not of this type, and is therefore subject to the further detailed controls as to content and form, is referred to as a **regulated hire advertisement**.

We may summarise by saying:

(1) that an 'advertisement for hire facilities' is any hire advertisement published for certain business purposes other than one which excludes consumer hire agreements;

(2) that every 'advertisement for hire facilities' must be free from false or misleading information; and

(3) that every such advertisement except one for business hire is a 'regulated hire advertisement' and subject to further controls as to content and form.

We now proceed to describe the controls as to *content*. The controls as to *form* relate to clarity and grouping. The clarity requirements are the same as for credit advertisements (see page 43). The grouping requirements correspond to those for credit advertisements (see pages 44 and 45) except that only exception (1) on page 45 applies.

*(d) Content of regulated hire advertisements*

The controls over the content of a **regulated hire advertisement** have the object of ensuring that the potential customer is not given a partial or one-sided view of the hire offer. Either:

(1) he must be given virtually no information other than that hire is available; or

(2) he must be given all relevant information; or

(3) if the information given is incomplete it must be balanced and contain essential items, and the customer must be told how to obtain the rest of it.

There is no parallel to the restriction of certain credit advertising expressions (except for 'no deposit' in the case of full advertisements, see below).

This object is affected by lengthy and complex provisions, which we now describe.

The provisions say that if an advertisement falls within the definition of 'regulated hire advertisement' its contents must comply with one or other of four alternative requirements. The advertiser can choose which one out of the four suits him best, but he must not go outside these categories. An advertisement giving virtually no information is called a *simple* advertisement. An advertisement giving all relevant information is a *full* advertisement. (There are two categories of full advertisement, one of which deals with the special case of an invitation to vary existing agreements.) An advertisement giving incomplete information is called an *intermediate* advertisement. We now describe each category in turn. Remember that your advertisement must comply with the requirements of one or other of them. A full advertisement may contain any additional hire information the advertiser chooses, but the other categories are restricted to what is specified in the legislation.

### (e) Simple hire advertisements

There are two requirements for this category, which are as follows:

(1) The only indication in the advertisement that the advertiser is willing to hire out goods must be a **simple indication of hire business**.

(2) The advertisement must not specify the cash price, or other price, of any goods.

The definition of a 'simple indication of hire business' is as follows. It is an indication that the advertiser carries on one of the types of business relevant for the purposes of the controls, being an indication which takes the form of:

(1) any name of his specified in his category B licence (or if he is not required to have a standard licence, any name under which he carries on business), and

(2) a statement either of an occupation of his or of the general nature of an occupation of his.

This is the official wording, but it is not altogether clear. It seems that it has the following meaning, bearing in mind that a simple advertisement is seen officially as a means of keeping the name of a business in the public eye. The name of the advertiser must appear. So must something about his 'occupation'. This is an odd word to describe the activities of what will usually be a limited company, but it must relate to the nature of the hire business. Examples are: 'office equipment hirer', 'television renter'. Examples of statements of the 'general nature' of an occupation are: 'contract car hire', 'plant rentals'.

The OFT consider that the typical simple advertisement is on objects like giveaway pens or bookmatches or on hoardings at sporting events.

> **Example 38** Television Hire Ltd, holders of a category B licence, present customers with diaries inscribed 'Television Hire Ltd Video rental'. This complies with the requirements of a simple hire advertisement.

Can more information be included? Three points arise. First, if the trader carries on two or more 'occupations' can they all be mentioned? It seems so. Secondly, can other information such as address and telephone number be included? Again, it seems so, provided the additional information does not in itself suggest that hire is available. Thirdly, can puffing descriptions be added to the words describing the occupation? Here the answer is no.

*(f)  Full hire advertisements (other than invitations to vary)*

The advertisement must not contain the expression 'no deposit' or any similar expression, except where no **advance payment** is payable.

*Basic information*    The basic information, which is also required to be given in an intermediate advertisement, comprises a statement that hiring of goods is being offered, the name and address of the owner or credit-broker and information where the owner requires insurance or security etc. The last two of these will now be explained in detail.

*Name and address of owner*    Where the prospective owner procures publication of the full advertisement, it must include his **name** and postal address unless it is displayed or (in the case of a sound advertisement) announced on the **premises** of the owner.

*Name and address of credit-broker*    Where a **credit-broker** procures publication, the advertisement must include his name and address and the fact that he is a credit-broker. Exceptions are that the name and address need not be given if the advertisement is displayed or announced on the credit-broker's premises and the fact that he is a credit-broker need not be stated where the prospective owner is an incorporated body and the credit-broker is its associate.

*Special requirements*    The advertisement must state the fact (if such is the case) that requirements are imposed concerning insurance, security or the opening of a deposit account.

*Additional information* Apart from the basic information described above, a full hire advertisement must also contain the following. If there is a requirement to make any **advance payment** this must be stated and particulars given. If the offer is *restricted* to certain persons this must be stated (eg 'not available to persons under twenty-one'). Where the goods are to be hired for a *fixed period* or a *minimum period* this must be stated. Certain information is required in relation to hire payments (other than advance payments). This comprises the *period* in relation to which each is to be made, the *amount*, and (if payments are variable in amount) particulars of variability. Similar information must be given about any **ancillary hire charge**. In all cases the details may be based on **representative information**, but if they are this fact must be stated.

## (g) Full hire advertisements (invitation to vary agreements)

This category applies to an advertisement which extends an invitation to individuals who are subject to existing hire agreements with the advertiser, the invitation being that they should agree to specified variations in those agreements. Here the advertisement must do two things in relation to the items given above as being required to be included in the ordinary category of full hire advertisements (disregarding irrelevant items).

(1) It must contain such of the information required by those items as will be *altered* if the invitation is accepted.

(2) It must indicate that the remaining items will remain unaltered (unless it repeats them in unaltered form).

The requirement is limited in this way because it is assumed that the hirer will know the terms of his existing agreement and only needs information about the proposed variations.

## (h) Intermediate hire advertisements

We have dealt with the simple advertisement, in which there must be a minimum of hire information. At the other extreme we have dealt with the full advertisement, specifying what hire information *must* be included (any other information being permissible in addition). Now we pass to the final category, where certain information is obligatory and additional optional hire information is strictly regulated. The potential customer *must* be offered an opportunity to secure a quotation completing the information required by a full advertisement.

*Obligatory information*    What is required to be given by an intermediate hire advertisement is the same as the basic information required for the ordinary category of full hire advertisement (page 124). There is one addition. The advertisement must contain an indication (for example 'Ask for our leaflet on hire terms') that individuals may obtain on request information in writing about the terms on which the advertiser is prepared to do business. It must also contain either a postal address to which or the number of a telephone by means of which such requests for a quotation may be made. (As to hire quotations see below.)

*Optional information*    Apart from the optional information about to be described, an intermediate advertisement must contain no other information indicating that the advertiser is willing to hire out goods. The advertiser is free to include one or more of the following items if he wishes. As always, **representative information** may be given provided this is stated.

(1)  A **simple indication of hire business**.
(2)  A statement that the hiring is restricted to certain persons (eg 'not available to persons under twenty-one').
(3)  Particulars of any restrictions imposed under **terms control**.

The advertiser has an additional option. He can also include *one only* of the following:

(1)  particulars of **advance payments** required (or a statement that no advance payment is required); or
(2)  the period for which hire may be provided; or
(3)  the frequency of **hire payments** (other than **advance payments**).

## 7  Quotations

The legislation gives consumers the right to obtain written quotations setting out the terms on which a trader is prepared to offer goods on hire. These supplement the incomplete information given in an intermediate advertisement, which must indicate that a quotation is available (see above). The right exists quite apart from any advertising there may have been. The trader is required to supply a quotation only if he receives an **obligatory hire quotation request**. If however he chooses to supply a quotation in response to a non-obligatory request he must observe the same standards. Breach of these requirements constitutes an offence. Conviction of the hire trader in the Crown Court carries a maximum penalty of imprisonment for one year and/or a fine of unlimited amount. In a magistrates' court the maximum penalty is a fine of £2,000.

### (a) Which requests are obligatory

A request for a quotation is obligatory only if it is made:
(1) by a qualifying individual;
(2) by a specified method; and
(3) to a **hire-trader** or **credit-broker** (or his representative). Furthermore it must
(4) ask for information in writing about the terms on which the hire-trader is prepared to do business with the individual, being business indicated in the request consisting of entry into certain types of hire agreement. These requirements are now examined in more detail.

*The qualifying individual* Any **individual** qualifies provided he is not a minor and is not resident outside the United Kingdom.

*The specified method* A request will not be obligatory unless it is made in writing, or is made orally on the trader's premises. A telephone request is however in order if made in response to an advertisement. No request is obligatory if made on the trader's premises in a case where a full advertisement is conspicuously displayed.

*The relevant agreements* The request will not be obligatory unless it relates to a regulated agreement. There is an exception if a full hire quotation in respect of the agreement in question was given by the trader to the **individual** within the preceding twenty-eight days. This is to prevent repeated requests which are unjustified.

### (b) The trader's response

The trader who receives an obligatory hire quotation request has two basic options. Either he must give a **full hire quotation** (the requirements for which are set out below and are much the same as for a full hire advertisement) or if he does not want the business (perhaps because he does not do business of that kind) he must notify the enquirer accordingly. If he only does business through a third party he must say so.

Suppose the trader, while not wishing to decline the business, has insufficient information on which to base a full quotation?

Here again he has two options. Either he may give an **estimated hire quotation** (see below) or he may ask for the missing information.

*(1) Full hire quotations*     A full hire quotation must be in writing, and may be framed as an offer capable by acceptance of ripening into a contract. If the trader does not wish to commit himself to this he is free to express the quotation accordingly.

> **Example 39** Rentaset Ltd do not wish their quotations to be capable of immediate acceptance as binding contracts since it is company policy to verify credit status in every case. On their quotation forms they therefore have printed the words 'This quotation is for information only and does not constitute a binding offer'.

The quotation must indicate the *minimum* period during which the information is to apply, so that the recipient knows how long he has to make up his mind. This can be expressed in any appropriate way, for example by saying 'This quotation is operative for fourteen days from the date hereof'. The information required by the regulations to be given must be presented *clearly* and *together as a whole*. The information required to be given is as follows:

(i) *Name and address*     The **name** and a postal address of the person giving the quotation. Where he is a **credit-broker** the name of the **hire-trader** must also be given (but his address need not be);

(ii) *Nature of transaction*     A statement indicating that the transaction to which the quotation relates is the hiring of goods;

(iii) *Special requirements*     The quotation must state the fact (if such is the case) that requirements are imposed concerning insurance, security or the opening of a deposit account.

(iv) *Additional information*     Apart from the basic information described above, the quotation must also contain the following. If there is a requirement to make any **advance payment** this must be stated and particulars given. If the goods are to be hired for a *fixed period* or a *minimum period* this must be stated and the duration given. The frequency and amount of hire payments must be stated, with particulars of variations. Finally the amount of any **ancillary hire charges** must be given.

*(2) Estimated hire quotations*    If the trader lacks some of the information needed for a full quotation he may, as explained above, give an **estimated hire quotation** instead. This contains just as much detail, except that some of it is based on assumptions which may not be correct in fact. They are comparable in principle to **representative information**, and must be reasonable in all the circumstances of the case. The quotation must indicate the assumptions made, and include a statement indicating that if any of them are incorrect the enquirer may make a request for another quotation based on additional information supplied by him.

### (c) Optional quotation requests

Where a request for a hire quotation does not comply with the requirements for an obligatory hire quotation request it may nevertheless have some legal effect. If it complies with the less strict requirements for an optional hire quotation request then, while the trader is not bound to respond to it, the legislation requires him, if he does decide to furnish a quotation, to do so in the same way as for an obligatory request. In other words there are three types of quotation request, as follows:

(1) Obligatory—the trader *must* respond as outlined above.
(2) Optional—the trader need not respond, but if he chooses to provide a quotation it must be a full hire quotation or (where he lacks sufficient information) an estimated hire quotation.
(3) Unregulated—the trader's response is not controlled by the legislation at all.

The requirements for an optional request are wider than for an obligatory request in the following ways:

(1) Requests from minors or foreign residents are not excluded.
(2) The request does not need to be made by any particular method.
(3) There is no exclusion of the case where a previous quotation was given within the preceding twenty-eight days.

In other respects the criteria are the same. The enquirer must be an **individual**, the trader must be a **hire-trader** or **credit-broker**, and the agreement in relation to which a quotation is requested must be a **regulated agreement**.

## 8 Steps prior to entry into hire agreement

This section deals with miscellaneous matters that may arise before your customer has entered into a hire agreement with you:

(a) his making with you of a contract to enter a future hire agreement;

(b) the suspension of linked transactions until the principal agreement is made;

(c) withdrawal by the customer from a prospective hire agreement, and

(d) your duties in relation to credit reference agencies consulted about the status of a prospective hirer.

### (a) Contracts to enter future hire agreements

The Act places restrictions on the effectiveness of contracts entered into by consumers purporting to bind them to enter into future hire agreements. This was done because it was thought desirable to limit the ability of hire traders to induce consumers to commit themselves to enter into possibly onerous future commitments. The only exception allowed concerns the case where the customer is himself carrying on a business, and requires goods on hire for use in that business.

Unless it is within this business exception (described in detail below), an agreement made on or after 19 May 1985 is therefore void if, and to the extent that, it purports to bind a person to enter as the **hirer** into a prospective **regulated agreement**.

### (b) The business exception

The business exception is somewhat complicated. To be within it, an agreement to enter into a future hire agreement must comply with the following conditions:

(1) It must be in writing;

(2) The goods must be required by the hirer for the purposes of a **business** carried on by him. Here it is sufficient if the hirer holds himself out as requiring the goods for such purposes;

(3) The earlier agreement must contain or refer to such information relating to the prospective hire agreement, presented clearly and together as a whole, as is required to be included in a **full hire quotation**.

In addition, there is a further requirement, expressed in the alternative. To be within the business exception, the earlier agreement must comply with one or other of the following conditions. *Either* it must not have been preceded by **antecedent negotiations** which included oral representations made when in the presence of the hirer by an individual acting as, or on behalf of, the **negotiator**, *or* (if it *was* preceded by such negotiations) it must be signed by the hirer at trade premises, that is **premises** at which any of the following is carrying on any business (whether on a permanent or temporary basis):

(a) the hire trader; or

(b) any party to a **linked transaction** to the prospective hire agreement (other than the hirer or a relative of his), or

(c) the negotiator in any antecedent negotiations.

*(c) Suspension of linked transactions until principal agreement made*

With certain exceptions, a linked transaction entered into before the making of the agreement to which it is linked has no effect until such time (if any) as the principal agreement is made. This is one aspect of the protection given by the Act in relation to linked transactions (as to the reasons for this protection see page 79). It applies only to linked transactions entered into on or after 19 May 1985.

The exceptions from this protection consist of the following linked transactions: collateral insurance policies, guarantees against defects in **goods**, and bank current or deposit account agreements.

*(d) Withdrawal from prospective hire agreement*

Part V of the Act contains two provisions concerned with withdrawal from prospective hire agreements. The first confers special protection on consumers contemplating entry into land mortgages, while the second deals with various aspects of the right to withdraw from any prospective regulated hire agreement. Each applies as from 19 May 1985.

*Duty to give notice of right to withdraw from prospective land mortgage*　The Act seeks to ensure that the prospective hirer under certain agreements to be secured on land receives notice of his right to withdraw from the agreement. Failure to comply means that the agreement, if made, will be treated as improperly executed (for the significance of this see page 137).

The duty to give this notice arises where a prospective regulated hire agreement (other than an **excepted agreement**) is to be secured on land. This is an unlikely, but possible, case. Where the duty applies, the hire trader, before sending the **unexecuted agreement** to the hirer for his signature, must give him a copy of it. This must include a box containing only a notice indicating the right to withdraw, and how and when it is exercisable.

*(e) Withdrawal from prospective hire agreements generally*

The Act lays down three rules relating to withdrawal from any propective regulated hire agreement. These:

- (a) make clear that a withdrawal notice need not be in any particular form;
- (b) specify persons who are deemed to be agents for the receipt of withdrawal notices, and
- (c) lay down the effect of a withdrawal notice. Each applies as from 19 May 1985.

*Giving of withdrawal notice*    The giving to a party of a written or oral notice which, however informally expressed, indicates the intention of the other party to withdraw from a prospective regulated hire agreement operates as a withdrawal from it. This provision does not apply to an **excepted agreement**. Since however the provision is declaratory of the common law the same result applies here too.

*Owner's agents for receipt of withdrawal notice*    Each of the following is deemed to be the agent of the **owner** for the purpose of receiving a notice to withdraw from a prospective regulated hire agreement (other than an excepted agreement):

- (a) a **credit-broker** who is the negotiator in antecedent negotiations;
- (b) any **person** who, in the course of a business carried on by him, acts on behalf of the **hirer** in any negotiations for the agreement.

*Effect of withdrawal*    Unless the hire agreement is an excepted agreement, then, whether or not it would if made have been a **cancellable agreement**, the withdrawal of the hirer operates to apply the cancellation provisions of the Act (for the effect of these see page 139). These apply not only to the agreement itself, but to any linked transaction, and to any other thing done in anticipation of the making of the hire agreement.

## 9 Form and content of hire agreements

### (a) Introductory

A central feature of agreement control relates to the form and content of **regulated agreements**. These provisions (contained in Part V of the Act) are basic to the concept of truth in lending, being aimed at ensuring that the consumer is given all the information he needs about the commitment he is undertaking, with adequate opportunity to withdraw if he has second thoughts.

The controls revolve round the concept of *proper execution* of agreements. If you as a hire trader fail to observe any statutory requirement, your agreement is treated as improperly executed. This has the routine consequence that you are unable to enforce it against the customer without a court order (known as an enforcement order).

This section therefore begins by explaining when a **regulated hire agreement** is improperly executed. Then we go on to consider the rules about the content, form and signing of hire agreements. This is followed by a description of the duties imposed on hire traders with regard to the supply of copies of agreements. Finally we look at what the exact consequences of improper execution are.

A further type of consumer protection given by agreement control, namely cancellation rights, is explained in a later section (see page 139).

### (b) When agreement is 'improperly executed'

Unless the requirements described below in this section are complied with in relation to a regulated hire agreement, other than an **excepted agreement**, the agreement is treated as improperly executed.

This rule is subject to the following alleviation. If, on an application made to the Director General of Fair Trading by a person carrying on a **consumer hire business**, it appears to the Director General impractical for the applicant to comply with any requirement concerning the *form* of the agreement in a particular case, he may direct that the requirement be waived or varied in relation to such agreements, and subject to such conditions (if any), as he may specify. He can do this only where he is satisfied that to do so would not prejudice the interests of hirers. Applications must be made on Form CCD 30/83, and be accompanied by supporting information on Form CCD 31/83. The application fee is £95.

For the detailed *consequences* of improper execution see the end of this section (page 137).

## (c)  Contents of agreement document

The Act and regulations lay down detailed rules about the form of the agreement. It must be expressed in a *document* complying with the following requirements. (If the agreement is a **modifying agreement** the requirements given below are adapted accordingly, the principle being that the hirer must be informed of changes from the original agreement.)

*Terms of the agreement*     The terms of any agreement may either be express or implied. When express, they may be set out in the agreement document or in some other document. The rules we are considering require the agreement document itself to contain certain basic terms (the 'prescribed terms'), namely the number, amount, frequency, and timing of hire payments, how the hirer is to discharge his obligations under the agreement, and any power of the hire trader to vary what is payable. Where further express terms are set out in some other document, this must be identified in the agreement document.

*Information for hirer*     The Act requires various further items of information to be set out in the agreement document. These consist of the heading 'Hire Agreement regulated by the Consumer Credit Act 1974', names and addresses of parties, description of goods hired, amount of any advance payment, duration of hire, description of any **security** provided, and indication of any default charges.

*Statement of protection and remedies*     The agreement document must also contain the prescribed form of statement describing the hirer's statutory protection and remedies. These forms, set out in Sched 4 to the Consumer Credit (Agreements) Regulations 1983, are too detailed and numerous to be reproduced here.

*Signature box*     The agreement document must contain a 'signature box' in the appropriate form set out in Sched 5 to the Consumer Credit (Agreements) Regulations 1983. The purpose is to ensure that in the place where he signs the document the hirer is reminded of the nature of the transaction he is committing himself to. Thus the signature box for ordinary hire agreements includes the words–

This is a Hire Agreement regulated by the Consumer Credit Act 1974. Sign it only if you want to be legally bound by its terms.

After the space allocated to the hirer's signature, the form goes on—

Under this agreement the goods do not become your property and you must not sell them.

*Lettering and layout of document* The lettering of the provisions required to be included in the agreement document must, apart from any signature, be easily legible, and of a colour which is readily distinguishable from the colour of the paper. The provisions must be shown together as a whole.

### (d) Signing of agreement document

Having ensured that the form and content of the agreement is correct, you must then consider the manner of signature. The agreement document must be signed by both parties. When presented or sent to the **hirer** for signature, the document must be in such a state that all its terms are readily legible.

The Act contemplates that the agreement document will either be presented for signature personally, that is face to face, or will be sent to the hirer by post. It does not contemplate that the hirer will himself fill in details and then present the document for signature to the trader.

Where an application form is used it is thus necessary for the hire trader, using the particulars filled in on the form by the customer, to draw up an agreement document for signature by him. It is an element in the Act's scheme of consumer protection that a hirer should always have an opportunity, when deciding whether or not to sign a regulated agreement, of being able to read it through and have before his eyes *all* its express terms. The unexecuted agreement is thus finally put forward by the hire trader, even though some of its terms may have been suggested by the consumer in filling in an application form.

The agreement document must be signed by the hirer in the space indicated for the purpose (the 'signature box' described above).

A date must also be inserted in the signature box. This will be the date of signing by the hirer, except that where the agreement is not a **cancellable agreement** the date on which the **unexecuted agreement** becomes an **executed agreement** may be inserted instead.

The agreement document must be signed by or on behalf of the **hire trader** outside the signature box in which the hirer signs. A date must also be inserted outside the signature box. This will be the date of signing by or on behalf of the hire trader, except that, as in the case of the hirer, where the agreement is not a cancellable agreement the date on which the unexecuted agreement becomes an executed agreement may be inserted instead.

The signature of a witness may be placed near the hirer's or hire trader's signature, provided it is not in the signature box.

In the case of a land mortgage where the duty arises to give a copy incorporating notice of withdrawal rights (see page 131 above), that duty must of course have been complied with. In addition, the agreement document must have been sent, for his signature, to the hirer *by post* not less than seven days after the copy was given to him.

The giving of the copy starts a 'consideration period', which goes on until either the hirer returns the agreement document signed by him or seven days elapses following the date on which the document was sent to the hirer for signature. The agreement will be improperly executed unless during this consideration period the hire trader refrains from approaching the hirer (whether in person, by telephone or letter, or in any other way) except in response to a specific request made by the hirer after the beginning of the consideration period. Furthermore no notice of withdrawal by the hirer must have been received by the hire trader before the sending of the agreement document.

### (e) Supply of copies of hire agreements

The statutory duty imposed on the **owner** to supply the hirer with a copy of a hire agreement differs according to whether signature by the hirer of the agreement document does or does not convert it into an 'executed agreement', that is a document which fully complies with the Act and regulations and is signed by *both* parties. If for example the document is sent by post to the hirer for signature, this question will depend on whether or not it had already been signed on behalf of the hire trader.

There are two principles. The first is that, at the time the agreement document is presented or sent to the hirer for his signature, he must at the same time receive for retention a copy of what he is being invited to sign. Furthermore if the document refers to other documents, copies of these also must be provided.

This first principle does not apply where the document is presented face to face, and on that occasion becomes an executed agreement. Here the case is fully covered by the second principle.

The second principle is that, except where the agreement document was sent to him and on signature by him became an executed agreement (in which case the first principle is deemed sufficient), the hirer must always receive a copy of the executed agreement, so that he can retain a document which completely embodies the contract he has committed himself to. If the agreement document is presented for signature face to face, and on that occasion becomes an executed agreement, the hirer must then and there be given his copy of the executed agreement. Otherwise it must be given to him within seven days after the second signature is added. In the case of a cancellable agreement it must be sent by post, so that the hirer is not pressurised by personal contact.

The regulations allow certain omissions. For example a copy of an unexecuted agreement may omit the name and address of the hirer. No copy need include information relating to the hirer or a surety which is for the use of the hire trader only and is not statutorily required to be included in the agreement document.

Equally there are various exceptions to the requirement to supply copies of documents referred to in the agreement document. If this were not so, every hirer would need to be supplied with a copy of the Consumer Credit Act for example.

## (f) Consequences of improper execution

As stated above (page 133), where the requirements outlined in this section are not complied with the result is that the agreement falls to be treated as 'improperly executed'. We now look at what this entails.

Where a hire agreement is to be treated as not properly executed it is enforceable against the hirer only where the county court makes an order (an 'enforcement order') to that effect. This means that if you fail to observe the rules you will be unable to enforce your agreement (including retaking the hired goods) until the court has had an opportunity to consider the matter and decide what would be the fair result.

Here the court does not have a free hand. Section 127 of the Act places fetters on its ability to grant an enforcement order. There must have been a document at least containing the 'prescribed terms' (see page 134 above), and it must have been signed by both parties, even though not in the correct manner.

The court has power to strike out a term of the agreement omitted from the signed document. It may also reduce or discharge any sum payable by the hirer in order to compensate him for prejudice suffered as a result of the contravention.

Where an application for an enforcement order is dismissed (except on technical grounds only) the **section 106 rules** apply to any security provided in relation either to the hire agreement or any actual or prospective **linked transaction**.

## 10 Secured hire agreements

Except for the final section relating to pawnbrokers, section 12 of Chapter 1 applies in exactly the same way to **consumer hire agreements** as it does to credit agreements. The Act's restrictions on taking security in relation to hire agreements, and its regulation of such securities, are not therefore described here. (See pages 61 to 64.)

### 11 Duties in relation to credit reference agencies consulted

The duties described in section 10 of Chapter 1 (pages 54 and 55) apply in exactly the same way to consumer hire businesses, and will not therefore be further described here. It may however be useful to explain the relevance of the duty (there described) to tell a credit-broker who introduces a customer the name and address of any credit reference agency consulted. As we shall see in the next chapter (page 151), the definition of 'credit-broker' includes a person who introduces customers requiring goods on hire to a firm carrying on a consumer hire business. Such firms will therefore be involved with credit-brokers and will often need to check the financial standing of customers introduced to them. The typical case is equipment leasing, where the customer selects goods from a supplier which are then sold to a finance house. In turn the finance house leases the goods to the customer. Here the supplier is deemed by the Act to function as a 'credit-broker', and the duty to give the supplier information about any credit reference agency consulted by the finance house will arise where the leasing arrangement is not proceeded with.

### 12 Liability for negotiator's acts or omissions

Section 14 of Chapter 1 (page 75) applies to **regulated consumer hire agreements** in the same way as to **credit agreements**. It is not possible, in other words, for the owner of **goods** to escape liability for acts or omissions of his employees or agents in negotiating a

**consumer hire agreement**. A clause in the agreement purporting to relieve the owner from such liability is void.

## 13 Cancellation of hire agreement by hirer

Except as mentioned below, section 15 of Chapter 1 applies as regards the cancellation of consumer hire agreements in the same way as it does to credit agreements. The Act's provisions in this respect are not therefore separately described here. (See pages 75 to 80.)

*Antecedent negotiations*      In relation to hire agreements, the meaning of 'antecedent negotiations' (pages 75 and 77) is much simpler, since only negotiations conducted by the **owner** or his staff are relevant. This means that categories (2) to (4) on pages 76 and 77 can be ignored.

*Non-cancellable agreements*      The only types of hire agreement not capable of being cancellable are:

(1) an agreement secured on land;

(2) an agreement which purports to bind a person to enter as hirer into a prospective regulated agreement made for business purposes; and

(3) a non-commercial agreement.

*Effect of notice of cancellation*      The special cases described on pages 79 and 80 do not apply to hire agreements.

*Incidental consequences*      The consequences listed on page 80 apply to hire agreements, except that the passage relating to part-exchange goods is not of course relevant.

## 14 Duties as to giving of information

The Act places on both parties to a hire agreement various duties in relation to the giving of information.

### (a) Information to be provided at request of hirer

The hirer of goods under a **regulated agreement**, other than a **paid-up agreement** or a **non-commercial agreement**, is entitled to request certain information from the owner of the goods. The request is effective only if certain conditions are complied with. It must be in writing, and accompanied by a fee of 50p. It must not be made within one month after compliance by the owner with a similar request from that hirer relating to the agreement in question. Failure to comply with the duty renders the agreement unenforceable by the owner while the default continues. If it continues for a month the owner commits an offence punishable on summary conviction with a fine not exceeding £1,000.

Within twelve **working days** after receiving an effective request, the owner must send the hirer a **prescribed copy** of the **executed agreement** (if any), and of any other document referred to in it (other than an **excepted document**), together with a signed statement which is binding on the owner. The statement must show, according to the information available to the owner, the total sum which has become payable under the agreement by the hirer but remains unpaid, showing the various amounts comprised in that total sum and the date when each became due.

### (b) Information as to whereabouts of goods

Where a **regulated agreement**, other than a non-commercial agreement, requires the hirer of goods to keep them in his possession or control, the Act gives the owner the right to information concerning them. Within seven **working days** after he has received a request in writing to that effect from the owner, the hirer must tell the owner where the goods are. The information need not be given in writing: a telephone call will do.

If the hirer fails to comply with this requirement, and the default continues for fourteen days, he commits an offence for which he is liable on summary conviction to a fine not exceeding £400.

### 15 Varying a hire agreement

The Act contains special provisions to deal with problems that may arise when the terms of a **consumer hire agreement** are altered after the agreement has been entered into. It deals differently with the case where the alteration is effected under a provision included in the agreement and the case where it is effected by the making of a further agreement.

### (a) Variation of regulated agreement under power contained in agreement

An agreement may include a power, exercisable by one party or both, to vary one of the terms of the agreement (eg a rental agreement may entitle the owner to raise the level of the rentals). In relation to consumer hire businesses, the only specific provision in the Act deals with the case where the **owner** has a right of variation. No comparable provision is made for rights of variation by the hirer. The Act prevents a variation by the owner from taking effect until the lapse of seven days after a notice in writing describing it has been given to the hirer.

**Example 40** A **regulated consumer hire agreement** made by O Ltd with Mr H contains the following terms:
'15. The rental under this agreement shall be £15 per month.
16. O Ltd may at any time determine to alter the rental current under this agreement.'
On 30 April O Ltd determine to increase the rental to £20 per month with immediate effect. They do not inform Mr H until 15 June, when a written notice is served on him specifying the increase and stating that it operates from 1 May. In fact, because of the Act, the increase does not operate until seven days have elapsed following service of the notice, ie it operates as from 23 June. If the meaning of the agreement is that the level of rental must apply uniformly throughout a calendar month the increase would operate as from 1 July.

Although this seven-day notice rule is the only specific provision in the Act dealing with alteration of a regulated agreement under a power contained in the agreement, it is possible, under the general provisions of the Act, for the use of such a power to lead to a change in the category into which an agreement falls.

**Example 41** A hire agreement covering a number of items is made between O Ltd and Mr H at a rental of £6,000 a year for three years. After six months, under a power to modify the agreement conferred on them (but not Mr H) by the agreement, O Ltd withdraw certain items with the result that the rental for the remaining two-and-a-half years drops to £3,600 a year. Since this means that Mr H is no longer bound to pay more than £15,000 in rental, the effect is to bring the agreement within the category of regulated agreements.

If the change had been the other way round there would not have been a change of category. Once protection is given to a hire agreement, changes in it will not withdraw the protection.

**Example 42** A hire agreement is made between O Ltd and Mr H for a fixed period of five years at a rental of £225 a month. Since the total rentals for the whole period will be under £15,000 this is a regulated agreement. After three years, under a power contained in the agreement, O Ltd raise the rental to £300. This brings the aggregate rent to £15,300. Since this is over the £15,000 limit for consumer hire agreements the effect would be to remove the agreement from the category of regulated agreements if it were not for the rule, applicable to all except running-account credit agreements, that 'once a regulated agreement, always a regulated agreement'.

### (b) Effect of a modifying agreement

We now pass to the second of the two types of case mentioned at the beginning of this section. A *new agreement* is made by which the earlier agreement is modified or added to. The Act calls this a **modifying agreement**, and lays down special rules governing its effect. These are explained in section 19 of Chapter 1 (pages 102 to 104). The following is an example in the hire field of the way a modifying agreement can move the earlier agreement into a different category.

> **Example 43** O Ltd make a hire agreement with Mrs H at a rental of £20 per month. The agreement is terminable by one month's notice on either side. It is a regulated consumer hire agreement. By a later agreement the parties vary the terms by adding an option for Mrs H to purchase the goods at any time after the hiring has subsisted for two years. The amendment brings the agreement within the **hire-purchase** definition and therefore removes it from the consumer hire category. From the time the amendment takes effect it becomes a **regulated consumer credit agreement**.

### 16 Restrictions on enforcement of agreement by owner

The Act places certain restrictions on your right as owner to enforce the contractual terms of a hire agreement. These are in addition to the Act's restrictions in relation to termination of the agreement, which are dealt with separately (see section 16 of this chapter, beginning on page 145).

### (a) Notice requirement

In certain cases, seven days' written notice is required before action under the agreement can be taken by the owner. If notice is not duly given, the action will be unlawful. (The provisions about to be explained do not apply in case of default, which is dealt with separately later in this section.)

*Cases where requirement applies*    The notice requirement applies to any **regulated agreement** (other than a **non-commercial agreement** in relation to which no **security** was provided), but only where the agreement specifies a period for its duration and that period is not yet ended. The requirement applies whether or not any party is entitled to terminate the agreement before the end of the specified period.

*Acts to which requirement applies*    The notice requirement applies where the owner intends to do any of the following, except by reason of a breach of the agreement:

(1) demand earlier payment of any sum; or

(2) recover possession of any **goods**; or

(3) treat any right conferred on the hirer by the agreement as terminated, restricted or deferred.

*What the notice must say*    To be effective, the written notice served by the owner must say that it is served under s 76(1) of the Consumer Credit Act 1974, and must contain prescribed information and advice as set out in Sched 1 to the Consumer Credit (Enforcement, Default and Termination Notices) Regulations 1983.

### (b) Default by hirer

The giving of a default notice in writing is usually necessary before action can be taken by the owner in the case of default by the hirer. If this notice is not duly given, the action will be unlawful. (The provisions about to be explained do not apply to *termination* of an agreement on grounds of default, which is dealt with separately in section 16 of this chapter, beginning on page 147.)

*Cases where requirement applies*    The default notice requirement applies to any **regulated agreement** (other than a **non-commercial agreement** in relation to which no security was provided).

*Acts to which requirement applies*    The default notice requirement applies where the owner intends to do any of the following (a 'restricted act') by reason of a breach of the agreement:

(1) demand earlier payment of any sum; or

(2) recover possession of any **goods**; or

(3) treat any right conferred on the hirer by the agreement as terminated, restricted or deferred; or

(4) enforce any security (including doing any act whereby a floating charge becomes fixed).

*What the default notice must say*    To be effective, the written default notice must say that it is served under s 87(1) of the Consumer Credit Act 1974, and must contain prescribed information and advice as set out in Sched 2 to the Consumer Credit (Enforcement, Default and Termination Notices) Regulations 1983 as amended.

*Where breach capable of remedy*    Where, in the case of a breach capable of remedy, the default notice specified what action was required to remedy it, and the date before which that action was to be taken, a restricted act must not be done by the **owner** before that date. (If the necessary remedial action was taken in time, the default is treated as not having occurred.) Where no such date was specified in the default notice, the restricted act must not be done by the owner until seven days have elapsed from the giving of the default notice.

*Where breach not capable of remedy*    Where, in the case of a breach not capable of remedy, the default notice specified the sum required to be paid as compensation for the breach, and the date before which it was to be paid, a restricted act must not be done by the owner before that date. (If the required sum was paid in time, the default is treated as not having occurred.) Where no such date was specified in the default notice, the restricted act must not be done by the owner until seven days have elapsed from the giving of the default notice.

*Default provisions in hire agreement*    The Act makes special provision as regards any term in the hire agreement which specifically relates to default (for example a penalty clause). Failure to comply with such a default provision is not in itself to be treated by the default notice as a breach of the agreement, but once the time restrictions relating to the default notice have expired the owner is free to enforce the default provision as well as doing any restricted act.

*Recovery of goods by owner*    The Act gives protection to goods held under a **regulated agreement**. The owner is precluded from entering on any premises to retake the goods without a County Court order (unless of course the occupier consents).

## (c) Death of hirer

The Act places certain restrictions on what the owner may do because of the death of the hirer under a regulated agreement. (The provisions about to be explained do not apply to *termination* of an agreement on the hirer's death, which is dealt with separately on page 148.)

*Acts to which restrictions apply*    The restrictions apply where the owner wishes to do any of the following (a 'restricted act') by reason of the hirer's death:

(1) demand earlier payment of any sum; or

(2) recover possession of any goods; or

(3) treat any right conferred on the hirer by the agreement as terminated, restricted or deferred; or

(4) enforce any security (including doing any act whereby a floating charge becomes fixed).

However, the restrictions do not affect any provisions concerning the payment of sums due under the agreement out of the proceeds of a policy of assurance on the hirer's life.

*The restrictions*     The restrictions depend on whether the hire agreement is fully secured. If it is, then the owner is not entitled to do any restricted act by reason of the death. (An act is treated as being done by reason of the death if it is done under a power conferred by the agreement which is either:

(a) exercisable on the hirer's death; or

(b) exercisable at will and exercised at any time after the hirer's death.)

If the hire agreement is *not* fully secured, then a County Court order is required before a restricted act can be done by reason of the death. To obtain such an order the owner must prove that he has been unable to satisfy himself that the deceased hirer's obligations are likely to be discharged.

## 17 Termination of hire agreements

The Act contains various provisions regarding the termination of **consumer hire agreements** which are **regulated agreements**.

### (a) Termination of agreement by hirer

The Act gives the hirer under certain agreements a right to terminate the agreement at any time he chooses.

*Agreements to which right applies*     The hirer's right to terminate applies to any regulated agreement *except*:

(1) an agreement which provides for the making by the hirer of payments which in total (and assuming no breach of the agreement) exceed £900 in any year; or

(2) an agreement for the purposes of the hirer's business.

An agreement is treated as being for the purposes of the hirer's business if it falls into either of the following categories:

(1) an agreement where the goods are hired for the purposes

of a business carried on by the hirer (or the hirer holds himself out as requiring the goods for those purposes) *and* the goods are selected by the hirer and then acquired by the owner at the request of the hirer from any person (other than the owner's **associate**); or

(2) an agreement where the goods are hired for the purpose of hiring them to other persons in the course of a business carried on by the hirer (or the hirer holds himself out as requiring the goods for those purposes).

What this rather clumsy provision amounts to is that whenever the hirer requires the goods so that he can in turn hire them out himself by way of business he can never terminate the agreement prematurely. If, however, he requires them for any other sort of business he is precluded from ending the agreement prematurely only where, for the hirer's benefit and at his choice, the owner has specially acquired the goods. Even then the owner is not protected if the acquisition was from an associated company.

*Method of termination*    The right of termination is exercised by giving notice in writing to any person entitled or authorised to receive payments under the hire agreement. The notice must not expire earlier than eighteen months after the making of the agreement. Furthermore the notice must be of a duration not less than the period between payments under the agreement (unless this exceeds three months, in which case the notice must be at least three months).

*Liabilities of hirer*    Termination of a hire agreement does not affect any liability under the agreement which has accrued (that is become due) before the termination.

## (b) Termination by owner (ordinary cases)

Seven days' written notice is usually required before a hire agreement can be effectively terminated by the owner. (The provisions about to be explained do not apply in case of default, which is dealt with separately later in this section.)

*Cases where requirement applies*    The notice requirement applies to any **regulated agreement** (other than a **non-commercial agreement** in relation to which no security was provided), but only where the agreement specifies a period for its duration and that period is not yet ended. The requirement applies whether or not any party is entitled to terminate the agreement before the end of the specified period.

*What the notice must say*    To be effective, the written notice

must say that it is served under s 98(1) of the Consumer Credit
Act 1974, and must contain prescribed information and advice as
set out in Sched 3 to the Consumer Credit (Enforcement, Default
and Termination Notices) Regulations 1983.

### (c)  Termination by owner (default cases)

The giving of a default notice in writing is usually necessary
before an agreement can be terminated on the ground of default
by the hirer.

*Cases where requirement applies*      The default notice requirement applies to any **regulated agreement** (other than a **non-
commercial agreement** in relation to which no **security** was
provided).

*What the default notice must say*      To be effective, the written
default notice must say that it is served under s 87(1) of the
Consumer Credit Act 1974, and must contain prescribed information and advice as set out in Sched 2 to the Consumer Credit
(Enforcement, Default and Termination Notices) Regulations
1983 as amended.

*Where breach capable of remedy*      Where, in the case of a
breach capable of remedy, the default notice specified what action
was required to remedy it, and the date before which that action
was to be taken, the agreement must not be terminated by the
owner before that date. (If the necessary remedial action was
taken in time, the default is treated as not having occurred.)
Where no such date was specified in the default notice, the agreement must not be terminated by the owner until seven days have
elapsed from the giving of the default notice.

*Where breach not capable of remedy*      Where, in the case of a
breach not capable of remedy, the default notice specified the
sum required to be paid as compensation for the breach, and the
date before which it was to be paid, the agreement must not be
terminated by the owner before that date. (If the required sum
was paid in time, the default is treated as not having occurred.)
Where no such date was specified in the default notice, the agreement must not be terminated by the owner until seven days have
elapsed from the giving of the default notice.

*Default provisions in hire agreement*      The Act makes special
provision as regards any term in the hire agreement which specifically relates to default (for example a penalty clause). Failure to
comply with such a default provision is not in itself to be treated
by the default notice as a breach of the agreement, but once the

time restrictions relating to the default notice have expired the owner is free to enforce the default provision as well as treating the agreement as terminated.

### (d) Termination by owner (death of hirer)

The Act places certain restrictions on what the owner may do because of the death of the hirer under a regulated agreement. Among these is one relating to the termination of the agreement by reason of the death.

*Cases where restriction applies* The restriction applies to any regulated agreement (other than a non-commercial agreement in relation to which no security was provided), but only where the agreement specifies a period for its duration and that period is not yet ended. The restriction applies whether or not any party is entitled to terminate the agreement before the end of the specified period.

*The restriction* The nature of the restriction depends on whether the hire agreement is fully secured. If it is, then the owner is not entitled to terminate the agreement by reason of the death. (An act is treated as being done by reason of the death if it is done under a power conferred by the agreement which is either:

    (1) exercisable on the hirer's death; or

    (2) exercisable at will and exercised at any time after the hirer's death.)

If the hire agreement is *not* fully secured, then a County Court order is required before the agreement can be terminated by the owner by reason of the death. To obtain such an order the owner must prove that he has been unable to satisfy himself that the deceased hirer's obligations are likely to be discharged.

### (e) Termination notices

The Act gives hirers the right to obtain from the owner written confirmation that a hire agreement (other than a non-commercial agreement) has come to an end.

To exercise this right, the hirer must give the owner a notice in writing stating that:

    (1) he was the hirer under a regulated agreement described in the notice, and the other party was the owner under the agreement; and

    (2) he has discharged his indebtedness to the owner under the agreement; and

(3) the agreement has ceased to have any operation,
and requiring the owner to give him a signed notice confirming that those statements are correct.

Within twelve **working days** after receiving the notice, the owner must either comply with it or serve a counter-notice. This must either say that the owner disputes the correctness of the hirer's notice (stating what is wrong with it) or say that the hirer is not indebted to him under the agreement. If the owner complies with the hirer's notice or states that the hirer is not indebted to him under the agreement, this is binding on the owner unless a court gives relief on the ground that a mistake has been made.

If an owner defaults in his duty under this provision for one month, he commits an offence and is liable on summary conviction to a fine not exceeding £400.

# Chapter 3

# Credit (and Hire) Brokerage

## 1 What 'credit brokerage' is

The Act is not content with regulating consumer credit and consumer hire traders and their agreements. It goes wider and covers **ancillary credit businesses**, with which we deal in this and the three following chapters. Here we examine what the Act calls 'credit brokerage', though it might more appropriately have used the term 'credit and hire brokerage' since introductions to hire traders are covered too. The scope is unexpectedly wide, and the definition covers most dealers in consumer durables as well as the more obvious trades such as mortgage-brokers.

### (a) Reasons for the controls

The extension of statutory control to this field began with a late-1960's survey by the Consumer Council into second-mortgage lending. The Council collected many complaints of abuse. Mortgage brokers were alleged to force more credit on the borrower than he wanted, or misrepresent the cost of credit, or overcharge on survey fees, or retain fees when the loan did not go through, or masquerade as principals when they were not. After examining this and other evidence, the Crowther Committee concluded that mortgage brokers needed statutory regulation, but went much wider than this particular trade. They advocated a system of control for all persons carrying on business as brokers or other agents in connection with the making of consumer loans, whether concerned with mortgages or not. In framing the Act the Government went wider still and included hire transactions as well. The result is that most retailers and other dealers in consumer durables who do not carry their own credit rank as credit-brokers.

*(b) The definition*

In the effort to include all cases it was desired to include and none it was not, the draftsman produced a complex definition of 'credit brokerage'. In essence it consists of the effecting of introductions of **individuals** desiring credit or goods on hire to firms offering such facilities or to other credit-brokers. The details of the definition are explained in section 3 below.

## 2 How the Act affects your business

If you carry on a credit brokerage **business** the Act affects you in various ways.

The following provisions apply now:

You must have a licence issued by the OFT unless you fall within a narrowly-defined excepted category.

You are restricted in the way you canvass for business.

You must observe the requirements relating to advertising and quotations (these go wider than the definition of credit brokerage).

You must give information about credit status enquiries made by you, or by traders to whom you introduce business.

In some cases you are subject to a £3 limit on your commission.

All these provisions are explained in the present chapter. Further provisions may be brought into force later and are outlined at the end of the chapter.

## 3 The definition in detail

In tackling the definition of '**credit brokerage**' it is best to break it up into compartments. First we look at the consumer, then at the intermediary and his function ('effecting introductions') and finally at the credit or hire trader. In brief we may say that it is credit brokerage to 'effect introductions' of specified types of individual to specified types of trader.

*(a) The individual*

First it is necessary to have an **individual** who desires to obtain **credit** of any kind (call him a credit-seeker) or who desires to obtain **goods** on hire (a hire-seeker). *It is irrelevant how much credit a credit-seeker desires.* The £15,000 limit does not apply here, and an individual is just as much a credit-seeker for the purposes of the definition of credit brokerage if he wants a loan of £100,000 as if he wants a loan of £100. Likewise the terms on which a hire-seeker desires to hire goods, and the value of those goods, are irrelevant. Also irrelevant is the purpose for which the individual requires the credit or goods, and whether it is a business or private purpose. Note that the primary object of a credit-seeker may not be to obtain credit as such, but rather to obtain goods or services which he will need credit to pay for. He may not be aware of needing credit, or indeed minded to seek the goods or services at all, until the idea is put into his head by a salesman or canvasser.

> **Example 44** A freelance agent, S, is in the practice of pushing through house doors leaflets advertising C Ltd's replacement windows and double-glazing service, which the leaflets say is available on cash or credit terms as the customer chooses. S pushes a leaflet through Mr D's front door, who fills in a coupon asking S to call on him and returns it. S calls, and as a result Mr D ultimately enters into an agreement with C Ltd for the supply of a replacement window on credit sale. S's activities constitute credit brokerage even though it had not occurred to Mr D to buy a replacement window (much less seek credit for it) until he read the leaflet.

### (b) The intermediary

A person will not be a 'credit-broker' within the meaning of the Act unless he carries on a **business** of credit brokerage. This means that introductions by relatives or friends do not fall within the statutory controls. It is irrelevant whether there are any pre-existing business arrangements between the intermediary and the credit or hire trader to whom introductions are effected. Also irrelevant are any connections between the intermediary and the credit-seeker or hire-seeker.

> **Example 45** E Ltd operate a staff house mortgage scheme by arrangement with BS, a building society, who advance the loans to members of E Ltd's staff applying on forms supplied by E Ltd's personnel department. By operating the scheme E Ltd are acting as credit-brokers, since what they are doing amounts to effecting introductions to one of the specified types of credit trader (described below).

The intermediary must not be acting in the course of his duties as an employee of the credit or hire trader. The employee of, say, a household goods supplier does not act as a credit-broker when in the course of his duties (perhaps as a canvasser) he tries to persuade people to take goods on credit from his employer. The employer and his employees, in this context, are one. If, however, the intermediary is the agent (though not the employee) of the trader he is what the law calls an independent contractor and will be a credit-broker in his own right unless he comes within the following exception provided for by the Act.

While, as we have seen, the Crowther Committee considered that persons carrying on business as brokers or other agents in connection with the making of consumer loans should be subject to control, they thought an exception should be made for canvassers operating from their own homes, such as housewives paid on commission by mail order firms. The Act gives effect to this, but in different terms. It limits the exception to **canvassing a regulated agreement off trade premises**. If the agreement canvassed is one for **restricted-use credit** financing a transaction between debtor and creditor (eg a hire-purchase or credit sale agreement), or is a **consumer hire agreement**, and if the canvasser is not acting in the capacity of an employee and does not by any other method effect introductions falling within the definition of credit brokerage, then the canvasser will not be a credit-broker. Note that it will destroy the exception if the canvasser also uses other methods to effect introductions to his principal, eg distributing circulars (see Example 44). As to debt counselling and debt collecting by such canvassers, see pages 176 to 177).

## (c) Effecting introductions

This apparently simple concept nevertheless presents problems. We all know what it is to effect an introduction between two people. Or do we? The following notes originate from queries traders have raised on the definition:

(1) An introduction falls within the definition whichever way round it is, ie whether the credit or hire trader's name is given to the credit-seeker or hire-seeker or the seeker's name is given to the trader.

(2) The seeker and the trader must be previously unknown to each other. You do not 'effect an introduction' between people who have dealt with one another before. This applies even where the previous dealing was with a different branch

of a limited company's business, though not where it was with a different company in the same group. (For the purpose of the Act, each company in a group is an entirely separate entity.) If however the previous dealing was a considerable time before, and the parties have lost touch with each other, current action by an intermediary will count as 'effecting an introduction'.

(3) The introduction must be for the purpose of making an agreement of the kind in question, even though not necessarily of precisely the same kind. An individual seeking equipment leasing may end up entering into a hire-purchase agreement for slightly different equipment with the finance house to which he is introduced. That is near enough to bring the introduction within the definition.

(4) Any method may be used for making the introduction. A common method is for the intermediary to supply the seeker with the name and address of the trader and leave the seeker to make the approach. The intermediary must however be aware of the seeker as an individual; it is not enough merely to advertise the trader's services generally.

**Example 46** A retail store which honours a certain credit card displays on its counters advertising material and application forms issued by the credit card company. The employees of the store do not give advice or information about the credit card to enquirers. The display does not amount to 'effecting introductions', and the store is not thereby made into a credit-broker. See also Example 44.

In *Brookes* v *Retail Credit Cards Ltd* [1986] CCLR 5 the Divisional Court confirmed the above Example, and indeed went further. They held it not to be credit brokerage under the Act even where the staff of the retail store helped customers fill in the credit application forms displayed.

(5) The intermediary need not receive a commission (or any other benefit) from the credit or hire trader. It is enough if he effects the introduction for any purpose of his business, eg to enable a customer to buy his goods or to improve relations with his own staff (see Example 44).

(6) It is immaterial that in effecting the introduction the intermediary is merely carrying out the instructions of a third party.

**Example 47** M, a manufacturer of television sets, arranges with F, a finance house, that F will enter into hire-purchase agreements with individuals who wish to purchase the sets from retail outlets. M instructs its retailers that if customers seek credit facilities they should be referred to F. In compliance with this instruction, R, an independent retailer, makes a practice of advising its customers accordingly. Prior to receiving the instruction from M, R had never heard of F and has had no contact with them. Nevertheless in advising its customers to approach F, R is acting as a credit-broker.

(7) It is immaterial whether the intermediary does anything to further the transaction, apart from merely effecting the introduction. Nor, on the other hand, does it matter if the intermediary does all the work. Traders such as car dealers often carry out all that is needed to complete a hire-purchase agreement between a customer and the finance house to which they have 'introduced' him. The dealer carries stocks of the finance company's forms, fills them out and, having obtained the customer's signature, forwards them to the company. The customer may never become aware of the finance company's name and address if he makes his instalment payments through the dealer. All this does not matter. The dealer is taken to have 'effected an introduction' if the result of his activities is that in law a credit agreement has been made between the customer and the finance company, or the possibility of such an agreement has arisen.

*(d)  The trader to whom the seeker is introduced*

We now come to the most complicated part of the definition of 'credit brokerage'. We have seen that in the case of a credit-seeker the amount of credit required is immaterial, and that a similar rule applies to hire-seekers. This does not however mean that all introductions of credit or hire-seekers are caught by the Act. If a man wishing to borrow £1,000,000 to float a company is introduced to a source of finance which would never contemplate a deal in less than six figures that will not be caught by the Act, and rightly so. It has nothing whatever to do with consumer credit.

What the complex provisions defining the relevant credit and hire traders are trying to do is identify those cases where regulation is appropriate and exclude the others. It will simplify matters if we do what the Act does not and deal with each type of trader separately. First we can get one straightforward case out of the way. If, instead of passing the credit- or hire-seeker on to a credit or hire trader, the intermediary introduces him to *another credit-broker* that in itself will count as credit brokerage by the intermediary.

*(e) The credit trader*

Introduction to a credit trader will be within the definition of credit brokerage if, but only if, the trade is in any one of the following categories (and if of course the other conditions we have described are satisfied):

(1) The trader carries on a **business** which comprises or relates to the provision of **credit** under regulated consumer credit agreements. As explained in section 1 of Chapter 1, see page 7). Such a business will be what the Act calls a consumer credit business and should hold a Category A licence unless run by an individual who does not grant credit exceeding £30. (To check whether a licence is held you can consult the Consumer Credit Public Register: see page 201.) It is still credit brokerage however even if the trader to whom the introduction is made does not need a licence, or has failed to get a licence when he should have one.

(2) The trader does not carry on a consumer credit business, but does carry on a business which comprises or relates to exempt **debtor-creditor agreements** which derive their exemption from the fact that the rate of the total charge for credit does not exceed the higher of the following: 13 per cent per annum or 1 per cent above bank base rate (for an explanation of this exemption see pages 14 and 15).

(3) The trader is a building society or local authority granting mortgage advances.

(4) The trader is one of the insurance companies, friendly societies, charities or statutory bodies whose mortgage advances are exempt from statutory control following an application made by them to the Department of Trade. (For a list of the first three of these see Appendix 2, page 232).

(5) The trader does not carry on a consumer credit business, and is not within paragraphs (2) to (4), but does carry on a business in the course of which he provides credit secured by a mortgage on land or buildings. (This category only

applies where the reason why the credit-seeker desires credit is to finance the purchase of a house, flat or other dwelling, or the provision of a dwelling by new building or conversion, and the dwelling is to be occupied by himself or his relative.)

(6) The trader does not carry on a consumer credit business, and is not within paragraphs (2) or (5), but does carry on a business which comprises or relates to consumer credit agreements which are:

(a) **exempt agreements** deriving their exemption from the fact that they are trade agreements with a foreign connection (see page 13), or

(b) **foreign agreements** which if they were United Kingdom agreements would be **regulated agreements** (because within the £15,000 limit).

It will be seen from the list of categories that the controls imposed by the Act on credit brokerage go considerably wider than the general system of trading control and agreement control imposed in relation to credit traders. The general system is limited to the trader who carries on a consumer credit business. Building societies, for example, and foreign traders escape. But brokers do not escape by confining their introductions to such exempt traders. The reason is simple. Loans by a building society or local authority are exempt from the Act because such bodies are closely controlled by other legislation, but brokers introducing business to them are not so controlled. Loans by a foreign credit trader are exempt because the British courts cannot reach such traders; but this does not apply to brokers operating in Britain to obtain custom for them.

**Example 48** To avoid control, a credit trader C (United Kingdom) Ltd establishes a subsidiary called C (Ireland) Ltd, registered in Dublin. It makes arrangements for agents in Britain to canvass (as independent contractors) on its behalf. Letters from C (Ireland) Ltd accepting credit proposals from individuals in the United Kingdom are invariably posted in Dublin, and credit contracts specify that they are to be governed by Irish law. C (Ireland) Ltd is not carrying on a consumer credit business within the meaning of the Act, but nevertheless the canvassers are '**credit-brokers**' and subject to the Act unless saved by the £30 exception described on pages 158 and 159.

Note that not all introductions to exempt credit traders are caught. If the trader limits himself to agreements falling within paragraphs (2) to (4) on page 12, an intermediary will not be a credit-broker because of introductions made to that trader—unless they fall within category (5) above. This category was inserted to give added protection in the case where complaints against mortgage brokers had been most vociferous, the market in second mortgages.

### (f)  The hire trader

When we come to hire traders the position is thankfully much simpler. Apart from foreign traders, the only type of hire trader introduction to whom constitutes 'credit brokerage' is one who carries on a **consumer hire business**. For reasons similar to those given above in relation to credit traders, the definition of credit brokerage also brings in introductions to a trader who does not carry on a consumer hire business but does carry on a business which comprises or relates to consumer hire agreements which are **foreign agreements** such that, if they were United Kingdom agreements, they would be regulated agreements (because conforming to the financial and duration requirements described on pages 115 and 116).

### 4  The Category C licence

If you carry on a credit brokerage business (and are not within the £30 exception mentioned below) then you need a licence from the OFT. Unless (which is most unlikely) you are covered by a group licence, the licence you need is a Category C standard licence issued to you or your firm individually. By the end of 1985, 144,889 Category C licences had been issued. The only groups generally licensed to carry on credit brokerage business by a group licence are solicitors, chartered accountants and certified accountants.

The details of the licensing system are explained in Chapter 8. A special authorisation in the licence is required if you wish to **canvass regulated agreements off trade premises**. For this an extra licence fee of £10 is payable. Canvassing restrictions are described in section 5 below.

The requirement to be licensed does not apply to a business carried on by an **individual** who limits himself to introductions of

persons desiring credit not exceeding £30 under **debtor-creditor-supplier agreements** where either:
(1) the credit is to finance a transaction in **goods** in a case where the creditor is also the **supplier** and would be willing to sell the goods to the prospective debtor for cash, or
(2) the credit-broker is the supplier.

*(a) Unenforceability of regulated agreements where broker unlicensed*

A unique feature applying only in the case of unlicensed **credit-brokers** is that their failure to take out a licence may render agreements made by *other traders* unenforceable. The need for an effective system of licensing control over credit-brokers was felt to be sufficiently great to require a penalty additional to the criminal penalty (see page 202) and the civil sanction whereby agreements for the services of any ancillary credit trader are unenforceable if he lacks a licence (pages 202 and 203). The result is in effect to make credit and hire traders part of the policing system for securing observance by credit-brokers of their duty to take out a licence.

The penalty operates in this way. If a **regulated agreement** is entered into by a consumer who, for the purpose of making that agreement, was introduced to the credit or hire trader by an unlicensed credit-broker, then the agreement is unenforceable against the consumer without a validation order by the OFT (though there is nothing to prevent the consumer himself enforcing the agreement if he wishes). A credit-broker is treated as **unlicensed** even where he actually holds a licence if it does not cover the introduction in question, eg where the introduction was effected through canvassing off trade premises and the licence did not contain a canvassing authorisation. In determining whether to make a validation order the OFT will be guided by the degree of culpability of the applicant in failing to obtain an adequate licence and the extent to which consumers have been harmed by the failure.

**Example 49** B, a banker, enters into loan agreements secured on house property following introductions by M, a mortgage broker to whom B pays commission. M is unlicensed. The OFT finds that M has made a practice of forcing more credit on borrowers than they need. In considering an application for a validation order, the OFT may find that the high-pressure techniques used by M have seriously prejudiced borrowers. They may refuse an order, or grant an order which excludes specified agreements from its operation or requires interest rates on validated agreements to be reduced.

The existence of this provision makes it essential for credit and hire traders to ensure that they do not accept business from unlicensed brokers. For this purpose a watch on the Consumer Credit Public Register may be necessary. By accepting introductions from an unlicensed broker, and entering into regulated agreements with the consumers introduced, the trader is enabling the unlicensed broker to carry on his illegal activities. If in such cases introductions were rejected the broker would quickly be driven out of business. The OFT is likely therefore to take a serious view of infringements and withhold validation orders where this seems justified for the protection of the consumer. In extreme cases the OFT may even go to the extent of suspending or revoking the Category A or B licence held by the trader (see page 207).

## 5 Canvassing restrictions

**Credit-brokers** are affected by all the canvassing restrictions imposed on credit traders (section 7 of Chapter 1, page 25) and on hire traders (section 5 of Chapter 2, page 118). Reference should therefore be made to the descriptions of those restrictions. The following points arise in addition.

### (a) Canvassing authorisation in licence

It is unlawful for a credit-broker to **canvass a regulated agreement off trade premises** unless he holds a Category C licence containing a specific canvassing authorisation, for which an additional fee of £10 is payable. It is immaterial that the trader whose agreements he is canvassing holds a Category A or B licence containing a canvassing authorisation. The OFT needs to be able to check that the credit-broker himself is fit to be allowed to engage in door-step canvassing.

The OFT must grant a canvassing authorisation if satisfied that the applicant is a fit person to engage in face-to-face canvassing (see page 199). The most obvious evidence that he is not a fit person is where he or his business associates have a record of intimidation or other harsh or oppressive conduct towards members of the public.

The consequence of engaging in face-to-face canvassing off trade premises when your Category C licence does not contain a specific canvassing authorisation is that you are guilty of unlicensed trading. (As to the penalties for this see page 202). Furthermore the agreements you negotiate will be unenforceable by the credit or hire trader without an order from the OFT (see pages 202 and 203). Note that this does not apply to canvassing by *employees* of the credit or hire trader or by exempted canvassers (see page 153) since they are not **credit-brokers** within the meaning of the Act.

## (b) Canvassing of credit-broker's own services

So far we have dealt with the canvassing by a credit-broker of agreements to be entered into by *other traders* (whether or not the broker acts as their agent in negotiating the agreement). Now we turn to another possible type of canvassing by a broker: attempting to persuade consumers to use the broker's services in obtaining for themselves a loan or other facility.

It is a criminal offence for any **individual** to canvass off trade premises the services of a credit-broker. It makes no difference whether the broker intends to charge for his services or not. On conviction in a Crown Court the maximum penalty is imprisonment for one year and/or a fine of unlimited amount. In a magistrates' court the maximum is a fine of £2,000. The crime is committed by the individual canvasser, though his employer (if any) would in most cases also be liable. The test of what constitutes canvassing off trade premises is virtually the same here as it is for canvassing regulated agreements. The latter test is described on pages 25 to 28, and the only difference (a very slight one) lies in the type of premises involved. For the purpose of canvassing the services of credit-brokers, 'trade premises' consist of any of the following:

(1) A place where the credit brokerage business is carried on;
(2) A place where any type of business is carried on by the individual canvasser;
(3) A place where any type of business is carried on by the canvasser's employer (whether he employs him as a canvasser or for any other purpose, including a purpose unconnected with credit or hire);

(4) A place where the individual who is canvassed carries on any type of business.

## 6 Advertisements

### (a) Advertising of trader's services

Credit-brokers, and persons carrying on a business which, while not within the definition of **credit-brokerage**, includes the effecting of introductions of **individuals** desiring credit to persons who provide credit secured on land or buildings, are affected by all the advertising restrictions imposed on credit traders (section 8 of Chapter 1, page 31) and on hire traders (section 6 of Chapter 2, page 120). Reference should therefore be made to the descriptions of those restrictions.

### (b) Advertising of credit-broker's own services

It is an offence to publish a brokerage advertisement if it conveys information which in a material respect is false or misleading. (For this purpose information stating or implying an intention on the advertiser's part which in fact he has not got is taken as false.) As with credit advertisements (see page 31), every type of advertising medium is covered. The rule applies to any advertisement published for the purposes of the business of, and advertising the services of, any **credit-broker** or any person who effects introductions of individuals desiring credit to persons who provide credit secured on land or buildings.

Conviction of the offence in a Crown Court carries a maximum penalty of imprisonment for one year and/or a fine of unlimited amount. In a magistrates' court the maximum penalty is a fine of £2,000. Apart from the advertiser himself, the publisher and any advertising agent may also be liable (see Chapter 7).

## 7 Quotations

**Credit-brokers** are affected by all the quotations provisions applying to credit traders (section 9 of Chapter 1, page 46) and to hire traders (section 7 of Chapter 2, page 126). Reference should therefore be made to the descriptions of those provisions.

## 8 £3 limit on brokerage fees

During the period between the publication of the Crowther

Report and the enactment of the Act, further complaints about brokers were brought to the Government's attention. Certain brokers had developed the practice of charging prospective borrowers large fees in advance. These were to cover such items as structural surveys and valuations of houses on which mortgages were sought, or were documentation fees, or were outright charges simply for introduction to a source of finance. Having collected such fees the broker made little real attempt to obtain a loan, or offered a loan on outrageously expensive terms. Sometimes a broker had a reputation such that no finance house would entertain his introductions. Some prospective borrowers put forward by brokers were such obviously poor security risks that no lender would look at them. In all such cases the consumer failed to obtain what he required and yet had parted with considerable sums which he could not get back. The Government adopted a remedy additional to those proposed by the Crowther Committee. This was to limit the brokerage fee to the purely nominal sum of £1 (now increased to £3) unless the brokers' efforts were successful within six months of effecting the introduction.

*(a) The consumer*

Four types of credit- or hire-seeker are given the protection of the £3 limit. The Act defines them in this way:

(1) An **individual** who seeks an introduction for a purpose which would be fulfilled by his entry into a **regulated consumer credit agreement or consumer hire agreement**. If he wishes to borrow £1,000 in cash, or buy a £3,000 car on hire purchase, or obtain equipment on hire for more than three months at total rentals not exceeding £15,000, he will be within this category. If he wishes to borrow an amount above the £15,000 limit by reference to which a consumer credit agreement is defined, he will not be within this category (but might be within the next).

(2) An individual who desires to obtain a house, flat or other dwelling for occupation by himself or his relative and needs credit (whether or not exceeding £15,000). This may be to finance (wholly or partly) the purchase of a dwelling, the erection of a dwelling, or the provision of a dwelling by conversion or other alteration of an existing building. The category does not cover finance required for the mere improvement of an existing dwelling. It does however cover a case where the dwelling is not the only property being acquired.

**Example 50** Mr B wishes to purchase a business consisting of a leasehold interest in premises comprising a lock-up shop with flat above, together with fixtures and fittings, stock and goodwill. He intends to reside in the flat. He seeks a loan of £17,000, secured by a mortgage of the lease, to enable him (with the addition of savings of his own) to purchase the business. Since the loan will partly finance the acquisition of the flat the case is within this category.

(3) An individual who seeks an introduction for a purpose which would be fulfilled by his entry into a consumer credit agreement or consumer hire agreement that would be a **regulated agreement** if it were not exempt. This does not however include the case where the exemption is one of those described in paragraphs (2) to (4) on page 12.

**Example 51** Mr D wishes to build a small commercial garage. He seeks an owner of building land costing not more than £15,000 who will sell it to him on credit terms allowing payment of the price (together with interest) in four equal six-monthly instalments. This is an exempt agreement falling within pargraph (2) on page 12. Mr D is not therefore within this category.

(4) An individual who seeks an introduction for a purpose which would be fulfilled by his entry into an agreement that would be a regulated consumer credit or consumer hire agreement but for the fact that it will be governed by a foreign law. This is an anti-avoidance category. A broker practising in the United Kingdom cannot avoid the £3 limitation on his fee by persuading his client to agree that a loan should be sought from an overseas moneylender.

*(b) The introduction*

If the consumer falls within one of the four categories listed above, the credit-broker will be restricted to a £3 fee if the introduction does not result in the consumer entering into a 'relevant agreement' (see below) within the six months following the introduction. A cancelled agreement is to be disregarded for this purpose. Also disregarded is the fact that it may be the consumer's own fault that no agreement results. If the consumer changes his mind about the deal and, although offered a perfectly good agreement within the six months, refuses it, the broker is still limited to £3. Nor will it help the broker to make a further introduction to a different source. If the first introduction fails for any reason the £3 limit applies, though there is nothing to prevent the broker making a fresh contract with the consumer and starting all over again. The £3 limit does not apply if no introduction is ever made, but in such a case the consumer is likely to be entitled to the return of his money as paid on a consideration which has wholly failed.

### (c) The 'relevant agreement'

It will not avail the credit-broker if the consumer enters into a credit or hire agreement which is not what the Act calls a 'relevant agreement'. In relation to the categories set out on pages 163 and 164, the following are relevant agreements:

Category (1)   Any regulated consumer credit or **consumer hire agreement**.

Category (2)   Any agreement for credit secured on land or buildings.

Category (3)   Any consumer credit or consumer hire agreement which is exempted from being a regulated agreement by the provisions described in paragraphs (1), (5) or (6) on pages 12 and 13.

Category (4)   Any agreement which would be a regulated agreement if it were not governed by foreign law.

### (d) What is included in the broker's fee

In all cases the £3 limit applies to what the Act calls 'a fee or commission' for the broker's services. (In addition, as explained in the next paragraph, it may in certain cases apply to other charges as well.) The broker cannot evade the Act by giving some other name to what is in essence a fee or commission for his services, but the services in question must be *brokerage* services. If he performs other services as well (eg a structural survey) the fee for them will not be caught by the £3 limit unless the provisions described in the next paragraph apply.

The amount which is subject to the £3 limit includes, in the case of an individual desiring to obtain credit under a **consumer credit agreement** (whether **regulated** or not), certain items in addition to any straightforward fee for the broker's services. These are the items which would be included in the **total charge for credit** if the agreement were made.

> **Example 52** B Ltd, a firm of mortgage brokers, agree to try and find a mortgage to advance 90 per cent of the price of £32,000 for a house Mr D wishes to purchase. B Ltd, at the outset, persuade Mr D to pay them £175, made up as follows:
>
> Fee for effecting an introduction       £25
> Documentation fee       £10
> Fee for surveying the house       £40
> Deposit (advance interest on loan)       £100
>
> Assuming Mr D desires the house for occupation by himself or a relative, this will fall within category (2). Does the £3 limit apply to the entire £175 or only part of it? This may not be altogether easy to determine. Anything which constitutes what the Act calls a fee or commission for the broker's services is clearly within the £3 limit. This applies to the first item and probably the second. The third item (the survey fee) is more difficult, for it depends on whether the mortgage agreement would require the borrower to pay this. Only in such a case would it be within the total charge for credit (see page 16). If a mortgage agreement has actually been made (but outside the six-month period, so that the £3 limit operates) the question will be decided by its actual terms. Otherwise it would be a matter for conjecture. Since mortgage agreements usually contain this requirement a court would probably hold that it was included. The advance interest of £100 certainly falls within the total charge for credit, so we conclude that the entire sum of £175 is subject to the £3 limit.

Where the £3 limit applies, it operates in this way. If, at the end of the six months immediately following the date on which the introduction is effected, no relevant credit or hire agreement has been entered into, the credit-broker must then repay the surplus over £3. Any part of the fee which has not by then been paid over to the broker by the credit- or hire-seeker ceases to be payable.

Is the broker therefore entitled to wait until the six months have expired before making repayment, even though it is obvious that no agreement will be made? As far as the Act is concerned, the answer is yes.

**Example 53** On 20 May, B Ltd, following a request by Mr D, introduce him to M, a moneylender. If this introduction does not lead to the making of a loan agreement within six months then, under the Act, £97 will be repayable by B Ltd to Mr D in respect of £100 paid by way of advance fees. On 1 June, Mr D informs B Ltd that his relative has just died leaving him some money and he no longer requires the loan. He demands the immediate return of his £100, or at least £97 of it. The Act however does not give Mr D any right to the payment of £97 before 20 November. To be successful, any claim by him before then would have to depend on the express or implied terms of his contract with B Ltd.

*(e) Contracting out*

The OFT takes the view that it is not possible for a broker to exclude the £3 limit by any contractual term. Moreover they would regard any attempt to do so as an unfair business practice endangering the broker's licence (see page 203).

## 9 Credit-brokers as statutory agents of credit traders

There are many cases where a retailer, dealer or other **supplier** of **goods** or services who is technically a **credit-broker** (because he passes customers who need **credit** so as to be able to acquire his goods or services on to sources of finance who can provide the credit) will be treated as the statutory agent of the credit trader to whom he makes introductions. This is mainly the concern of the credit trader rather than the credit-broker, and is described in section 13 of Chapter 1 on pages 65 to 74. Note that the only case which the Act lays down by reference to credit-brokers as such is the first of the two basic cases dealt with in section 13, ie where the credit is to finance a transaction between the creditor and the debtor (eg a **hire-purchase agreement**, which the Act treats as credit) and the goods are sold to the creditor for this purpose by a dealer who is also a credit-broker. (This case is fully described on pages 66 to 69.)

The other basic case dealt with in section 13 of Chapter 1 is in terms of a **supplier** as statutory agent of a connected lender. However, such a supplier will frequently also be a credit-broker. His position is described in pages 69 to 73. Note that in certain instances he may be under a duty to indemnify a credit trader who suffers loss through his default (see page 73).

## 10  Liability for credit-broker's acts or omissions

An agreement, whenever made, is void if it purports to relieve a **credit-broker** from liability in a case where he sells **goods** to a credit grantor so that they can be the subject of a hire-purchase, credit sale or **conditional sale agreement**. Nor can an agreement effectively make the credit-broker the agent of the consumer in such cases. These rules only apply however where the credit-broker is the statutory agent of the credit trader under the provisions just described.

## 11  Duties in relation to credit reference agencies consulted

As explained in Chapter 1 in relation to **credit-traders** (page 138) and in Chapter 2 in relation to **hire-traders** (page 54), these traders are under a duty to give **credit-brokers** certain information. This duty arises where as a credit-broker you have introduced a consumer to the trader and the trader has consulted a **credit reference agency** about the consumer's financial standing. If the trader decides not to proceed with the proposed credit or hire agreement, and he does not inform the consumer of his decision directly, he is under a duty, not later than the time he informs you of his decision, also to tell you the name and address of the credit reference agency in question.

### (a)  Duty to inform consumer

Where you have received from the credit or hire trader the name and address of a credit reference agency consulted by him, the consumer has a right to obtain this information in turn from you. The same applies if you yourself have applied to a credit reference agency for information about the consumer during the period leading up to the making of a regulated credit or hire agreement or the breaking off of negotiations for the agreement. The consumer need pay no fee for obtaining the information from you.

To be entitled to the information, the consumer must comply with the procedure laid down. He must make the request in writing, and give you his own name and address so that you know where to send the information. His request must reach you before the end of the prescribed period. This runs from the time negotiations for the credit or hire agreement are commenced (whether by you or the credit or hire trader). If the agreement is made, the period expires twenty-eight days after it is made. If it is not made, the period expires twenty-eight days after the negotiations for it end. They are taken to end on the date the trader gives notice to the consumer (or to you) that he does not intend to proceed with the making of the agreement. If no such notice is actually given, the negotiations end at such time as it would be reasonable for the consumer to conclude that the intention to make an agreement has been abandoned.

If you receive a request which complies with these requirements, your duty is to give the consumer notice in writing of the name and address of the credit reference agency within seven days after receiving the request. Except in one case, this does not apply if you do not hold a Category C licence. The exceptional case is where the introduction was for the purpose of entering into the type of credit arrangement where you, as a dealer, sell goods to a finance house so that they can be disposed of on hire-purchase or similar terms to the consumer (see page 66). In this type of case the duty applies whether or not you are licensed, and breach of it is punishable (in a magistrates' court only) by a fine of up to £1,000. In all other cases the duty only applies if you are licensed, and there is no criminal penalty for its breach. The sanction is limited to disciplinary action by the OFT (ie suspension or revocation of your licence, or a warning that this may follow any further infringement).

### (b) Agents and employees

If you employ canvassers or other agents, or have numerous branches, you should take steps to ensure that head office is kept informed about approaches to credit reference agencies. An enquiry made by an agent in the course of his authorised activities is treated as made by his principal. Similar precautions should be taken in relation to information received from credit and hire traders.

### 12 Provisions not yet in force

All the provisions so far described in this chapter are operative (in relation to a **credit brokerage business**) at the date of going to press. There are further provisions of the Act which have not yet been applied in relation to businesses of this type. When this happens they will be accompanied by detailed regulations. Until these regulations are produced, only a bare outline can be given of the additional controls which will apply to your credit-brokerage business if and when the Act is fully applied.

*(a) Trading control*

There are wide powers to specify how a Category C licence-holder is to operate his business, though breach of the regulations will not be criminal except where they relate to the seeking of custom.

*(b) Agreement control*

The power to regulate **credit** and **hire agreements** is echoed in relation to agreements entered into in the course of a credit brokerage business. If such agreements are themselves credit or hire agreements (which the broker makes as agent of the credit or hire trader) the main controls will of course apply directly. The further powers are mainly concerned with agreements for the broker's services, under which he may be entitled to commission from the consumer. Regulations may specify the pre-contract information which must be given to the consumer, and the documentation requirements. As with credit and hire agreements, control will not be enforced by use of the criminal law. Instead, infringing agreements will be treated as 'improperly executed'. Enforcement against the consumer will then require a court order.

# Chapter 4

# Debt Counselling and Debt Adjusting

## 1 What 'debt counselling' and 'debt adjusting' are

Despite the apparent generality of the terms 'debt counselling' and 'debt adjusting', the definitions in the Act severely limit their width. The first limitation is that they only apply to activities in relation to a **consumer credit agreement** or **consumer hire agreement** (though it makes no difference in this connection whether it is a **regulated agreement**, an **exempt agreement** or a **foreign agreement**). The second limitation is that the Act excludes from the definitions a wide variety of *excepted persons*. Finally, the activity is only subject to control if it is carried on by way of **business**.

The difference between the two terms lies in the fact that an activity is 'debt counselling' when it is confined to advising the consumer on how to settle his debts, while it is 'debt adjusting' if it goes further and involves something like the taking over and settlement of the various debts in return for regular payments to the debt adjuster by the consumer. The definitions are explained in more detail below (see section 3 on page 172).

### (a) Reasons for the controls

The Crowther Committee received evidence of serious abuses by persons holding themselves out as debt counsellors or debt adjusters. They offered a 'multiple debtor' the service of taking over responsibility for payment of all his debts, the debtor undertaking to pay back the sum involved, with charges, to the person offering the service. This procedure was held out to the debtor as greatly to his advantage in that it saved him the trouble and anxiety of having to reach an accommodation with each of a number of different creditors, all his liabilities being refinanced and converted into a single debt to one person. Unfortunately, the Committee found, some people offering this service, after collecting substantial sums from debtors, absconded or became insolvent without paying a penny towards discharge of the liabilities of the debtors whose interest they were supposed to be safeguarding. The Committee added that they did not doubt that, when conducted by reputable concerns, debt counselling and debt adjusting provide a valuable and much-needed service. Nevertheless they felt the opportunities for exploitation of hard-pressed debtors were such that the protection of a licensing system was needed.

The Crowther Committee did not mention another aspect justifying control. A debt adjuster, without being dishonest, may nevertheless require payments from the debtor which are exorbitant. For example he may buy up the debts very cheaply as bad debts, but charge the debtor on the basis of their full face value. He may fail to pass on rebates for early settlement, or may, in other ways, make exorbitant charges.

## 2 How the Act affects your business

If your business is or includes a business of debt counselling or debt adjusting the following provisions apply now:

You must have a licence issued by the OFT.

You are restricted in the way you canvass for business.

Your advertisements must not be misleading.

These provisions are explained in the present chapter. Further provisions may be brought into force later and are outlined at the end of the chapter.

## 3 The definitions in detail

### (a) Debt counselling

It is 'debt counselling' for any person other than an excepted person (see below) to give advice to the debtor or hirer about the liquidation of a debt due under a **consumer credit agreement** or **consumer hire agreement**. Note that the debt must be 'due', so advice limited to debts which will become due under the agreement at a future time is not caught.

*(b) Debt adjusting*

Here the definition is more complicated. It falls into three parts, each limited to activity in relation to a consumer credit agreement or consumer hire agreement. It is debt adjusting for any person other than an excepted person to do any of the following:

(1) Negotiate with the creditor or owner, on behalf of the debtor or hirer, terms for the discharge of a debt due under the agreement.

(2) Take over, in return for payments by the debtor or hirer, his obligation to discharge a debt due under the agreement.

(3) Carry out any similar activity concerned with the liquidation of a debt due under the agreement.

Note that, as with debt counselling, the debt must be 'due'. Although debt adjusting is likely to include debts which will only become due under the agreement at a later date, it does not fall within the definition unless there are current obligations also.

The open-ended nature of paragraph (3) may cause doubts as to exactly how wide it goes. It should be remembered that the purpose of the definition is to describe in precise terms a well-known and recognised commercial function; it is not meant to impose controls on areas going beyond that function. One particular point on which doubt has arisen concerns part-exchange transactions. It is common for used-car dealers, for example, to settle outstanding hire-purchase commitments when taking a customer's old car in part-exchange. The cost of doing this is reflected in the financial arrangements governing the purchase of the new car. Is it debt-adjusting within the definition? The answer is no, at least where the customer is not in financial difficulty (and he is not likely to be in difficulty over payments on his old car if he is engaged in buying a new one). Debt adjusting is essentially concerned with helping people who are financially embarrassed. Where this element is absent, the activity is unlikely to fall within the definition.

*(c) Excepted persons*

In a further attempt to limit the terms 'debt counselling' and 'debt adjusting' to their generally-accepted commercial meaning, the Act lists a number of persons whose activities do not fall within the definitions of these terms. The same list applies to the definition of 'debt collecting', which is dealt with in Chapter 5.

First, certain lawyers are excepted. A barrister (in Scotland an advocate) is excepted if he is acting as such. This is not likely to apply in relation to debt adjusting, since it would be unprofessional for a practising barrister to engage in this activity. A solicitor is excepted if he is engaging in contentious business, ie business for the purpose of legal proceedings in any court or proceedings before an arbitrator. (Solicitors are in any case covered by group licence—see page 209.) Next there is a general exception for the type of canvasser who is excepted from being a credit-broker by the provision designed to exclude such people as housewives who canvass from their own homes (see page 153). This exception only applies where the credit or hire agreement in relation to which help is given was made in consequence of an introduction by such a canvasser. It allows for the fact that people like mail-order canvassers build up a connection and not only procure the making of credit or hire agreements but also collect debts arising under them and advise debtors who get into difficulties. It was felt the exception from being a credit-broker should extend to such linked activities also.

The remaining exceptions are best dealt with separately according to whether the agreement in question is a credit or hire agreement. If it is a **consumer credit agreement** the following are excepted persons:

(1) The **creditor**, if he does not hold that position by virtue of an assignment (other than an assignment made in connection with the transfer to the assignee of a **business** which is not a **debt collecting** business). This ensures the common-sense result that the original creditor is not treated as an ancillary credit trader when collecting debts due under the agreement or advising or co-operating with the debtor where he has got into financial difficulties. It also lets out a person who by operation of law has succeeded to the creditor's position, eg the trustee in bankruptcy in whom the property of a bankrupt sole trader vests automatically under the Insolvency Act. It does not however let out the finance house discounting receivables, or any other trader who takes over as creditor by accepting an assignment. The words in brackets provide a saving however for the creditor who holds that position by virtue of an assignment made in connection with the transfer to the assignee of a business (other than a debt-collecting business). Again the object of this is a commonsense one. If the whole business of the original creditor has been transferred as a going concern,

the trader receiving it should be in the same position as the original creditor. This will not apply however if that trader is in business as a debt-collector (when in any case he will need a Category E licence—see page 181).

(2) The **supplier**, in a case where the credit is provided to finance a transaction under which goods, services or land are supplied to the debtor. If the supplier, whether or not acting as the creditor's agent, advises the debtor about liquidating his indebtedness under the agreement or does any of the acts falling within the definition of debt adjusting, he will be let out by this exception.

(3) A **credit-broker**, where the credit-broker has acquired the business of a supplier falling within paragraph (2). This is likely to be a rare case.

If the agreement is a **consumer hire agreement** then, in addition to the lawyers and canvassers mentioned on pages 173 and 174, the *owner* is an excepted person, provided he does not hold that position by virtue of an assignment (other than an assignment made in connection with the transfer to the assignee of a **business** which is not a **debt collecting** business). This exception corresponds to the first exception applying to credit agreements (paragraph (1) on page 174), and the same explanation covers it.

### 4 The Category D licence

If you carry on a **business** which comprises or relates to debt counselling or debt adjusting or both, you need a licence from the OFT. Unless you are covered by a group licence, the licence you need is a Category D standard licence issued to you or your firm individually. This covers both types of activity. By the end of 1985, 48,929 Category D licences had been issued. The details of the licensing system are explained in Chapter 8.

Note that a debt adjuster who operates by, in effect, making loans to debtors will require a Category A licence as well. If a debt counsellor or debt adjuster introduces debtors to credit grantors he will also need a Category C licence as a credit-broker.

No fee is payable for the Category D licence where the applicant makes no charge, and requires no commission, in connection with those or any other business activities (whether in the field of credit or not).

**Example 54** As part of its personnel welfare services, a large retailing company regularly gives advice to staff about their financial problems. It needs a Category D licence, and must pay a fee for it because, although it does not charge employees for this service, it does of course charge for the goods it sells.

Where an organisation, such as a voluntary advice service, makes no charge to its clients, it is probably not carrying on a business, and therefore does not need a licence anyway.

*(a)  Group licences*

These are explained on pages 209 to 212. So far, a group licence covering debt counselling and debt adjusting has been issued in respect of each of the following groups:
   (1) *Solicitors* This is needed only in respect of non-contentious business, since in respect of contentious business solicitors are excepted persons (see page 174).
   (2) *Chartered accountants and certified accountants.*
   (3) *Citizens Advice Bureaux* It is doubtful if this licence was necessary since these Bureaux are probably not carrying on a business.
   (4) Certain persons such as *liquidators, executors and trustees,* but only where they or their firm are already licensed in respect of other activities.
   (5) *Age Concern/Old People's Welfare Committee in England* It is most unlikely that these charities would be regarded as giving advice and help by way of business, so that the group licence is almost certainly unnecessary.

## 5 Canvassing restrictions

A person carrying on a business which comprises or relates to debt counselling or debt adjusting is not allowed to canvass for business as a debt counsellor or debt adjuster if the canvassing is done off trade premises. This prohibition only applies to face-to-face canvassing. Contravention is a criminal offence, and it makes no difference whether the trader intends to charge for his services or not. This is a serious matter for charities and other voluntary bodies. If (contrary to this author's belief) they were held to be carrying on a business it would follow that their helpers might, in offering their services to people in need, inadvertently commit a technical offence.

Conviction of this offence in a Crown Court carries a maximum penalty of imprisonment for one year and/or a fine of unlimited amount. In a magistrates' court the maximum is a fine of £2,000. The crime is committed by the individual canvasser, though his employer (if any) would in most cases also be liable. The test of what constitutes canvassing off trade premises is virtually the same here as it is for canvassing regulated agreements. The latter test is described on pages 26 to 27, and the only difference (a very slight one) lies in the type of premises involved. For the purpose of canvassing the services of debt counsellors or debt adjusters, 'trade premises' consist of any of the following:

(1) A place where the business of debt counselling or debt adjusting is carried on.

(2) A place where any other type of **business** is carried on by the individual canvasser.

(3) A place where any other type of business is carried on by the canvasser's employer (whether he employs him as a canvasser or for any other purpose, including a purpose unconnected with credit or hire).

(4) A place where the **individual** who is canvassed carries on any type of business.

## 6 Advertisements

It is an offence to publish a debt-counselling advertisement if it conveys information which in a material respect is false or misleading. (For this purpose information stating or implying an intention on the advertiser's part which in fact he has not got is taken as false.) As with credit advertisements (see page 31), every type of advertising medium is covered. The rule applies to any advertisement published for the purposes of the business of, and advertising the services of, any person if:

(1) It indicates that he is willing to advise on debts or engage in transactions concerned with the liquidation of debts, and

(2) It does not indicate that he is unwilling to act in relation to **consumer credit agreements** and **consumer hire agreements**.

Conviction of the offence in a Crown Court carries a maximum penalty of imprisonment for one year and/or a fine of unlimited amount. In a magistrates' court the maximum penalty is a fine of £2,000. Apart from the advertiser himself, the publisher and any advertising agent may also be liable (see Chapter 7).

## 7 Provisions not yet in force

All the provisions so far described in this chapter are operative (in relation to debt counselling and debt adjusting) at the date of going to press. There are further provisions of the Act which have not yet been brought into operation in relation to activities of this type. If and when this happens they will be accompanied by detailed regulations. Until these regulations are produced, only a bare outline can be given of the additional controls which will apply to your debt counselling or debt adjusting business when the Act is fully operative.

### (a) Trading control

There are wide powers to specify how a Category D licence-holder is to operate his business, though breach of the regulations will not be criminal except where they relate to the seeking of custom.

### (b) Agreement control

There is power to make regulations specifying the pre-contract information which must be given to debtors engaging the services of debt counsellors and debt adjusters, and prescribing documentation requirements. As with credit and hire agreements, control will not be enforced by use of the criminal law. Instead, infringing agreements will be treated as 'improperly executed'. Enforcement against the consumer will then require a court order.

# Chapter 5

# Debt Collecting

## 1 What 'debt collecting' is

For the purposes of the Act, a person is a debt collector if he 'takes steps to procure payment of a debt due'. This includes *any* steps to procure payment, from merely asking for it, to the bringing of court proceedings to enforce it. However, as with debt counselling and debt adjusting, the Act severely limits the way it applies to debt collecting.

The first limitation is that the term only applies to collecting debts due under **consumer credit agreements** or **consumer hire agreements** (though it makes no difference in this connection whether an agreement is a **regulated agreement**, an **exempt agreement** or a **foreign agreement**).

The second limitation is that the Act excludes from the definition a wide variety of *excepted persons*. These are the same as for debt counselling and debt adjusting, and are described on pages 173 to 175.

The third limitation is that the activity is only subject to control by the Act if it is carried on by way of **business**. This may fall into any of three distinct categories. First, the debt collector may simply be acting as the agent of the creditor in collecting debts as they fall due (employees of the creditor do not count as debt collectors in their own right). Second, the debt collector may be a *factor* who acquires good debts (including debts not yet due) in return for payment to the creditor. (This gives the creditor a steady cash flow, often in anticipation of receipts from his customers, and may also provide a sales account and supervisory service.) Third, the debt collector may buy up *bad debts*, or debts which are probably bad, for very much less than their nominal

179

value in the hope that by rigorous collection methods full payment can be obtained.

## 2  Reasons for the controls

Unlike debt counsellors and debt adjusters, debt collectors are not employed directly by the public. The OFT is not therefore concerned with the methods they use to *obtain* business, but only with the methods they use in collecting debts—where of course they do enter into relations with consumers. Note however that a contract for his services made by an **unlicensed** debt collector with a trader will be unenforceable by the debt collector without an OFT order—see page 202. This is somewhat illogical, but helps to reinforce the licensing system.

The Crowther Committee expressed concern at various forms of improper pressure which are put on debtors. In this they echoed the views of an earlier official enquiry, the Payne Committee, which reported in 1969. The findings of that Committee were summarised by the present author in his book *Tangling with the Law*, as follows:

Some creditors carry ruthlessness to the limits of legality, or even beyond. Rather than waste time in court procedure they take direct action, either themselves or by assigning the debt to professional debt-collectors. Unofficial methods of debt collection include a number of questionable tactics. There is the 'blue frightener', a notice of intention to start County Court proceedings printed on blue paper so as to resemble a County Court summons. This may be followed by the 'red frightener', which is a printed notice in red lettering headed 'You have four days in which to reduce your debt'. If these devices fail they are likely to be followed by more concrete threats, rather than actual court proceedings. The threat to tell a man's neighbour or his employer, or to send round a van boldly painted 'Bad Debt Collection Van', can be very effective. So also can constant personal visits or telephone calls, particularly early in the morning or very late at night. More serious are actual threats of force, or personal calls accompanied by a fierce-looking dog. The Payne Committee found that some creditors were prepared to use any method and to go to unacceptable lengths to harass and intimidate debtors, instilling in them fear and panic.

In 1970, s 4 of the Administration of Justice Act was passed to clamp down on the practices described by the Payne Committee. This makes harassment of debtors a criminal offence punishable in a magistrates' court by a fine. The following acts are singled out as criminal:

(1) Harassing the debtor with demands for payment calculated to inflict alarm, distress or humiliation because of their frequency, the way they are made, or any threat or publicity accompanying them.

(2) Falsely representing that criminal proceedings lie for non-payment of the debt.

(3) Falsely representing that the debt collector has official authority.

(4) Serving a document falsely appearing to be of an official nature (eg a 'blue frightener').

The effect of the Consumer Credit Act is to add the support of the licensing system to the criminal sanctions imposed by the Administration of Justice Act. In his annual report for 1979, the Director General of Fair Trading said:

Debt collecting is, by its nature, an area which must be kept under close scrutiny. Practices which have been regarded as unfair include the charging of collection fees when there was no provision for this in the original agreement; the use of letter headings and trading names which mislead the consumer as to the identity of the person seeking to collect the debt; and the use of official-looking documents which might be taken for summonses.

### 3 How the Act affects your business

The only way in which the Act affects you if you carry on a debt collecting business is through the licensing system. You need a licence issued by the OFT. Unless you are covered by a group licence, the licence you need is a Category E standard licence issued to you or your firm individually. Up to the end of 1985, 16,489 Category E licences had been issued. Group licences for debt collecting have so far been issued only in respect of solicitors and persons acting as liquidators, receivers, etc. The latter are only covered if they hold or are covered by a licence in some other capacity. For details of the licensing system, see Chapter 8.

# Chapter 6

# Credit Reference Agencies

## 1 What a 'credit reference agency' is

The Act defines a 'credit reference agency' as a **business** which furnishes information relevant to the financial standing of **individuals**. The information need not have anything to do with a credit or hire transaction. Information does not fall within the definition, however, unless it is collected by the agency for the purpose of being passed on to enquirers.

> **Example 55** In the course of dealing with its customers, a bank accumulates information about their financial standing. In replying to credit status enquiries, the bank draws on this information. It does not however gather such information *for the purpose* of answering enquiries. The bank is not a credit reference agency within the meaning of the Act.

Even where a business does collect information for the purposes of passing it on, this does not necessarily mean it will be treated as a credit reference agency. The statutory definition is intended to identify a well-known type of business which is carried on under different descriptions (a common one is 'credit reference bureau'). It is not designed to go wider than this.

> **Example 56** In the course of his practice, a solicitor specialising in conveyancing frequently has occasion to make enquiries about the financial standing of individuals who are prospective tenants of property owned by the solicitor's clients. The information is passed on to the client so that he may judge whether a prospective tenant is suitable. The solicitor is not a 'credit reference agency' despite the fact that he may appear to fall within the literal meaning of the definition.

A credit reference agency may be non-profit-making (usually operated by a trade protection society) or a business run for profit. The Crowther Committee found there were about forty in each category, the largest being British Debt Services Ltd and the United Association for the Protection of Trade Ltd. However, by the end of 1984, 4,196 Category F (credit reference agency) licences had been issued under the Consumer Credit Act. This remarkable discrepancy can only be attributed to excess of caution on the part of traders who did not in fact need a licence.

## Reasons for the controls

Like debt collectors, credit reference agencies are not normally employed directly by consumers. The OFT is not therefore concerned with the methods they use to obtain business. Note however that a contract for an agency's services made with a trader will, if the agency is unlicensed, be unenforceable by the agency against the trader without an OFT order—see page 202. This appears illogical, but reinforces the effectiveness of the licensing system. The reason why the Act applies to credit reference agencies at all is to check breach of privacy and the spreading of incorrect or misleading information about consumers.

## 2 How the Act affects your business

The Act places duties on a wide variety of businesses to disclose when they have consulted a **credit reference agency** about the financial standing of a would-be customer—see page 54 (credit traders), page 138 (hire traders) and page 168 (credit-brokers). In addition, this duty of disclosure is placed on a connected **supplier**. This arises where in the course of negotiations for the type of **debtor-creditor-supplier agreement** where the creditor is not also the supplier (ie one falling within paragraph (2) or (3) on page 11), the supplier has applied to a credit reference agency for information about the financial standing of the consumer. If the consumer makes a written request not more than twenty-eight days after negotiations for the credit agreement have ended (whether on the making of the agreement or otherwise), the supplier must within seven days give the consumer written notice of the name and address of the credit reference agency consulted. Breach of this duty is a criminal offence, punishable (in a magistrates' court only) by a fine of up to £1,000. (This is the only case where the provisions of the Act impose a duty on a supplier as such.)

If you act as a credit reference agency, the Act affects you as follows:

You must have a licence issued by the OFT.

You must give any **individual** about whom you hold information notice of what the information is, and correct it where it is shown to be erroneous.

### 3  The Category F licence

If you carry on a credit reference agency, you need a licence from the OFT. Unless you are covered by a group licence, the licence you need is a Category F standard licence issued to you or your company individually. Up to the end of 1985, 4,786 Category F licences had been issued. The details of the licensing system are explained in Chapter 8. The only group licence so far issued which covers credit reference agencies is one which applies to the liquidator, receiver, etc of a credit reference agency where he or his firm is already covered by a licence under the Act (see page 210).

### 4  The duty to give consumer a copy of his file

*(a)  The file*

The Act calls the information kept by a credit reference agency about a consumer his 'file'. The Act says that the 'file' includes *all* the information kept but probably this should be treated as limited to information relevant to financial standing. This may include information about other people (eg the consumer's wife) if this is considered relevant to the credit status of the consumer himself. Note that an agency may keep information on more than one actual file. In the case of a sole trader, for example, the agency may keep one file on the trader in his private capacity and another under his trade name. On any request by the trader for a 'copy of his file', *both* files are subject to disclosure.

It is immaterial whether the information is kept in an actual file or in other ways. It may, for example, be kept in machine-readable form for computer use. Where the Act requires the consumer to be given a copy of his file, or of any part of it, the material given must be in plain English. If it is kept in abbreviated form, or in code, or on computer tape or disc, or in a language other than English, it must therefore be turned into a form of English which can be readily understood by the ordinary person.

## (b) The application

The duty of the credit reference agency only arises where the consumer (which means any **individual**) gives it proper notice requesting a copy of the file. It must be notice in writing, including the name and address of the consumer. The consumer must pay a fee of £1. No reason for the request need be given. If the agency reasonably requires further particulars to enable it to identify the file, the consumer must supply these. The agency may ask for any trade names of the applicant, and previous addresses, so as to be sure that all its relevant files are disclosed.

It is immaterial whether or not the consumer has been told that the agency has been consulted about him, or whether indeed it has been consulted in fact. If no file is kept on that particular consumer, the agency must tell him so in writing within seven **working days**. The fee of £1 need not be returned.

Where the agency does keep a file on the applicant, its duty depends on whether the normal procedure applies or s 160 of the Act is relevant.

The normal procedure will always apply where the applicant does not carry on a **business**, ie is a private individual. Even where the applicant does carry on a business, the normal procedure will apply unless the agency has obtained a 's 160 direction' (see below) and chooses to act under it. If it wishes, the agency can always use the normal procedure even though the case is covered by a s 160 direction.

## (c) The normal procedure

Where the normal procedure applies the agency must, within seven **working days** after the notice requirements set out above are complied with, give the applicant a copy of his file together with a notice in the prescribed form setting out his rights (see Notice A in Appendix 3, page 238).

## (d) Section 160 procedure

This was designed for the case where business contacts of a trader supply information about him to a credit reference agency. If a copy of the trader's entire file were supplied to him he might learn which of his contacts supplied such information and what its nature was. The likelihood of this could deter the contacts from supplying information to the agency and thus adversely affect the service it provided to its customers. Accordingly s 160 empowers the OFT to make a direction in favour of a credit reference agency (on payment of a fee of £25) designed to avoid this difficulty. Before doing so the OFT must be satisfied that, having regard to the methods employed by the agency and to any other relevant factors, it is probable that business consumers will not be prejudiced by the making of the direction. This is a safeguard against the possibility that an agency might use unscrupulous methods to gather information, in which case it might be wiser to let business consumers see everything that was held on their files. (The possibility appears remote, in view of the OFT's disciplinary powers against licence holders.) There is power to vary or revoke the direction.

By the end of November 1980, thirty agencies had been granted s 160 directions. Typically, these permit the agency to delete from the copy supplied to the consumer any report (whether written or otherwise) submitted to the agency by an individual or organisation if the report 'would, either directly or indirectly, disclose the source of the information supplied'. The direction requires the agency to disclose to the enquiring consumer (unprompted) the *number* of reports so deleted 'together with information based on the material deleted that will enable the consumer to understand the general view of his business presented by the deleted reports'. The s 160 direction tells the agency which information it is entitled to withhold. Where the s 160 procedure applies therefore the agency need only give the applicant such information included in, or based on, entries in his file as conforms to the OFT direction. This must be accompanied by a special notice of the applicant's rights (see Notice B in Appendix 3, page 240). The agency must tell the consumer that it is proceeding under s 160 of the Consumer Credit Act 1974. As with the normal procedure, the response of the agency must be by notice in writing given to the consumer within seven **working days** after the consumer complies with the notice requirements described on page 185.

It is the essence of the s 160 procedure that the applicant is only told *part* of the story. He may well feel dissatisfied, and wish to know more. The Act provides for this. First, the applicant must take such steps in relation to the agency as may be reasonable with a view to removing the cause of his dissatisfaction. In other words he must ask the agency to tell him what he wants to know. If it refuses, he may apply to the OFT for help. The OFT has power to direct the agency to give them a copy of the entire file. They can thus inspect the material which the agency is withholding from the applicant. If the OFT feels that on balance the material, or part of it, should not be withheld it may make the appropriate disclosure to the applicant itself. Otherwise the OFT will tell the applicant that he is not entitled to the information. Normally the OFT will not disclose further information without first inviting the agency to submit observations.

*(e) Penalties*

If a credit reference agency fails to comply with any of the duties outlined above it commits a criminal offence for which it is liable on summary conviction in a magistrates' court to a fine of up to £1,000.

## 5  Amendment of consumer's file

We have described in section 4 part of the machinery the Act provides to safeguard **individuals** about whom credit reference agencies keep information. That part of the machinery enables the individual to find out what information relative to him the agency has on its files, and is therefore presumed to be passing on to enquirers. If the information is factually correct then, although it may be detrimental to the individual, there is nothing he can do about it. The efficient working of the credit industry depends on an accurate supply of information about the financial standing of would-be borrowers. But suppose the information held on the agency's files is incorrect? Here a further part of the machinery provided by the Act comes into play.

*(a) Notice requiring removal or amendment*

We have the situation where an applicant has been given by the agency a copy of his file (where the normal procedure applies) or has been given by the agency, and perhaps to a further extent by the OFT, notice of information kept on his file (where the s 160 procedure applies). The applicant can only take further action where he considers:
  (1) that one or more entries in his file is factually incorrect, and
  (2) that if they are not corrected he is likely to be *prejudiced*.

In other words he cannot complain merely because an entry is mistaken. The mistake must be of a kind that is likely to prejudice the applicant in his future attempts to obtain credit. The applicant's remedy is to give the agency written notice requiring it either to delete the offending entry or entries altogether or to amend them so that they no longer contain prejudicial errors.

In response, the agency must within twenty-eight days serve on the applicant a *counter-notice*. In relation to each of the entries in question, this may be a counter-notice of removal, a counter-notice of amendment, or a counter-notice of non-action.

### (b) Counter-notice of removal

If the counter-notice states that the agency has removed the offending entry from the applicant's file, the agency must, within ten **working days** after serving the counter-notice give a written notice to those of its *customers* to whom since the date six months before the agency received the original application from the consumer, the agency has furnished information relevant to the consumer's financial standing.

If the information furnished to the customers did *not* include the entry which has been removed, but (whether in the form of a rating or opinion or otherwise) was based on the removed entry and therefore falls to be modified, the notice to the customers must give particulars of the modified information and state that it has been modified because of the removal of the entry from the file.

If, on the other hand, the information furnished to the customers did include the removed entry, the notice to the customers must tell them that entry has been removed, giving particulars of it, so that they can identify it.

Note that in neither case is there any requirement to tell the customers *why* the entry was removed.

### (c) Counter-notice of amendment

If, instead of stating that the incorrect entry has been removed from the file, the counter-notice to the consumer states that the agency has *amended* the entry, it must include a copy of the entry in its amended form. Within ten **working days** after serving the counter-notice, the agency must give written notice to its *customers* in the same way as described above in relation to a counter-notice of removal.

*(d) Counter-notice of non-action*

If the agency does not agree that the entry is incorrect, or, while admitting the error, does not accept that its nature or importance is such as to prejudice the consumer, the agency may serve a counter-notice on the consumer simply informing him that it is taking no action. Here there is no need for the agency to give any notice to its customers.

*(e) Penalties*

The Act provides no penalty for failure by the credit reference agency to serve a counter-notice on the consumer, though he is given a remedy in such cases (explained in section 6 below). Nor does the Act lay down any penalty where the agency serves a counter-notice of removal or amendment but fails to carry out what is stated in the counter-notice, or fails to notify its customers as required. For all these breaches, the only sanction available is, as so often under the Act, the enforcement of the disciplinary powers possessed by the OFT in relation to licensees.

## 6 Notices of correction

Where a counter-notice of removal of an entry has been served on the consumer he should have no further cause for anxiety. Since the incorrect entry has been removed altogether from his file, information based on it will no longer be passed to the agency's customers. Those customers who in the recent past have been given incorrect information will have been told the true position. Accordingly, the Act provides no further remedy to the consumer in such cases. A further remedy is, however, provided where the agency has served on the consumer either a counter-notice of amendment of the file, or a counter-notice of non-action, or has failed to serve any counter-notice at all within the twenty-eight day time limit. Where a counter-notice of amendment is served, the amendment may fail to satisfy the consumer; in the other two cases he will clearly be unsatisfied. Accordingly the Act provides for what it calls a 'notice of correction' in such cases.

*(a) Description of a notice of correction*

The notice of correction is added by the agency to the consumer's file. It is designed to offset the incorrect entry remaining on the file by showing in what way it is incorrect. It is drawn up by the consumer himself, and must not exceed two hundred words in length. Nor must it be of such a nature that it would be improper to publish it because:

(1) it is incorrect, or
(2) it unjustly defames any person (eg because it says something about an individual or company which is both derogatory and untrue), or
(3) it is scandalous (eg because it is obscene or blasphemous, or displays racial prejudice), or
(4) it is frivolous (eg because it is clearly not meant to be taken seriously), or
(5) it is for any other reason unsuitable.

*(b) Requirement to add notice of correction*

Within a specified time limit, the consumer may require the agency to add the notice of correction to his file and include a copy of it when furnishing information included in or based on the entry to which it relates. The time limit is as follows: Where a counter-notice of amendment or a counter-notice of non-action is served by the agency on the consumer, he has twenty-eight days following the day on which the counter-notice is received by him within which to require (in writing) the notice of correction to be added by the agency to his file. Where on the other hand no counter-notice was received by the consumer he can send the requirement at any time during the period which *begins* on the expiry of twenty-eight days from the receipt by the agency of his notice requiring removal or amendment of the entry and *ends* on the expiry of a further twenty-eight days.

> **Example 57** On Monday 1 October an individual sends by first class post to a credit reference agency a written notice requiring removal or amendment of an entry in his file. The agency does not reply. It is taken to have received the notice on 2 October, so the period within which the consumer may serve a further notice this time requiring a notice of correction to be added to his file commences at the beginning of 31 October and expires at the end of 27 November.

*(c) Compliance with requirements to add notice of correction*

Unless the agency thinks it would be improper to publish the notice of correction (for any of the reasons stated above), it must, within twenty-eight days after receiving the requirement, give the consumer written notice informing him that it has received it and intends to comply with it. (If it fails to do this there is no criminal penalty, but the consumer can apply to the OFT—see below.) Within a further ten **working days** the agency must give notice in writing to each of its customers to whom (at any time since the date six months before the consumer originally applied for a copy of his file) the agency has furnished information about the consumer's financial standing. If the information furnished included the entry referred to in the notice of correction, the customer must be sent particulars of the entry, together with a copy of the notice of correction. Otherwise, it suffices if the customer is given particulars of the modified information and a statement that the information has been modified by reason of the notice of correction.

### (d) Procedure where notice of correction improper

If the agency considers that it would be improper to publish the notice of correction and is unable to settle the matter by negotiating with the consumer (eg by agreeing a revised wording) it too can apply to the OFT. There is no time limit for this application, and no fee is payable. The application must be made on form CC/314/77 and accompanied by the information required by form CC/315/77. (For details of where to obtain these forms see Appendix 5, page 247.)

### (e) Consumer's right to apply to OFT

If, after the expiry of twenty-eight days from the agency's receipt of his requirement that a notice of correction be added to his file, the consumer has not been told of the agency's compliance, he can apply to the OFT for an order determining the matter. This is so whether or not the agency is making its own application to the OFT. There is no time limit, and no special forms are provided.

### (f) Order by OFT

On an application by the credit reference agency or the consumer in relation to a proposed notice of correction, the OFT can make whatever order it thinks fit for settling the matter. Normally the OFT, before making an order, will attempt conciliation between the parties. An order will be made only after the views of both sides have been obtained. If an order is eventually made it may require the agency to add the notice of correction in the form drafted by the consumer or in a form modified to remove any improper feature. Alternatively (where the OFT considers the consumer is not justified in asking for a notice of correction to be added to his file) the order may quash the notice of correction and dispense with any action by the agency. A further possibility is that the order may direct the agency to remove the entry from the file altogether, in which case the notice of correction would no longer be relevant.

The order will specify the period within which any action by the agency must be taken. If the agency does not comply it will be guilty of a criminal offence for which it will be liable on summary conviction in a magistrates' court to a fine not exceeding £1,000.

## 7 Conclusion

In view of the complexity of the provisions of the Act relating to credit reference agencies it may be helpful to give an example showing how the normal procedure operates.

**Example 58** Mr X suspects that incorrect information about his financial status is held on the files of A Ltd, who hold a Category F licence as a credit reference agency.

| | |
|---|---|
| 3 March | Mr X sends a written request for a copy of his file to A Ltd, together with £1.00. |
| 7 March | A Ltd ask Mr X for particulars to enable them to identify his file. |
| 10 March | Mr X sends the particulars requested. (A Ltd must complete the next step within seven **working days** after the day on which they receive the particulars.) |
| 15 March | A Ltd send Mr X a copy of his file and a notice of his rights in the form set out on page 238. |
| 20 March | Mr X writes to A Ltd pointing out that his file contains an entry to the effect that a judgment debt of £500 is unpaid. He states that the judgment debt was in fact for £100 and was paid one month after judgment. He asks that the entry either be removed altogether or amended to accord with the facts. (A Ltd must complete the next step within twenty-eight days after receiving this letter.) |

| | |
|---|---|
| 4 April | A Ltd write to Mr X informing him that they have amended the entry, enclosing a copy of the amended entry. It states that the judgment debt was paid after one month but still gives its amount as £500. (A Ltd must complete the next step within ten working days after the day on which Mr X is taken to receive this letter.) |
| 7 April | A Ltd send notices giving particulars of the amendment to all customers to whom, since the previous 3 September, they have furnished information about Mrs X's financial standing. |
| 20 April | Mr X sends A Ltd a notice of correction stating that the true amount of the judgment debt was £100 and requiring them to include a copy of this notice when furnishing information based on the entry. (He had twenty-eight days to send this, starting with the date of receipt of the letter posted on 4 April.) |
| 11 May | A Ltd apply to the OFT for an order quashing the notice of correction on the ground that it is factually incorrect. |
| 20 May | Mr X applies to the OFT for an order directing A Ltd to act on the notice of correction. |
| 30 June | After investigating the matter, the OFT determines that A Ltd are right and quash the notice of correction. A Ltd ask for costs, but are informed that the OFT has no power to award costs. Mr X seeks to appeal, but is told that there is no right of appeal. |

# Chapter 7

# Advertising Agencies and Publishers

In relation to advertising offences, the Consumer Credit Act is not content merely to impose penal sanctions on the advertiser himself. In addition, advertising agencies and the publishers of advertisements are also penalised. In this respect therefore they too are types of business required to take notice of the provisions of the legislation.

## 1 The cases

These secondary penalties only arise where the advertiser is himself guilty of an offence (or would be guilty if he were not able to claim the benefit of the defence of mistake etc—see page 220). The offences in question are those relating to advertisements for *credit* (section 8 of Chapter 1, page 120), *goods on hire* (section 6 of Chapter 2, page 31), *credit-brokerage* (section 6 of Chapter 3, page 162) and *debt-counselling* (section 6 of Chapter 4, page 177).

## 2 Persons and penalties

The Act does not use the term advertising agency. Instead it speaks of a person who, in the course of a **business** carried on by him, devised the advertisement in question. If different people devised different parts of the advertisement then the person guilty of the secondary offence is the one who devised the part relevant to the primary offence committed by the advertiser.

There is even less said in the Act about who the publisher is. Nevertheless it is clear that, according to the medium in which the advertisement appears, the person indicated in the table below would be treated as the publisher.

| Medium | Publisher |
|---|---|
| Newspaper or magazine | Proprietor |
| Poster | Owner of site |
| Radio or television | Owner of station |
| Cinema | Exhibitor |

In other types of advertisement, for example catalogues, circulars and price-tickets, the publisher and the advertiser would be the same person and the secondary liability would not arise.

The penalties for the secondary offence are the same as for the primary offence. Conviction in a Crown Court carries a maximum penalty of imprisonment for one year and/or a fine of unlimited amount. In a magistrates' court the maximum penalty is a fine of £2,000.

## 3 Special defence for publishers

In addition to the defence of mistake etc which is available in relation to all offences created by the legislation (see page 220), the Act gives publishers a special defence when charged with a secondary offence in relation to an advertisement. The publisher is entitled to be acquitted if he proves (on a balance of probabilities) that the advertisement was published in the course of a **business** carried on by him (as it normally would be), that he received the advertisement in the course of that business (as again would be normal), and that he did not know, and had no reason to suspect, that its publication would be an offence. This reproduces a defence provided (for other purposes) by s 25(3) of the Fair Trading Act 1973.

While this defence may be of some help to publishers, it does not protect them as much as might appear. It is no use the publisher saying, for example, that he was unaware of the law laid down by the Consumer Credit Act. Ignorance of the law is no excuse. Nor will it avail him to plead that it was a member of his staff, and not he himself, who made the wrong decision (see page 220). The practical question is whether it is necessary for the publisher to check the copy at all, or whether he can go ahead and publish without any check. The answer must be that some check is necessary or the purpose of Parliament in providing the offence would be nullified. On the other hand the pubisher's staff cannot be expected to carry out detailed investigations. More precise guidance must await a court decision on the extent of this defence or the similar one in s 25(3) of the Fair Trading Act 1973.

Chapter 8

# The Licensing System

## 1 Introduction

The scale of the licensing system can be gauged from the fact that more than a quarter of a million licences have been issued since licensing got under way in 1976. This figure refers to categories, and many traders have licences of more than one category. Still, the system is enormous. It has been criticised as being too cumbersome, but the answer to this was given by the Director General of Fair Trading in his annual report for 1979:

The licensing provisions of the Consumer Credit Act have been criticised by some as a sledgehammer to crack a nut, but I am convinced that they have already proved valuable and that their value will be increasingly demonstrated in the future. Before the Act, various sectors were controlled by different agencies of Government, and in some cases the control was very stringent indeed. In other areas of credit, there was no control whatever—with the result that some very undesirable people were concerned with credit activity, seeking a quick profit and having little regard for the trail of financial misery which they left behind. Even in apparently reputable sectors, the licensing process has revealed that, over the years, unacceptable working practices had grown up—sometimes without the knowledge of senior management. The need for firm action at the beginning of the 1970s was recognised by the credit industry itself, and the licensing powers conferred by the Act have enabled me to discover, and start to deal with, a variety of unfair and harmful practices.

There are two types of licence—standard licences and group licences. This chapter is mainly about standard licences, which are the only ones that concern ordinary trading businesses. A section on group licences appears at the end of the chapter.

There are six licence categories:

197

Category A    consumer credit business
Category B    consumer hire business
Category C    credit brokerage
Category D    debt adjusting and debt counselling
Category E    debt collecting
Category F    credit reference agency

A licence covering two or more categories is nevertheless embodied in one document.

The licence is required by the person carrying on the business in question. It may be a sole trader, partnership, limited company, or other corporate or unincorporated body. If you run the business as a sole trader you yourself need the licence. If your business is in the form of a limited company it is the company which needs the licence. In the case of a partnership or unincorporated body the licence should be applied for in the name of the partnership or body. Except in this case, a standard licence cannot be issued to more than one person. If your business is organised as several separate limited companies or partnerships, each company or partnership which comes within the scope of the Act must be separately licensed. However, a licence covers all the branches of a licensee's business no matter how numerous they are and regardless of where in the United Kingdom they are situated.

Details of the licensing system which are common to all categories of licence are outlined in this chapter. Features which only apply to one of the six categories are dealt with in the chapter on the type of business covered by that category.

## 2 Applications

Apply on forms CC1/84 and CC2/84 obtainable from OFT, Consumer Credit Licensing Branch, Government Buildings, Bromyard Avenue, Acton, London W3 7BB, or from local authority trading standards departments (sometimes called consumer protection or weights and measures departments). For the names and addresses of these see Appendix 5, page 247. If your firm is a limited company, or is otherwise incorporated, and has a **controller**, you also need to complete form CC79B/75. The fee for a licence is £80 for a sole trader and £150 in all other cases with a further £10 if you require a canvassing authorisation (see below). If more than one category of licence is required there is an extra £10 fee for each additional category. The application must be correctly made out, and accompanied by the necessary fee, or it will be treated as not having been made. (For rights of appeal see page 208.)

### 3 Qualification for a licence

Not every trader is entitled to a licence. The OFT must be satisfied that the applicant is a 'fit person' to carry on the type of business in question and also that the trade name is not misleading or otherwise undesirable. If it is so satisfied it must grant the licence. Persons whose conduct is relevant in assessing fitness include the applicant's employees, agents and business associates, past and present. Acts indicating unfitness include fraud, other dishonesty, violence, contravention of consumer protection legislation, sex or race discrimination and any deceitful, oppressive, unfair or improper business practices (whether unlawful or not). Some business practices are currently causing anxiety to the OFT. These include the following. When engaged in they may endanger the licence.

### (a) General

In many sectors of business, agreements are drawn up which do not take into account recent legislation such as the Unfair Contract Terms Act 1977, the Supply of Goods (Implied Terms) Act 1973, and the Consumer Transactions (Restrictions on Statements) Order 1976. Clauses are included in agreements which could mislead or confuse the consumer, or unjustifiably limit his rights.

### (b) Moneylending

Interest is charged on money not advanced (for example by advancing part only of the agreed loan initially, but charging interest from the outset on the full amount). Interest rates charged are increased by more than the agreement allows (for example by stating in the agreement that the rate will never exceed a recognised published base rate, then later increasing it to a level above that rate). Borrowers' signatures are obtained before forms are fully completed (so that, for example, the borrower is misled about the duration of his loan).

*(c) Motor trade*

Some aspects give serious cause for concern, and the behaviour of a number of dealers has fallen below an acceptable level. The number of complaints and the criminal convictions of members of the trade continue to excite comment from the OFT. The most common problem is the 'clocking' of secondhand cars (falsifying the odometer so that the vehicle appears to have done fewer miles than is the case), and the sale of cars previously 'clocked'. The proper practice is to disclaim the reading to prospective purchasers where the dealer has any doubt of its accuracy.

Another abuse is the sale of unroadworthy vehicles and vehicles of unmerchantable quality. This constitutes an offence under the Road Traffic Acts, the Trade Descriptions Acts or the Motor Vehicles (Construction and Use) Regulations.

Anxiety is also caused by the failure of dealers who supply credit to discharge their responsibilities properly. Dealers do not always ensure that customers understand the nature of the transaction and the extent of their rights under the statutory Consumer Credit Act.

*(d) Television traders*

There continue to be complaints in this field. On rentals, these include the increasing of charges (other than VAT) when the rental agreement does not allow for any increase, failing to maintain sets properly despite a service contract, failing to have a proper complaints procedure, and the unauthorised charging for the collection of sets on the termination of hire contracts. Ex-rental television sets are sometimes sold as 'new', or as having been reconditioned when this is not the case.

*(e) Home improvement trades*

These include such services as the supply and fitting of double-glazing, replacement windows, patio doors, central heating and solar heating. Over-persuasive sales techniques (particularly by doorstep salesmen) are complained of. So too are inadequate methods of measurement and fitting, and defective components.

Cancellation rights are often not observed, and unjustified cancellation fees demanded. Sometimes these include claims for work not in fact carried out. Agreed discounts are not honoured. Deposit refunds are refused when proposed work is not proceeded with because of difficulty in obtaining credit.

## 4 What a licence covers

A licence covers all lawful activities done in the course of the business, whether by the **licensee** or his employees or agents, though an agent will require his own licence in addition. If the licence is to cover **canvassing off trade premises** this must be referred to expressly in it. If the licence category extends to a part only of the actual business carried on, the licence will not cover the activities of other parts of the business.

**Example 59** A company carries on a credit and hire business, but only holds a Category A licence. The licence will cover all lawful activities done in the course of the credit side of the business, but not the hire trade.

A licence does not authorise trading under any name not specified in the licence.

## 5 The Consumer Credit Public Register

The OFT is required to keep a Register showing details of licence applications, licencees granted and other information relating to licensing. The Register may be inspected on any **working day** between 10.00 and 16.00 hours. An index listing applicants and licensees by true name and business name can be examined free of charge. This enables you to see whether a file exists on the person or firm in which you are interested. There is a fee of £1 for each file of entries inspected. Copies may be taken. Alternatively copies will be supplied by the OFT on payment of £0.75 per sheet for copies certified to be correct (these may be needed for court proceedings) or £0.30 for uncertified copies. Copies will be sent by post on payment of a further £1.50 for five copies or less. No charge is made to enforcement officers. In addition, the OFT publishes the weekly *Consumer Credit Bulletin* giving details of licences issued, varied etc. The Register can be inspected at the Consumer Credit Licensing Branch, OFT, Government Buildings, Bromyard Avenue, Acton, London W3 7BB. Copies of Register entries, and of the *Consumer Credit Bulletin*, are obtainable from the same address.

For the duty imposed on licensees to notify changes in registered particulars see page 204.

### 6 Penalties for unlicensed trading

The Act penalises unlicensed trading in three ways: by making it a criminal offence, by rendering the trader's agreements unenforceable by him (though not by the customer), and by putting at risk his ability to obtain or retain a licence. In relation to unlicensed **credit-brokers** there is an additional penalty, since **regulated agreements** made on their introduction are unenforceable against the debtor or hirer without an OFT order (see page 159).

### (a) Criminal offences

To trade without a licence or beyond the scope of the licence you hold is punishable in a Crown Court by imprisonment for up to two years, or a fine of any amount, or both. In a magistrates' court the maximum penalty is a fine of £2,000. The same penalties apply to the offence of trading under a name not specified in the licence.

### (b) Unenforceable agreements

Apart from the special case of unlicensed credit-brokers (mentioned above), there are two types of agreement that are rendered unenforceable: (1) a **regulated agreement** and (2) an agreement for the services of an **ancillary credit trader**. In each case the OFT may however grant a validation order restoring enforceability.

(1) A regulated agreement which is made by an unlicensed trader or is beyond the scope of a licence held by the trader is unenforceable by him unless a validation order is obtained from the OFT. This does not apply where the trader does not need a licence (see page 25).

(2) Similarly, an agreement for the services of an unlicensed **credit-broker, debt collector, debt counsellor, debt adjuster** or **credit reference agency** is unenforceable by the trader unless a validation order is obtained. This applies even though the customer is a limited company and not an **individual**. It does not of course apply to a credit-broker who does not need a licence because he is an individual covered by the £30 exception (see pages 158 and 159).

Application for a validation order must be made to the OFT at the same address as for a licence (see page 198). The fee is £10. In deciding whether to grant the order the OFT will consider how far customers were prejudiced by the failure to obtain the necessary licence and the extent of the trader's culpability. An order will not be made where the trader is of bad character or would for any other reason be refused a licence.

### (c) Risking existing or future licences

Since a record of contravening consumer protection legislation is a factor to be considered by the OFT in deciding whether to grant or renew a licence it follows that to be detected in unlicensed trading is to put the retention or obtaining of a licence in jeopardy. Accidental omissions will not be penalised in this way, provided steps are taken to ensure they do not recur.

## 7 Duration of licence

Normally a standard licence lasts fifteen years, and can then be renewed. The OFT sends renewal reminders to the licensee's registered address. The following may end a licence prematurely: revocation (see page 207); the occurrence of a 'terminating event' (not applicable to limited companies); change in composition and name of a partnership.

### (a) Terminating events

Where the licensee is a sole trader any of the following is a 'terminating event', though the licence does not end at once: death of the licensee; his becoming incapable through mental illness of managing his business affairs; his adjudication as a bankrupt; court approval of a composition or scheme of arrangement; registration of a deed of arrangement. Where the licensee is a partnership the following are 'terminating events' if applying to all the partners: bankruptcy; approval of a composition or scheme of arrangement; registration of a deed of arrangement.

After the 'terminating event' the business can be carried on *for twelve months only* under the same licence by the 'interim successor' (ie the executor, trustee or other person to whom management of the licensee's business affairs has passed). This applies even though the licence would have expired earlier. Notice must be given to the OFT within two months of the occurrence of the terminating event, or the right of the interim successor to carry on the business will cease.

## (b) Partnership changes

Where a change in a partnership has the result that the business ceases to be carried on under the name, or any of the names, specified in the licence this brings the licence to an end immediately. A new licence must therefore be obtained in advance of any such change becoming effective.

## (c) Limited companies

There is no provision for 'terminating events' in relation to the insolvency of limited companies and other incorporated bodies because the liquidator, receiver or manager in a winding up acts on behalf of the company, which continues to be the licensee.

## (d) Renewal of licence

Exactly the same principles apply to the question whether a licence will be renewed as apply to the grant of a licence. The OFT must be satisfied, in others words, that the applicant for renewal is a fit person to carry on the business and that the trade name is not undesirable.

For rights of appeal see page 208.

The first licences were issued for three years only. Just before the first of them were due to expire the Government announced (on 10 July 1979) that to achieve a saving in manpower at the OFT the licence period would be extended to ten years without the need for individual renewal applications. A similar decision in 1986 further extended the period to fifteen years.

## 8 Duty to notify changes

The Act places heavy duties on licensees to notify the OFT of changes affecting them. Breach is punishable in a Crown Court by imprisonment for up to two years, or a fine of any amount, or both. In a magistrates' court the maximum penalty is a fine of £2,000. Notifiable changes are those in:

(1) particulars entered in the Consumer Credit Public Register (see page 201);
(2) members of a licensed partnership;
(3) **officers** of a licensed company;
(4) control of a licensed company;
(5) officers of a controlling company.

No fee is charged.

*(a) Changes in registered particulars*

Within twenty-one **working days** after a change takes place in any particulars entered in the Register relating to the officers or partners of the licensee firm, or the address of its registered office or principal place of business, written notice must be given to the OFT. Form CC8/79 may be used.

*(b) Change in partnership members*

Within twenty-one working days after a change takes place in the members of a licensed partnership, written notice must be given to the OFT. Form CC8/79 may be used.

*(c) Changes in company officers*

Within twenty-one working days after any change takes place in the **officers** of a licensed limited company or other body (whether incorporated or not) written notice must be given to the OFT. Form CC8/79 may be used.

*(d) Changes in control of company*

Within twenty-one working days after a licensed limited company or other incorporated body becomes aware that a person has become or ceased to be its **controller** it must give written notice to the OFT. Form CC12/80 may be used. Since otherwise the licensee might remain ignorant of such changes, the Act requires the person becoming or ceasing to be its controller to notify it within fourteen working days.

*(e) Changes in officers of controlling company*

Within twenty-one working days after any change takes place in the **officers** of an incorporated body which is a controller of a licensed incorporated body the latter (whether it knows of the change or not) is under a duty to give written notice to the OFT. Form CC12/80 may be used. The controller must give the licensee written notice of the change within fourteen working days.

## 9 Variation of licence

The Act provides for both compulsory and voluntary variation of licences. The same rules apply to variation as to grant of a licence, eg a new trade name cannot be added unless it is not misleading or otherwise undesirable.

*(a) Compulsory variation*

This is one of the three weapons available to the OFT when it becomes apparent that the trading methods or character of a licensee or his associates are such that he should no longer be allowed to carry on business in accordance with the terms of the licence. Compulsory variation is the least drastic remedy; the others being suspension and revocation (see below).

> **Example 60** A mail order trader holds a Category A licence containing a canvassing authorisation. Complaints reach the OFT that his canvassers use oppressive methods. On investigation the complaints prove justified. The trader fails to give satisfactory assurances that he will not in future use oppressive canvassing methods. The OFT varies the licence by removing the canvassing authorisation.

For rights of appeal see page 208.

*(b) Variation at licensee's request*

If it thinks fit, the OFT can vary a licence at the request of the licensee. This is often done, usually to include a further category of business (fee £10), to add a canvassing authorisation (fee £10), or to change the trade name or add an additional trade name (fee £5). A further reason might be to remove a restriction contained in the licence. There is power to impose such restrictions, but in practice this is done rarely, if at all. Apart from the changes just mentioned, changes in particulars mentioned in the licence, eg the trading address, do not require a formal variation of the licence, though they may need to be notified to the OFT (see page 204). Note that the same person must remain the licensee, even though the trade name is changed. This is because licences are not transferable.

> **Example 61** A sole trader is licensed under the name Apex Decorating Co. The trader decides to turn his business into a limited company, Apex Decorating Co Ltd. It is not possible to vary the licence by substituting the new name. The limited company is a new legal person, which must obtain a licence in its own name.

The position is different where ownership of a company changes by transfer of shares. Thus if the trader in the previous example, after incorporating his business, later decided to sell it by transferring his shares in Apex Decorating Co Ltd to someone else that person will not need to obtain a licence. The licence held by the company will continue to cover its activities, though the change of control must be notified (see page 205).

## 10 Suspension or revocation of licence

If the OFT learns facts that, if it had known them when the licence was applied for, would have caused refusal of the application, it may suspend or revoke the licence. Information adverse to the licensee may come to light where a change is notified to the OFT, eg where a company passes under the control of an undesirable holding company, or the court may find the licensee to have been entering into extortionate credit bargains (see page 87), or an enforcement officer making a routine inspection may report adversely on the trading methods of the licensee, or enforcement authorities may receive complaints from the public which on investigation prove justified (for example see page 206). The OFT will usually start by warning the licensee to improve his trading methods. If this is ineffective it may seek convincing assurances that the necessary improvements will be made. Finally it may resort to suspension of the licence for a stated period or indefinitely. If the case is more serious, eg where a sole trader is sentenced to imprisonment for fraud, the licence may be revoked.

Suspension does not terminate the licence but, except in relation to an application for renewal (which may be made during suspension), the **licensee** is treated as if the licence had not been issued. In other words he is **unlicensed** until the suspension comes to an end. This applies to all his activities, even though complaints were centred on conduct at one branch of the business only. However, the OFT may deal with this type of case by compulsory variation of the licence.

> **Example 62** The licensee operates a large business with many branches. The OFT becomes aware that, while the business as a whole is conducted on proper lines, the personnel at one of the branches have developed an unacceptable form of trading which cannot be remedied quickly. The OFT varies the licence by adding a limitation preventing the business being carried on at the offending address.

## 11  Rights of appeal

The Act lays down a uniform procedure for protecting the rights of traders in relation to adverse decisions by the OFT on licensing matters. The procedure confers rights to make oral or written representations (or both), rights of appeal from OFT decisions to the Secretary of State for Trade and Industry and a further right of appeal (on points of law only) to the courts. The procedure comes into operation whenever the OFT official dealing with the matter is minded to refuse any application, grant it in different terms from those sought, or vary, suspend or revoke a licence. This provisional view of the OFT official must be notified to the person affected. The notice gives the reasons for the view and states the facts on which it is based.

### (a)  Representations

At least twenty-one days must be allowed to the aggrieved person to submit written and/or oral representations showing why the adverse decision should not be made. If the person asks for an oral hearing, a time and place will be fixed and not less than twenty-one days' notice given. The hearing is informal, and witnesses can be called. The person affected may present the case himself or use a professional or lay representative. He can support his case with documents, books, letters and sworn or unsworn written statements. Witnesses appearing in person are not sworn or cross-examined. Evidence must be relevant, but will not be excluded merely because it is hearsay or otherwise inadmissible in a court of law.

### (b)  Appeal to Secretary of State

If, despite any representations made, the OFT notifies an adverse determination the person aggrieved may appeal to the Secretary of State for Trade and Industry within twenty-eight days of receiving the determination. The grounds of appeal must be stated, and the OFT will put in a reply to them. The appellant in turn can submit a rejoinder. If, which is unlikely, the appeal is not contested by the OFT the Secretary of State must allow it. Otherwise there will be a hearing before an appeal tribunal (unless the appellant indicates that he does not wish this). The tribunal then reports its findings to the Secretary of State, who may give such directions as he thinks just. He must however observe the rules of natural justice (as indeed must the OFT). The directions may require the appellant to pay costs. If a point of law arises during the proceedings a case may be stated for the opinion of the court.

### (c) Appeal to Court

On a point of law only, an appeal lies from the Secretary of State's decision to the Divisional Court of the Queen's Bench Division (in Scotland the Court of Session; in Northern Ireland the High Court).

## 12 Group licences

Instead of requiring traders to apply individually for standard licences covering their activities, the OFT has power to grant a group licence if it appears that the public interest is better served by doing so. As its name implies, the standard licence is the normal type. Since the requirements that the licensee is a 'fit person' and the trade name suitable do not apply to group licences it follows that the public interest test can be satisfied only where the nature of the group is such that it is safe to assume that all persons within it are fit to carry on the activities in question and will not do so under unsuitable names. This particularly applies where there is a system of statutory or professional control over members of the group. It does not apply to a group of commercial companies since the OFT does not consider the Companies Act controls to be adequate protection. The fee for a group licence varies according to the number of members of the group, as follows:

| | |
|---|---|
| 1,000 members or less | £2,000 |
| over 1,000 but not over 5,000 | £5,000 |
| over 5,000 | £10,000 |

No fee is charged where the group's 'business' is limited to free debt-adjusting and debt-counselling (category D). Canvassing off trade premises is not authorised by a group licence. Group licences (usually of fifteen years' duration) have so far been issued to the following:

(1) The Law Society (licence in respect of all solicitors who for the time being hold a practising certificate which is in force issued by the Law Society under the Solicitors Act 1974, s 10, to carry on the business of consumer credit, credit

brokerage, debt adjusting, debt counselling and debt collecting limited to activities arising in the course of practice as a solicitor). The Law Reform Committee of the Law Society take the view that the scope of the group licence extends to solicitors who act as agents for building societies and who may carry out the activity of credit brokerage as part of their agency.

(2) The Law Society of Scotland (licence in respect of all solicitors in the same terms, with necessary changes, as the licence referred to in head (1) above).

(3) The Incorporated Law Society of Northern Ireland (licence in respect of all solicitors in the same terms, with necessary changes, as the licence referred to in head (1) above).

(4) The National Association of Citizens' Advice Bureaux (licence in respect of all bureaux which are from time to time registered with the Association, to carry on the business of debt adjusting and debt counselling).

(5) Individuals appointed to certain specified posts (licence in respect of any individual who already holds a standard licence of any description under the Act, or who is a member of a partnership holding such a licence or who is covered by any group licence, and who is appointed to be:

(a) a liquidator, receiver, or manager, of a body corporate or an unincorporated body;

(b) an executor, administrator, trustee, receiver, manager or judicial factor of the estate of a deceased person;

(c) a trustee in bankruptcy or sequestration;

(d) a person authorised under the Mental Health Act 1983, ss 95 or 96, to carry on the business of a person becoming a patient under Part VII of that Act, or (in Scotland) a curator bonis or judicial factor appointed to carry on the business of a person;

(e) a person authorised in Northern Ireland under the Lunacy (Ireland) Act 1871, ss 15 or 68, to carry on the business of a person who is of unsound mind or incapable of managing his person or property;

(f) a trustee under, or in pursuance of (i) a composition or scheme of arrangement proposed under the Bankruptcy Act 1914, s 16, and approved by the court, (ii) a deed of arrangement registered under the Deeds of Arrangement Act 1914, (iii) a deed of arrangement produced under the Bankruptcy (Scotland) Act 1913 and approved by the court, (iv) a voluntary trust deed of arrangement registered in Northern Ireland under the Deeds of Arrangement Act 1887.

The group licence covers the business or businesses of consumer credit, consumer hire, credit brokerage, debt adjusting, debt counselling, debt collecting and credit reference agency, but is limited to activities carried on by members of the group in pursuance of the duties imposed upon them by virtue of an appointment or appointments above mentioned. (The licence is specified to run for an indefinite period.)

(6) Age Concern England (licence in respect of a group consisting of the National Old People's Welfare Council together with all Age Concern/Old People's Welfare organisations registered as charities by the Charities Commission who have as their object the promotion of the welfare of the aged in any manner deemed at any time to be charitable and who together with and through membership of the National Old People's Welfare Council, make up the movement of Age Concern/Old People's Welfare Committee in England, to carry on the business of debt adjusting and debt counselling).

(7) The Institute of Chartered Accountants in England and Wales (licence in respect of a group consisting of all chartered accountants who for the time being hold a practising certificate which is in force, issued by the Institute of Chartered Accountants in England and Wales, to carry on the business of consumer credit, credit brokerage, debt-adjusting and debt-counselling. The licence is limited to activities arising in the course of practice as a chartered accountant established (whether in whole or in part) within the United Kingdom and carried on there by the member either as a sole practitioner or in partnership with others who for the time being hold the like qualification or a qualification authorising such activities as a chartered or certified accountant in partnership under any other licence.)

(8) The Institute of Chartered Accountants of Scotland (licence in the same terms, with necessary changes, as the licence referred to in head (7)).

(9) The Institute of Chartered Accountants in Ireland (licence in the same terms, with necessary changes, as the licence referred to in head (7)).

(10) The Association of Certified Accountants (licence in the same terms, with necessary changes, as the licence referred to in head (7)).

# Chapter 9

# The Enforcement Machinery

## 1 Enforcement authorities

The Consumer Credit Act depends for its effectiveness on a policy of active policing. Like many modern regulatory systems, it does not merely rely on giving people private rights of action and creating criminal offences. By conferring on certain public authorities both the duty to see that the Act is obeyed and the necessary back-up powers to enable them to carry out the duty, the Act creates the machinery to ensure its effectiveness. We have seen in Chapter 8 that the licensing system is the principal means of securing fair trading in the credit and hire industries. To promote effective working of the licensing system, and the other protective features of the Act, central and local enforcement authorities are equipped with power to enter premises, to inspect and seize books and documents, to bring legal proceedings and so on.

### (a) Central authorities

We begin at the top with the Secretary of State for Trade and Industry who is the Government Minister in charge of the working of the Act, though in practice this task is performed by a Minister of State. Next comes the OFT, headed by the Director General of Fair Trading. This is a semi-independent department of the civil service. Although the Act refers to the Director General rather than the OFT when conferring powers and duties, it is in practice an official of the OFT and not the Director General himself who will exercise a particular executive function. Accordingly, since this is a practical handbook, we refer throughout to the OFT.

The Act says it is the duty of the OFT to administer the licensing system and generally to *superintend* the working and enforcement of the Act and regulations made under it. Where 'necessary or expedient' the OFT must actually enforce the Act itself, though in general this task is left to local enforcement authorities. In addition, the OFT must keep under review, and advise the Secretary of State about, social and commercial developments at home and overseas so far as they relate to the provision of credit and hire facilities to individuals. The OFT must publish information and advice to consumers and traders about the operation of the Act, credit facilities available, and other relevant matters. Each year the OFT publishes an annual report describing its activities.

The Secretary of State can give directions to the OFT about how it is to carry out its functions, but in practice a large degree of independence is allowed. The Secretary of State is answerable to Parliament for any administrative failures by the OFT, and its activities are subject to surveillance by the Parliamentary Commissioner for Administration (Ombudsman) and the Council on Tribunals.

*(b) Local authorities*

The local enforcement authorities under the Act are the trading standards departments of local councils. In some areas they are called the consumer protection department or the weights and measures department. A list of them, with addresses, is given in Appendix 5 (page 247). The Act places upon these local authorities a duty to enforce the Act and regulations made under it, though in most cases they must notify the OFT before actually starting a prosecution. Whenever the OFT requires, the local authority must send it a report on the local authority's activities under the Act. In case of complaint the Secretary of State has power to hold a local inquiry.

## 2 Powers of enforcement officers

The Act gives officers employed by the OFT or a local enforcement authority extensive powers to aid them in carrying out their functions.

*(a) Test agreements*

If an enforcement officer has reason to suspect that a trader is in the habit of contravening the Act he will need to gather legally effective evidence of this. One way of doing so is to pose as a private individual seeking the services the trader provides. The Act specifically empowers enforcement officers to do this. The officer (if so authorised by his employing authority) can even go the length of borrowing money, entering into a hire-purchase agreement, or making any other contract with the suspected trader. If a prosecution later ensues, the officer's evidence will have the same effect as if he had been a private individual acting on his own behalf. (If the Act did not say this, the defence could plead that the contract was effectively made by the authority through its servant the officer. A local enforcement authority is not an **individual** within the meaning of the Act and so would not be covered by the Act's protective provisions.) Test agreements may of course establish that there is nothing wrong with the trader's practices. Or, while not proving that actual criminal offences are committed, they may show that the trader is guilty of improper business practices such as call for the exercise of disciplinary powers under the licensing system.

*(b) Entry of premises*

An enforcement officer may need to enter trading premises so as to gather evidence of criminal or improper conduct (or satisfy himself that no contravention of the Act has been committed). The Act contains two sets of entry provisions, one of which involves the obtaining of a magistrates' warrant. Both permit the officer entering premises to take with him such other people and equipment as he thinks necessary.

The first set of provisions, which does not involve obtaining a warrant, is simply designed to ensure that the officer is not liable to an action for trespass if he enters premises without the occupier's permission. The officer is not required to have any firm grounds for suspicion, but the following conditions apply.

(1) The officer must be authorised by his employing authority to act as an enforcement officer under the Act.

(2) He must enter at a 'reasonable' time, which probably means during the trader's business hours.

(3) He must produce his credentials if so asked.

(4) The 'premises' must not be in use as a dwelling, but can be any other place (eg a trailer or booth). A place is not 'used as a dwelling' for this purpose if it is partly used for business purposes as well.

(5) If any person resists the entry, the officer must not use force against him. The officer may take any necessary steps to

gain entry (as by unlocking a door), though he may not cause damage. If the premises are in use as a dwelling, or forcible resistance is feared, or the occupier is away, or the premises are vacant, it may be necessary to use the alternative procedure and apply for a magistrates' warrant. Two conditions must be satisfied before a warrant can be issued. One relates to the premises and the other to the question of the occupier's permission to enter.

The first condition (relating to the premises) is satisfied only if there are *in fact* (whatever the enforcement officer may reasonably think) grounds for believing *either*:

(1) that goods, books or documents which the officer has power to inspect (see below) are on the premises and are likely to disclose a breach of the Act or regulations, *or*

(2) that a breach of the Act or regulations has been, is being, or is about to be committed on the premises.

The second condition (relating to the occupier's permission) is satisfied if any of the following apply:

(1) admission to the premises has been refused and written notice of intention to apply for the warrant has been given to the occupier; or

(2) admission to the premises is likely to be refused (eg because the occupier has shown hostility) and written notice of intention to apply for the warrant has been given to the occupier; or

(3) an application for admission, or the giving of such a notice of intention, would defeat the object of the entry (eg because the previous conduct of the occupier has shown he would be likely to remove or destroy records if given warning); or

(4) the premises are unoccupied (as opposed to the occupier being temporarily absent); or

(5) the occupier is temporarily absent and it might defeat the object of the entry to wait for his return (if the proprietor of a one-man business is on holiday permission must be sought on his return unless paragraph (3) applies).

If the conditions (relating to the premises and the occupier's permission respectively) are both satisfied the officer who desires entry by warrant must draw up a statement (known as an 'information') which sets out the facts showing that the two conditions are satisfied and swear it (or affirm its truth where this is permissible) before any solicitor holding a practising certificate. The magistrate has a discretion whether to issue a warrant, even though the information satisfies the two conditions. When issued, a warrant continues in force for a month and allows reasonable force to be used against persons and property. If, however, the premises are unoccupied, or the occupier is temporarily absent, the inspecting officer on quitting the premises must leave them as effectively secured against trespassers as he found them. A warrant permits one entry only.

What can the enforcement officer do when he has lawfully entered the premises, whether under a warrant or not? Clearly he can inspect the premises and anything that is in them, though he cannot use force against persons or property unless armed with a warrant. He cannot in either case remove any property except under specific powers mentioned below. Normally he will only be interested in account books and other business records, but his powers extend to the inspection, seizure and testing of goods as well. Conditions (1) to (3) on page 215 apply to the exercise of powers in relation to books, documents and goods, but Condition (1) applies in modified form in relation to a book or document which relates to a bank, to a document embodying a **consumer hire agreement** under which the **owner** is the Post Office, and to a file kept by a **credit reference agency** about an individual. In all these cases a local enforcement officer needs OFT authority.

## (c) Inspection and seizure of books and documents

If, but only if, there are *in fact* grounds for suspecting breach of any provision made by or under the Act, the enforcement officer, in order to find out whether the breach has actually occurred, may require the production of books or documents for his inspection. The requirement may be made of the trader himself or any of his employees. The books or documents must relate to the business, and the officer may take copies of them. If any information is not in the form of a readable document (eg if it is on computer tape or microfilm) the officer can demand to be supplied with a documentary version in readable form. If the officer has reason to believe that a book or document may be required as evidence in proceedings for an offence under the Act he may seize and detain it (breaking open any container in which it is kept if the occupier refuses). There is a saving for privileged documents in the possession of a barrister or solicitor. No book or document must be removed without notifying the owner.

### 3 Obstruction, deception and impersonation

The Act lays down a number of criminal offences designed to secure the effectiveness of the enforcement machinery. It is an offence *wilfully* (ie intentionally and without lawful excuse) to *obstruct* an enforcement officer or fail to comply with his directions. This includes failing to give the officer any information or assistance he may reasonably require, though a person is not bound to incriminate himself or his spouse. An offender is liable on summary conviction by a magistrates' court to a fine not exceeding £1,000.

Severer penalties are laid down for deception or impersonation of an enforcement officer. A person who makes any statement which he knows to be false can be punished in a Crown Court with imprisonment for up to two years, or a fine of any amount, or both. In a magistrates' court the maximum penalty is a £2,000 fine. The same penalties apply where an individual who is not in fact a duly authorised officer of an enforcement authority acts as if he were one. As well as an imposter, this would cover a genuine enforcement officer who inadvertently exceeded his authority (eg by seizing consumers' files from a credit reference agency when he lacked OFT authority). The same penalties again apply where, in connection with any application or request to the OFT, or in response to any invitation or requirement made by the OFT, a person knowingly or recklessly gives false information.

### 4 Disclosure of information

Where by the use or threatened use (either express or implied) of powers conferred by the Act, or otherwise in the exercise of their functions under the Act, the OFT or a local enforcement authority has acquired information about an **individual** or a **business** there are restrictions on its disclosure without consent. Where the information relates to an individual, the consent required is that of the individual himself. Where however it relates to a business, the restrictions only apply while the business continues to be carried on and the consent required is that of the person who is currently carrying it on. This is because the restrictions on business information are designed to safeguard trade secrets, and those affected by their disclosure are presumed to be the current proprietors. All information is protected, except where it has previously been made public by including it in the Consumer

Credit Public Register. However, it is not possible to 'disclose' information to someone who already knows it (or is by law deemed to know it, eg because it has been passed to one of his employees).

Disclosure is not caught by these protective provisions if it is effected by entering particulars in the Consumer Credit Public Register. Nor is it caught if made for the purpose of facilitating the performance of statutory functions, or in connection with the investigation or prosecution of *any* criminal offence, or for the purpose of civil proceedings brought either under the Act or under Part III of the Fair Trading Act 1973.

A person who contravenes the disclosure restrictions is liable on conviction by a Crown Court to imprisonment for up to two years, or a fine of any amount, or both. On summary conviction by a magistrates' court, the maximum penalty is a fine of £2,000.

## 5 Criminal proceedings

The Act contains some general provisions relating to criminal offences and proceedings.

### (a) Liability of a company and its directors etc

A corporation, being a legal fiction, can only act through the agency of individuals, but it is not necessarily responsible for the criminal acts or omissions of those individuals. If the crime requires a mental element (eg giving information to an enforcement officer which is 'known to be false'), a company cannot be liable unless the necessary element was present in the mind of an individual who can be treated as the embodiment of the company. This will be the case where the individual had the status and authority necessary to make his acts those of the company (eg a director or company secretary, or an employee to whom the duty in question was specifically delegated).

In the case of an offence of strict liability, where no mental element is required, the company will always be liable for the acts and omissions of its officers and employees. By a provision frequently found in modern legislation, the Act extends this liability to an officer himself where the company's offence was committed with his consent or connivance, or because of his neglect. ('Connivance' here means shutting one's eyes to the fact that the offence was being committed, or in other words tacitly approving it.) The people to whom this liability extends are the following:

(1) Any director of the company;
(2) The company secretary;
(3) Any manager having general authority (but not a mere branch manager);
(4) Any similar officer of the company;
(5) Anyone purporting to act as such an officer, even though in fact he is not one;
(6) In the case of a corporate body which is managed by its members collectively, any member.

Any such individual is treated as having committed a similar offence to that of the company, and is therefore liable to the same penalties.

*(b) Defence of mistake etc*

A further provision relating to offences of strict liability mitigates hardship where a person other than the accused was really responsible for the contravention, or the contravention was due to accident or mistake. It is a complete defence for the person charged with any act or omission constituting an offence under the Act to prove that his act or omission was due to any of the following:

(1) Reliance on information supplied to him by another person, or any other act or omission by another person. (If the accused is an **individual**, the 'other person' may be any other individual or corporate body; but if the accused is a corporate body it cannot escape by blaming any person listed in paragraphs (1) to (6) above.)
(2) A mistake by the accused. (If the mistake was by another person, the accused must rely on the ground set out in the previous paragraph.)
(3) Accident or other cause beyond the accused's control. (This does not cover an act or omission by the accused's employee or agent.)

However, the defence is not established unless the accused also proves that he took all reasonable precautions, and exercised all due diligence, to avoid the commission of his own act or omission and any relevant act or omission by a person under his control. The prosecutor must be given details of the identity of any person upon whom proof of the defence depends.

## 6 Prohibition of contracting-out

A key factor in the enforcement machinery is the provision which renders void any attempt to contract out of the protection given by the Act to those who enter into a **regulated agreement** or **linked transaction**. Without this, unscrupulous traders could persuade consumers to sign away their rights.

The provision does not only apply to terms in the credit or hire contract itself, but to any other agreement made with the **debtor** or **hirer** or his relative. A **surety** is also precluded from contracting-out of the protection the Act gives him. Where a provision of the Act or regulations specifies the duty or liability of the consumer in certain circumstances, a contractual term is inconsistent with that provision (and therefore void) if it imposes an additional duty or liability on him in those circumstances. Equally, an agreement for **security** is void in so far as it secures an obligation rendered ineffective by the Act.

The Act makes it clear, however, that this protective provision does not go so far as to preclude the consumer from effectively agreeing to waive the need for the trader to apply for an order from the court or the OFT where this is required by the Act. Such agreement cannot however be given in advance of the time when it operates. This means that it cannot be included in the credit or hire contract itself.

> **Example 63** A finance company enter into a **hire-purchase agreement** with an **individual** for goods priced at £300. The agreement is a **regulated agreement**. The individual was introduced to the finance company by an unlicensed **credit-broker**. This means that the agreement is unenforceable against the consumer without an OFT order. The consumer falls into arrears, and the company desire to repossess the goods. They ask the consumer if he will allow this, and he agrees. The agreement to allow repossession is effective even though no OFT order is obtained.

# Appendix 1

# Dictionary of Technical Terms

## Note

Where a term is fully defined in the main part of the book, and the definition is too lengthy to be repeated in this dictionary, the reader is referred to the relevant place. Otherwise the dictionary contains definitions of all technical terms used in the book. To indicate that they are defined or mentioned here, the terms are printed in bold type whenever they occur in the text. Terms italicised in this Appendix are themselves defined in this dictionary. Definitions of terms marked with an asterisk are given in simplified form.

| | |
|---|---|
| **advance payment** | (1) in relation to a *credit agreement*, any payment to be made by the *debtor* before drawing credit (other than an insurance premium or a payment included in the *total charge for credit*) (2) in relation to a *consumer hire agreement*, any payment to be made by the *hirer* before obtaining possession of the goods. |
| **advertisement for credit facilities** | see page 32. |
| **advertiser** | any person indicated by the advertisement as willing to enter into transactions to which it relates. |
| **ancillary credit business** | a business of *credit brokerage, credit reference agency, debt adjusting, debt collecting* or *debt counselling*. |
| **ancillary hire charge\*** | a charge under a *consumer hire agreement* or related transaction (not being an *advance payment*, ordinary hire charge, default charge, insurance premium, |

maintenance charge or pre-existing obligation).

**annual percentage rate of charge**  see page 17.

**antecedent negotiations**  see pages 75–77.

**approximate rate**  see pages 19–21.

**associate***  relative, fellow partner, company under the same *controller*, company (in relation to its controller), controller (in relation to his company).

**assumption that the account is fully used**  assumption that the customer immediately draws the full credit allowed and then repays it by instalments in accordance with the agreement (not subsequently drawing any further credit).

**assumption that the account is one-third used**  assumption that the customer immediately draws one-third of the credit allowed and then repays it by instalments in accordance with the agreement (not subsequently drawing any further credit).

**bona fide small agreement***  a credit or hire agreement not exceeding £50, other than:
    (a) a secured agreement (disregarding security by guarantee or indemnity):
    (b) a *hire-purchase* or *conditional sale* agreement;
    (c) an agreement which is one of several, all of which would have been combined in one agreement but for the desire to avoid the Act.

**budget account agreement**  a *debtor-creditor-supplier agreement* for *running-account credit* with a credit limit, where instalments include either a fixed charge for each transaction or a charge proportionate to the price.

**business***  a trade (or other commercial activity) or profession, other than one only conducted occasionally

**cancellable agreement**  see pages 77–78.

**canvassing a regulated agreement off trade premises**  see pages 25–28.

| | |
|---|---|
| **cash price** | the price for cash prevailing at the relevant time, ignoring discounts (unless applicable in the stated circumstances). |
| **charge per pound lent** | the *total charge for credit* divided by the total amount advanced. |
| **conditional sale agreement** | an agreement for the sale of goods or land where the price is payable by instalments and ownership remains with the seller until specified conditions are fulfilled. |
| **consumer credit agreement** | see page 9. |
| **consumer credit business** | see page 7. |
| **Consumer Credit Tables** | Tables published by HMSO in 1977 in 15 separate parts, as modified by correction slips published in December 1978. A one-volume edition of the official Tables is published by Longman Professional, as part of the present author's *Consumer Credit Control*. |
| **consumer hire agreement** | see pages 115–117. |
| **consumer hire business** | see page 114. |
| **controller** | a person in accordance with whose instructions (direct or indirect) the directors of a company act, or who (alone or with *associates*) controls, whether directly or indirectly, one-third of the voting power. |
| **credit** | any form of financial accommodation (including cash loans and hire purchase, but excluding accommodation over any item making up the *total charge for credit*) |
| **credit agreement** | a *personal credit agreement* secured on land or buildings, or a *consumer credit agreement*. |
| **credit-brokerage** | see pages 151–158. |
| **credit reference agency** | see page 182. |
| **credit-token** | see pages 83–85. |
| **credit-trader** | a person who carries on a *consumer credit business* and/or a *business* in the course of which he provides *credit* to *individuals* secured on land or buildings. |

| | |
|---|---|
| **creditor** | the person providing credit under a *consumer credit agreement*. |
| **dealer** | (1) in relation to a *hire-purchase agreement, credit-sale agreement* or *conditional sale agreement* (where he is not the creditor) the person selling the goods etc to the creditor. <br> (2) in relation to any other *credit agreement*, the *supplier*. |
| **debt adjusting** | see page 173. |
| **debt collecting** | see page 179. |
| **debt counselling** | see page 172. |
| **debtor** | the *individual* receiving credit under a *consumer credit agreement*. |
| **debtor-creditor agreement** | a *consumer credit agreement* which is a *regulated agreement* but is not a *debtor-creditor-supplier agreement*. |
| **debtor-creditor-supplier agreement** | see pages 11 and 12. |
| **embodies** | a document 'embodies' a provision if the provision is set out either in the document itself or in another document referred to in the document. |
| **estimated credit quotation** | see pages 49 and 50. |
| **estimated hire quotation** | see page 129. |
| **excepted agreement** | an agreement excepted from most of Part V of the Act, namely: |

(a) a bank overdraft agreement; or
(b) a *non-commercial agreement*; or
(c) an unwritten *bona fide small agreement* being a *debtor-creditor-supplier agreement* for *restricted-use credit*; or
(d) a *regulated agreement* which purports to bind a person to enter as debtor or hirer into a prospective regulated agreement made for business purposes; or
(e) an agreement allowing a temporary excess on a *running account agreement*; or

(f) an unwritten *debtor-creditor agreement* to finance the payment of taxes and fees arising on death.

**excepted document\***

(1) a public document such as an enactment, a certified register copy, or a document published by an official body, or (2) a private document supplied by the debtor or hirer, a catalogue, a document of title, or a document to be retained by the debtor or hirer.

**excepted linked transaction\***

a contract of insurance, guarantee of goods, or current or deposit account.

**executed agreement**

a document which *embodies* the terms of a *regulated agreement*, or such of them as have been reduced to writing, and is signed by the parties.

**exempt agreement**

see pages 11–13 (credit agreements) and page 117 (hire agreements).

**extortionate**

see pages 88–91.

**file**

see page 184.

**fixed-sum credit**

*credit* which is not *running-account credit*.

**flat rate**

a uniform percentage charge on the original amount advanced, regardless of repayments of principal embodied in the instalments already paid by the debtor.

**foreign agreement**

an agreement governed by the law of a country outside the United Kingdom.

**full credit quotation**

see page 47.

**full hire quotation**

see page 128.

**goods**

movable property of any kind; crops etc which are to be severed from the land and delivered separately.

**group licence**

see page 209.

**hire-purchase agreement**

an agreement (other than a *conditional sale agreement*) by which possession of *goods* is transferred in return for instalment payments, and the property in the goods will pass on the happening of a specified event (eg exercise of an option to purchase).

**hire-trader**

a person who carries on a *consumer hire business*.

**hirer**

the *individual* who receives possession of *goods* under a *consumer hire agreement*.

**identified dealer**

a *dealer* who is named or identified in an advertisement, or upon whose *premises* the advertisement is published.

**improperly executed**

see page 56.

**individual**

one or more natural persons, or a partnership including at least one natural person (even though it may also include a company or other body corporate), or any other unincorporated body of persons.

**licensee**

(1) in relation to a standard licence, the person to whom the licence was issued or his interim successor (see page 203).
(2) in relation to a group licence, any person covered by the licence.

**linked transaction***

a transaction entered into in relation to a *regulated agreement* by the *debtor* or *hirer*, or his relative, which is required by a term of the agreement or is otherwise connected with it.

**modifying agreement**

an agreement which varies or supplements an earlier agreement.

**multiple agreement**

an agreement which, because it falls into several categories relevant under the Act, is to be treated as a number of separate agreements.

**name**

(1) where the person is covered by a *standard licence*, any name of his specified in the licence.
(2) where the person is not covered by a standard licence, any name under which he carries on business.

**non-commercial agreement**

an agreement not made in the course of a business carried on by the creditor or hirer.

**obligatory credit quotation request**

see page 46.

| | |
|---|---|
| **obligatory hire quotation request** | see page 126. |
| **officer** | a director, secretary, or other person who exercises control over the general policy of a company. |
| **optional credit quotation request** | see page 50. |
| **optional hire quotation request** | see page 124. |
| **owner** | the person who gives possession of goods under a *consumer hire agreement*. |
| **paid-up agreement** | an agreement under which no sum is, or may become, payable by the debtor or hirer. |
| **period rate of charge** | a percentage rate of charge for a period being a rate comprising all items included in the *total charge for credit*. |
| **personal credit agreement** | an agreement by which an *individual* is provided with *credit* of any amount. |
| **premises** | any place, stall, vehicle, vessel, aircraft or hovercraft at which a person is carrying on any *business* (whether on a permanent or temporary basis). |
| **prescribed copy\*** | a true copy, easily legible, with or without officially-sanctioned omissions. |
| **rate of the total charge for credit** | the *annual percentage rate of charge*, determined to one decimal place (further decimal places being disregarded). |
| **recognised bank** | an institution recognised by the Bank of England as a bank for the purposes of the Banking Act 1979. |
| **regulated agreement** | a *consumer credit agreement* or *consumer hire agreement* which is neither an *exempt agreement* nor a *foreign agreement*. |
| **regulated credit advertisement** | see page 34. |
| **regulated hire advertisement** | see page 122. |
| **representative information** | information an *advertiser* may reasonably expect to be representative of transactions of the class in question (being |

transactions he might reasonably contemplate entering into).

**representative total charge for credit**

see page 19.

**restricted-use credit\***

a credit facility intended to finance a specific transaction, or finance a transaction with a specific person, or refinance any transaction, and provided in a way which does not leave the *debtor* free to use it as he chooses.

**running-account credit\***

a facility enabling the *debtor* to receive from time to time cash, goods or services to an amount such that (taking into account payments made by him) the credit limit (if any) is not exceeded.

**section 106 rules**

see page 61.

**security**

a mortgage, charge, pledge, bond, debenture, indemnity, guarantee, bill, note or other right securing the carrying out of the obligations of the *debtor* or *hirer* under a *consumer credit agreement* or *consumer hire agreement*.

**simple credit advertisement**

see page 36.

**simple hire advertisement**

see page 123.

**simple indication of credit business**

see page 36.

**simple indication of hire business**

see page 123.

**standard licence**

see page 197.

**supplier\***

the person (whether the *creditor* or a third party) who supplies goods, services or land under a transaction financed by a *consumer credit agreement*.

**surety**

the person by whom any *security* is provided.

**total amount payable by the debtor**

the aggregate of:
(1) any *advance payment*,
(2) the amount of *credit* repayable, and
(3) the *total charge for credit*.

**total charge for credit**

see pages 15–17.

**trade premises**

see pages 26, 27, 161 and 177.

**unexecuted agreement**

a document which *embodies* the terms of a prospective agreement, or such of them as it is intended to reduce to writing.

**unlicensed**

not a *licensee* in relation to the activity in question.

**unrestricted-use credit**

a credit facility which is not a *restricted-use* credit.

**working day**

any day except Saturday, Sunday or a bank holiday.

## Appendix 2

# List of Exempt Insurance Companies, Friendly Societies and Charities

*Bodies whose agreements of the specified description are exempt agreements*

### Insurance Companies

Abbey Life Assurance Company Limited

Abbey Life Pension and Annuities Limited

Albany Life Assurance Company Limited

Alliance Assurance Company Limited

Allied Dunbar Assurance plc

Ambassador Life Assurance Company Limited

American International Life Assurance Company of New York

American Life Insurance Company

Ansvar Insurance Company Limited

Atlas Assurance Company Limited

Australian Mutual Provident Society

Avon Assurance PLC

Black Horse Life Assurance Company Limited

Bradford Insurance Company Limited

Britannic Assurance plc

The British & European Reinsurance Company Limited

British Equitable Assurance Company Limited

The British Life Office Limited

The British Oak Insurance Company Limited

British Reserve Insurance Company Limited

Caledonian Insurance Company

The Cambrian Insurance Company Limited

The Canada Life Assurance Company

Cannon Assurance Limited

Car and General Insurance Corporation Limited

Citibank Assurance Company Limited

City of Westminster Assurance Company Limited

City of Westminster Assurance Society Limited

Clerical, Medical and General Life Assurance Society

The Colonial Mutual Life Assurance Society Limited

Commercial Union Assurance Company plc

Commercial Union Pensions
Management Limited
Commercial Union Life
Assurance Company Limited
Confederation Life Insurance
Company
The Contingency Insurance
Company Limited
Co-operative Insurance Society
Limited
Cornhill Insurance plc
Criterion Insurance Company
Limited
Crown Life Assurance Company
Limited
Crown Life Insurance Company
Crown Life Pensions Limited
Crusader Insurance plc

The Dominion Insurance
Company Limited

Eagle Star Insurance Company
Limited
Ecclesiastical Insurance Office plc
Economic Insurance Company
Limited
English & American Insurance
Company Limited
The Equitable Life Assurance
Society
Equity & Law Life Assurance
Society plc
Essex and Suffolk Insurance
Company Limited
Excess Insurance Company
Limited

Federation Mutual Insurance
Limited
Fine Art and General Insurance
Company Limited
Friends' Provident Life Office
FS Assurance Limited

General Accident Life Assurance
Limited

General Accident Fire and Life
Assurance Corporation plc
Gisborne Life Assurance
Company Limited
Gresham Life Assurance Society
Limited
Guardian Assurance plc
Guardian Royal Exchange
Assurance plc

Hill Samuel Life Assurance
Limited

The Ideal Insurance Company
Limited
The Imperial Life Assurance
Company of Canada
Irish Life Assurance plc
The Iron Trades Employers
Insurance Association Limited

Langham Life Assurance
Company Limited
Legal and General Assurance
Society Limited
The Licences and General
Insurance Company Limited
The Life Association of Scotland
Limited
London Aberdeen & Northern
Mutual Assurance Society
Limited
London and Manchester
Assurance Company Limited
London and Manchester
(Pensions) Limited
London & Scottish Assurance
Corporation Limited
The London Assurance
The London Life Association
Limited

The Manufacturers Life Insurance
Company
Marine and General Mutual Life
Assurance Society
Maritime Insurance Company
Limited

Medical Sickness Annuity & Life
Assurance Society Limited
The Mercantile and General
Reinsurance Company plc
Midland Assurance Limited
The Motor Union Insurance
Company Limited
Minster Insurance Company
Limited
Municipal Life Assurance Limited
Municipal Mutual Insurance
Limited

NALGO Insurance Association
Limited
National Employers' Life
Assurance Company Limited
National Employers' Mutual
General Insurance Association
Limited
The National Farmers' Union
Mutual Insurance Society
Limited
The National Insurance and
Guarantee Corporation plc
The National Mutual Life
Association of Australasia
Limited
National Mutual Life Assurance
Society
National Provident Institution
National Vulcan Engineering
Insurance Group Limited
N.E.L. Pensions Limited
The New Zealand Insurance plc
North British & Mercantile
Insurance Company Limited
The Northern Assurance
Company Limited
Norwich Union Fire Insurance
Society Limited
Norwich Union Insurance Group
(Managed Funds) Limited
Norwich Union Insurance Group
(Pensions Management)
Limited
Norwich Union Life Insurance
Society

NRG London Reinsurance
Company Limited

Oaklife Assurance Limited
The Ocean Accident & Guarantee
Corporation Limited
The Orion Insurance Company plc

The Parcels & General Assurance
Association Limited
Pearl Assurance plc
Pensions Management (SWF)
Limited
Permanent Insurance Company
Limited
Phoenix Assurance plc
Pioneer Mutual Insurance
Company Limited
Property Growth Pensions &
Annuities Limited
Provident Life Association of
London Limited
Provident Mutual Life Assurance
Association
Provincial Insurance plc
Provincial Life Assurance
Company Limited
The Prudential Assurance
Company Limited

Railway Passengers Assurance
Company
Refuge Assurance, plc
The Reliance Fire and Accident
Insurance Corporation Limited
The Reliance Marine Insurance
Company Limited
Reliance Mutual Insurance
Society Limited
Royal Exchange Assurance
Royal Insurance plc
Royal Insurance (Int.) Limited
Royal Insurance (U.K.) Limited
Royal Life Insurance Limited
Royal Life (Unit Linked
Assurances) Limited
Royal Life (Unit Linked Pensions
Funds) Limited

The Royal London Mutual
Insurance Society Limited
The Royal National Pension Fund
for Nurses
Royal Reinsurance Company
Limited

Schroder Life Assurance Limited
Scottish Amicable Life Assurance
Society
Scottish Equitable Life Assurance
Society
Scottish General Insurance
Company Limited
Scottish Insurance Corporation
Limited
The Scottish Life Assurance
Company
The Scottish Mutual Assurance
Society
The Scottish Provident Institution
Scottish Union and National
Insurance Company
Scottish Widows' Fund and Life
Assurance Society
The Sentinel Insurance Company
Skandia Life Assurance Company
Limited
Standard Life Assurance
Company
Standard Life Pension Funds
Limited
The State Assurance Company
Limited
Suffolk Life Annuities Limited
Sun Alliance and London
Assurance Company
Limited
Sun Insurance Office Limited
Sun Life Assurance Company of
Canada
Sun Life Assurance Society plc

Target Life Assurance Company
Limited

The Teachers' Assurance
Company Limited
Transinternational Life Insurance
Company Limited
Trident General Insurance
Company Limited
Trident Investors Life Assurance
Company Limited
Trident Life Assurance Company
Limited

U.K. Life Assurance Company
Limited
United British Insurance
Company Limited
United Friendly Insurance plc
United Kingdom Temperance and
General Provident Institution
United Standard Insurance
Company Limited
The University Life Assurance
Society

The Victory Reinsurance
Company Limited

Wesleyan and General Assurance
Society
The Western Australian Insurance
Company Limited
Westgate Insurance Company
Limited
The White Cross Insurance
Company Limited
World-Wide Assurance Company
Limited

The Yorkshire Insurance
Company Limited

Zurich Life Assurance Company
Limited

## Friendly Societies

The Ancient Order of Foresters
Friendly Society
Anglo-Saxons Friendly Society

Blackburn Philanthropic Mutual
Assurance Society
British Benefit Society
British Order of Ancient Free
Gardeners' Friendly Society
British United Order of
Oddfellows Friendly Society
Brunel Assurance Society

Cirencester Benefit Society
City of Glasgow Friendly Society
Civil Servants' Annuities
Assurance Society
Colmore Friendly Society
Coventry Assurance Society

Dentists' Provident Society
Devon and Exeter Men's
Equitable Benefit Society
Devon and Exeter Women's
Equitable Benefit Society

Grand United Order of
Oddfellows Friendly Society

The Hampshire and General
Friendly Society
Harvest Friendly Society
Hazel Grove Provident Burial
Society
Hearts of Oak Benefit Society
Hoddesdon Provident and
Annuity Society

The Ideal Benefit Society
The Independent Order of Odd
Fellows Manchester Unity
Friendly Society
The Independent Order of
Rechabites, Salford Unity,
Friendly Society

Leeds District of the Ancient
Order of Foresters Investment
Association
Leek Assurance Collecting
Society
The Leicester District Foresters'
Investment Society
Liverpool Victoria Friendly
Society
The Loyal Order of Ancient
Shepherds (Ashton Unity)
Friendly Society
Loyal Past and Present Officers'
Lodge, Norwich District,
Independent Order of
Oddfellows M.U. Friendly
Society

The Manchester and Districts of
the Ancient Order of Foresters
Investment Association

National Deposit Friendly Society
National Equalized Druids
Friendly Society
National United Order of Free
Gardeners Friendly Society
New Tab Friendly Society
Northumberland and Durham
Miners' Permanent Relief Fund
Friendly Society
Nottingham Oddfellows Friendly
Society
Nottingham Permanent Mutual
Money Society

The Order of Druids Friendly
Society
The Order of the Sons of
Temperance Friendly Society
Original Holloway Society

Pioneer Benefit Society
Preston Catholic Collecting
Society

Preston Shelley Assurance Collecting Society
Provident Reliance Friendly Society

Rational and County Assurance Society
Royal Liver Friendly Society

Scottish Friendly Assurance Society
The Scottish Legal Life Assurance Society
Sons of Scotland Temperance Friendly Society
Stepney District Distressed Members' Pension Benevolent Fund
Suffolk Friendly Society
The Sussex Widow and Orphans Society

The Teachers' Provident Society
Time Assurance Society
Tunbridge Wells Equitable Friendly Society
Tunstall and District Assurance Collecting Society

United Ancient Order of Druids Friendly Society
United Kingdom Civil Service Benefit Society
United Patriots' National Benefit Society

West Surrey General Benefit Society
Widow and Orphan Fund of the Woolwich District of the Independent Order of Odd Fellows, Manchester Unity Friendly Society
Widow and Orphans' Fund, Stepney District of the Independent Order of Odd Fellows, Manchester Unity Friendly Society
Widows' and Orphans' Society, Ware District of Odd Fellows
Widow, Widowers' and Orphans' Fund of the Godalming District of the Independent Order of Oddfellows, Manchester Unity Friendly Society
Wiltshire Holloway Benefit Society

## Charities

The Central Board of Finance of the Church of England
Church Commissioners
The Church of England Pensions Board
The Church of Scotland
The Church of Scotland General Trustees

Church of Scotland Trust
The Winchester Diocesan Board of Finance
York Diocesan Board of Finance Limited

# Appendix 3

# Credit Reference Agency Notices

## *Notice A*

(1) With this statement is a copy of the credit reference agency's file on you.

*Your rights if an entry is wrong*
(2) If you think that anything in the file is wrong and you are likely to suffer as a result, you have the following rights.

(3) If you think that there is no basis at all for the entry, you may write to the agency requiring it to remove the entry.

(4) If the entry is incorrect you may write to the agency requiring it to remove or amend the entry. When writing to the agency, you should say why you think that the entry is incorrect.

*What happens then?*
(5) Within 28 days of receiving your letter the agency should write and tell you that it has removed the entry from the file, or amended it, or taken no action. If the entry has been amended, the agency must send you a copy of the amended entry.

*What can you do if you are not satisfied?*
(6) If the agency tells you that it has taken no action, or if it does not reply to your letter within the 28 days, or if it makes an amendment which you think is unsatisfactory, you may write a note correcting the entry and send it to the agency with a letter requiring the agency—
to add the note to its file about you
*and*

238

to include a copy of it when furnishing information included in or based on the entry which it corrects.

(7) Your note of correction should give a clear and accurate explanation of why you consider the entry to be incorrect. It must not be more than 200 words long. You can prepare the note yourself or with the help of, for example, a citizens advice bureau, a consumer advice centre or a solicitor.

NB: If the agency considers that your note of correction is incorrect, or defamatory, or frivolous, or scandalous, or unsuitable for any other reason, it can ask the Director General of Fair Trading to give a ruling as to what it must do.

IMPORTANT

(8) If the agency has replied to the first letter in which you objected to the entry, you must send your note of correction within 28 days of receiving its reply.

(9) If the agency did not reply to your first letter within 28 days, your note of correction must be sent within the next 28 days.

(10) If the agency accepts your note of correction (ie is not seeking a ruling from the Director General), it must tell you within 28 days that it intends to comply with your request.

*Your rights if the agency does not accept your note of correction within 28 days*

(11) You may write to the Director General of Fair Trading at the Office of Fair Trading, Field House, Bream's Buildings, London EC4A 1PR, who may make whatever order he thinks fit. You should say that you are writing under Section 159(5) of the Consumer Credit Act 1974 and give:

your full name and address (and telephone number, if any);

name and address of the credit reference agency;

the agency's reference number (if any);

details of the entry you consider incorrect, including,

why you consider it incorrect,

why you consider it prejudicial to your interest, and

an indication of when you sent to the agency the note of correction mentioned in paragraph 6.

Before deciding what to do, the Director General may ask the agency for its side of the case by sending it a copy of your letter. In return, you will be sent any comments the agency makes.

NOTE: The various periods of 28 days referred to in this statement start with the day following receipt and end with that of delivery, so in order to avoid any risk of losing your rights you should allow for postal delays.

# *Notice B*

CREDIT REFERENCE AGENCY FILES
BUSINESS CONSUMER'S RIGHTS UNDER SECTIONS 159 AND
160 OF THE CONSUMER CREDIT ACT 1974

(1) You requested a copy of the file kept by the credit reference agency about you and your business. Under a direction given by the Director General of Fair Trading the agency need not give you a complete copy of its file about you but is allowed to withhold certain information in it (for example, the source of the information), the disclosure of which might adversely affect the service of the agency to its customers.

(2) Sections 159 and 160 of the Consumer Credit Act 1974 give you certain rights about your file and the correction of wrong information in it. You should read the notes below carefully to see what your rights are.

RIGHTS UNDER SECTION 160(4)

(3) These rights apply if you are dissatisfied with the information sent to you, for example, because you cannot judge its accuracy without information which has apparently been withheld under the Director General's dispensation. (If the information is *incorrect*, as opposed to *incomplete*, your rights under Section 159 (not 160) are relevant—see below.) You should first get into touch with the agency, setting out the reasons for your dissatisfaction and asking it to help you.

*What if the agency cannot help you?*
(4) You may write to the Director General of Fair Trading, Office of Fair Trading, Field House, Bream's Buildings, London EC4A 1PR, giving him a copy of the information you have received, the date you received it and notice that you are dissatisfied with it. He will also need to know what steps you have taken with the agency to remove the cause of your dissatisfaction.

(5) You should do this within 28 days of originally receiving the information from the agency's file. If you cannot write within 28 days then write as soon as possible giving the reasons for the delay.

(6) It will be helpful if, in your letter to the Director General, you say that you are writing under Section 160(4) of the Consumer Credit Act and include the following information—
name, address (and telephone number, if any) of your business;
name and address of the credit reference agency;
the agency's reference number (if any).

(7) If the Director General is satisfied that you have taken all reason-

able steps with the agency, he may obtain disclosure to you of further information on your file.

## RIGHTS UNDER SECTION 159

(8) Whether or not you have applied to the Director General under Section 160, you have the following rights.

*Your rights if information is wrong*
(9) If you think any of the information is wrong and you or your business are likely to suffer as a result, you have the following rights.

(10) If there is no basis at all for the entry, you may write to the agency requiring it to remove the entry.

(11) If the information is incorrect you may write to the agency requiring it to remove or amend the entry. When writing to the agency, you should say why you think the information is incorrect.

*What happens then?*
(12) Within 28 days of receiving your letter, the agency should write and tell you that it has removed the entry from the file, or amended it, or taken no action. If the entry has been amended, the agency must send you a copy of the amended entry.

*What can you do if you are not satisfied?*
(13) If the agency tells you that it has taken no action, or if it does not reply to your letter within the 28 days, or if it makes an amendment which you think is unsatisfactory, you may write a note correcting the information and send it to the agency with a letter requiring the agency—
to add the note to its file about you
*and*
to include a copy of it when furnishing information included in or based on the entry which it corrects.

(14) Your note of correction should give a clear and accurate explanation of why you consider the information to be incorrect. It must not be more than 200 words long. You can prepare the note yourself, or you may care to obtain professional assistance, for example, from a solicitor.

NB If the agency considers that your note of correction is incorrect, or defamatory, or frivolous, or scandalous, or unsuitable for any other reason, it can ask the Director General of Fair Trading to give a ruling as to what it must do.

## IMPORTANT
(15) If the agency has replied to the first letter in which you objected to the information, you must send your note of correction within 28 days of receiving its reply.

(16) If the agency did not reply to your first letter within 28 days, your note of correction must be sent within the next 28 days.

(17) If the agency accepts your note of correction (ie is not seeking a ruling from the Director General), it must tell you within 28 days that it intends to comply with your request.

*Your rights if the agency does not accept your note of correction within 28 days*

(18) You may write to the Director General of Fair Trading at the address mentioned in paragraph 4 explaining the situation. He may make whatever order he thinks fit.

(19) You should say that you are writing under Section 159(5) of the Consumer Credit Act 1974 and give—
    name, address (and telephone number, if any) of your business;
    name and address of the credit reference agency;
    the agency's reference number (if any);
    details of the entry you consider incorrect, including—
        why you consider it incorrect,
        why you consider it prejudicial to your interests, and
        an indication of when you sent to the agency the note of correction mentioned in paragraph 13.

Before deciding what to do, the Director General may ask the agency for its side of the case by sending it a copy of your letter. In return, you will be sent any comments the agency makes.

NOTE: The various periods of 28 days referred to in this statement start with the day following receipt and end with that of delivery, so in order to avoid any risk of losing your rights you should allow for postal delays.

# Appendix 4

# List of Regulations, Orders etc

### *Note*

The following is a complete list of statutory instruments and general notices made or issued under the Consumer Credit Act 1974. Those printed in italics are revoked.

### *Statutory Instruments*

The Consumer Credit Act 1974 (Commencement No 1) Order 1975 (SI 1975 No 2123)

The Consumer Credit (Period of Standard Licence) Regulations 1975 (SI 1975 No 2124)

The Consumer Credit Licensing (Representations) Order 1976 (SI 1976 No 191)

The Consumer Credit Licensing (Appeals) Regulations 1976 (SI 1976 No 837)

The Consumer Credit (Termination of Licences) Regulations 1976 (SI 1976 No 1002)

The Consumer Credit Act 1974 (Commencement No 2) Order 1977 (SI 1977 No 325)

*The Consumer Credit (Exempt Agreements) Order 1977 (SI 1977 No 326)*

*The Consumer Credit (Total Charge for Credit) Regulations 1977 (SI 1977 No 327)*

The Consumer Credit (Notice of Variation of Agreements) Regulations 1977 (SI 1977 No 328)

The Consumer Credit (Credit Reference Agency) Regulations 1977 (SI 1977 No 329)

The Consumer Credit (Conduct of Business) (Credit References) Regulations 1977 (SI 1977 No 330)

The Consumer Credit (Entry and Inspection) Regulations 1977 (SI 1977 No 331)

The Consumer Credit Act 1974 (Commencement No 3) Order 1977 (SI 1977 No 802)

*The Consumer Credit (Exempt Agreements) (Amendment) Order 1977 (SI 1977 No 1493)*

The Consumer Credit Act 1974 (Commencement No 4) Order 1977 (SI 1977 No 2163)

*The Consumer Credit (Exempt Agreements) (Amendment) Order 1978 (SI 1978 No 126)*

*The Consumer Credit (Exempt Agreements) (Amendment No 2) Order 1978 (SI 1978 No 1616)*

*The Consumer Credit (Notice of Variation of Agreements) (Amendment) Regulations 1979 (SI 1979 No 66).*

*The Consumer Credit (Notice of Variation of Agreements) (Amendment No 2) Regulations 1979 (SI 1979 No 667)*

*The Consumer Credit (Period of Standard Licence) (Amendment) Regulations 1979 (SI 1979 No 796)*

*The Consumer Credit (Exempt Agreements) (Amendment) Order 1979 (SI 1979 No 1099)*

The Consumer Credit Act 1974 (Commencement No 5) Order 1979 (SI 1979 No 1685)

The Consumer Credit Act 1974 (Commencement No 6) Order 1980 (SI 1980 No 50)

The Consumer Credit (Total Charge for Credit) Regulations 1980 (SI 1980 No 51)

*The Consumer Credit (Exempt Agreements) Order 1980 (SI 1980 No 52)*

*The Consumer Credit (Exempt Advertisements) Order 1980 (SI 1980 No 53)*

The Consumer Credit (Advertisements) Order 1980 (SI 1980 No 54)

*The Consumer Credit (Quotations) Regulations 1980 (SI 1980 No 55)*

The Consumer Credit Act 1974 (Commencement No 7) Order 1981 (SI 1981 No 280)

The Consumer Credit (Running-Account Credit Information) Regulations 1983 (SI 1983 No 1570).

The Consumer Credit (Increase of Monetary Amounts) Order 1983 (SI 1983 No 1571)

The Consumer Credit (Advertisements and Quotations) (Amendment No 2) Regulations 1983 (SI 1983 No 1721)

The Consumer Credit (Increase of Monetary Limits) Order 1983 (SI 1983 No 1878)

*The Consumer Credit (Exempt Agreements) (Amendment) Order 1984 (SI 1984 No 434)*

The Consumer Credit (Negotiable Instruments) (Exemption) Order 1984 (SI 1984 No 435)

The Consumer Credit Act 1974 (Commencement No 9) Order 1984 (SI 1984 No 436)

The Consumer Credit (Entry and Inspection) (Amendment) Regulations 1984 (SI 1984 No 1046)

The Consumer Credit (Advertisements and Quotations) (Amendment) Regulations 1984 (SI 1984 No 1055)

The Consumer Credit (Local Acts) Order 1984 (SI 1984 No 1107)

The Consumer Credit Cancellation Notices and Copies of Documents (Amendment) Regulations 1984 (SI 1984 No 1108).

The Consumer Credit (Enforcement, Default and Termination Notices) (Amendment) Regulations 1984 (SI 1984 No 1109)

The Consumer Credit (Agreements) (Amendment) Regulations 1984 (SI 1984 No 1600)

The Consumer Credit (Exempt Advertisements) Order 1985 (SI 1985 No 621)

The Consumer Credit (Agreements and Cancellation Notices and Copies of Documents) (Amendment) Regulations 1985 (SI 1985 No 666)

The Consumer Credit (Exempt Agreements) (No 2) Order 1985 (SI 1985 No 757)

The Consumer Credit (Total Charge for Credit) (Amendment) Regulations 1985 (SI 1985 No 1192)

The Consumer Credit (Exempt Agreements) (No 2) (Amendment No 2) Order 1985 (SI 1985 No 1918)

## *General Notices*

*General Notice No 1—Consumer Credit Fees*

*General Notice No 2—Form of Application for a Standard Licence*

General Notice No 3—Form of Application for a Direction under Section 160(1)

General Notice No 4—Form of Application for a Group Licence

General Notice No 5—The Public Register

*General Notice No 6—Form of Application to vary a Standard Licence*

General Notice No 7—Form of Application to end the Suspension of a Standard Licence

*General Notice No 8—Form of Application for an Order under Section 148(2) of the Act in respect of Ancillary Credit Business Services other than Credit Brokerage*

*General Notice No 9—Form of Application for an Order under Section 40(2) of the Act*

*General Notice No 10—Form of Application for an Order under Section 149(2) of the Act*

General Notice No 11—Form of Application by a Consumer for an Order under Section 159(5)

General Notice No 12—Form of Application by a Credit Reference Agency for an Order under Section 159(5)

*General Notice No 13—Form of Application for an Order under Section 148(2) of the Act in respect of the Services of a Person Carrying on an Ancillary Credit Business*

General Notice No 14—Period of, and Form for, Application for Standard Licence

General Notice No 15/15A—Consumer Credit Fees

General Notice No 15(b)—Consumer Credit Fees (Credit Unions)

General Notice No 16—Application to Renew a Group Licence

# Appendix 5

# Official Addresses

## Department of Trade and Industry

*CCC Division*
Millbank Tower
Millbank
London SW1P 4QU

(01–211 3000)

## Offices of Fair Trading

*Consumer Credit Division*
Field House
Bream's Buildings
London EC4A 1PR

(01–242 2858)

*Consumer Credit Licensing Branch*
Government Building
Bromyard Avenue
Acton
London W3 7BB

(01–749 9151)

Consumer Credit Publications
Branch
Government Building
Bromyard Avenue
Acton
London W3 7BB

(01–749 9151)

*Scottish Branch*
9 Hope Street
Edinburgh EH2 4EL

(031–225 3185)

## Local enforcement authorities

### City of London & London Boroughs

*London, Corporation of*
Department of Trading Standards
Milton Court
Moor Lane
London EC2Y 9BL

*Barking and Dagenham*
Trading Standards Division
Town Hall
Barking
Essex IG11 7LU

*Barnet*
Chief Inspector of
Trading Standards
Town Hall
The Burroughs
Hendon NW4 4BG

*Bexley*
Consumer Services Department
Bexley Civic Offices
Broadway
Bexleyheath Kent DA6 7LB

*Brent*
Trading Standards Service
249 Willesden Lane
London NW2 5JH

*Bromley*
Trading Standards Service
Bromley Civic Centre
Rochester Avenue
Bromley
Kent BR1 3UH

*Camden*
Weights and Measures
Department
Endsleigh Gardens
London WC1H 0EB

*Croydon*
Consumer Affairs
119 Canterbury Road
Croydon CR0 3HH

*Ealing see Brent*

*Enfield*
Trading Standards Department
341A Baker Street
Enfield EN1 3LF

*Greenwich*
Department of Consumer
Protection and
Environmental Health
Riverside House

Woolwich High Street
Woolwich SE1 6DN

*Hackney*
Comprehensive Consumer Affairs
Service
136/142 Lower Clapton Road
London E5 0JQ

*Hammersmith see City of
Westminster*

*Haringey*
Weights and Measures
Department
590 Seven Sisters Road
Tottenham N15 6HR

*Harrow see Brent*

*Havering*
Trading Standards Office
Langtons Cottage
Billet Lane
Hornchurch
Essex RN11 1XL

*Hillingdon*
Trading Standards Division
Department of Public Protection
Services
Barra Hall Wood End
Green Road
Hayes
Middlesex UB3 2SA

*Hounslow*
Trading Standards Department
Hounslow Borough Offices
Great West Road
Brentford
Middlesex TW8 9BZ

*Islington*
Trading Standards Department
159–167 Upper Street
London N1 1RE

*Islington see Camden*

*Royal Borough of Kensington
and Chelsea see City of
Westminster*

*Royal Borough of Kingston upon
Thames*
Trading Standards Department
Guildhall
Kingston upon Thames
Surrey KT1 1EU

*Lambeth*
Environmental Health and
Consumer Services
138–146 Clapham Park Road
London SW4 7DD

*Lewisham see Southwark*

*Merton Environmental Health and
Trading Standards Department*
Park Place
54 Commonside West
Mitcham
Surrey CR4 4HB

*Newham*
Consumer Protection Services
495 High Street North Manor Park
London E12 6TH

*Redbridge*
Weights and Measures
Department
Woodbine Place Wanstead
London E11 2RH

*Richmond upon Thames*
Public Protection Division
Elmsfield House High Street
Teddington
Middlesex TW11 8EJ

*Southwark*
Trading Standards Office
23 Harper Road
London SE1 6AW

*Sutton Trading Standards Service*
Civic Offices
Sutton
Surrey SM1 1EA

*Tower Hamlets*
Trading Standards Office
5 Calvert Avenue
London E2 7JZ

*Waltham Forest*
Trading Standards Service
8 Buxton Road
Walthamstow
London E17 7EJ

*Wandsworth*
Trading Standards Office
Town Hall
Wandsworth High Street
London SW18 2PU

*City of Westminster*
Trading Standards Service
Westminster Council House
Marylebone Road
London NW1 5PT

## Metropolitan County Councils

*Greater Manchester*
County Consumer Services
PO Box 435 County Hall
Piccadilly Gardens
Manchester M60 3HX

*Merseyside*
Trading Standards Department
62 Great Crosshall Street
Liverpool L3 2AT

*South Yorkshire*
Consumer Protection Department
BAC Building
Regent Street
Barnsley
South Yorkshire S70 2MG

*Tyne and Wear*
Consumer Service Department
Sandyford House
Archbold Terrace
Newcastle upon Tyne NE2 1ED

*West Midlands*
Consumer Protection Department
County Hall 1 Lancaster Circus
Queensway
Birmingham B4 7DJ

*West Yorkshire*
Department of Trading Standards
Nepshaw Lane
Gildersome
Morley LS2 0QW

## Non-Metropolitan County Councils

*Avon*
Trading Standards Department
Rackhay
Queen Charlotte Street
Bristol BS1 4HY

*Bedfordshire*
Trading Standards Department
1 Peel Street
Luton LU1 2QR

*Berkshire*
Trading Standards Department
Shire Hall
Shinfield Road
Reading RG2 9XA

*Buckinghamshire*
Consumer Protection Department
County Hall
Aylesbury HP20 1UP

*Cambridgeshire*
Consumer Protection Department
Hinchingbrook Cottage
Brampton Road
Huntingdon PE18 8NA

*Cheshire*
Department of Trading Standards
Backford Hall
Chester CH1 6EA

*Cleveland*
Trading Standards Department
Cannot Street
Middlesbrough TS1 5JJ

*Cornwall*
Trading Standards Department
County Hall
Truro TR1 3BQ

*Cumbria*
Department of Trading Standards
County Offices
Kendal LA9 4RQ

*Derbyshire*
Trading Standards Department
Ivon Brook
South Darley
Nr Matlock DE4 2JW

*Devon*
HQ Trading Standards
Department
Broadwalt House
Southernhay West
Exeter EX1 1TX

*Dorset*
Trading Standards Department
2 Commercial Road
Poole
Dorset BH14 0JL

*Durham*
Consumer Protection Department
County Hall
Durham DH1 5UB

*East Sussex*
Trading Standards Department
PO Box 5 County Hall
St Anne's Crescent
Lewes BN7 1SW

*Essex*
County Consumer and Public
Protection Department
Beehive Lane
Chelmsford CM2 9SY

*Southend-on-Sea*
Trading Standards Office
Civic Centre
Southend-on-Sea SS2 6ER

*Gloucestershire*
Trading Standards Department
Hillfield House
Denmark Road
Gloucester GL1 3LD

*Hampshire*
Trading Standards Department
HQ
2nd Floor Ashburton Court
The Castle
Winchester SO23 8TB

*Hereford and Worcester*
Trading Standards Department
Morton House
Fernhill Heath
Worcester WR3 7UR

*Hertfordshire*
Trading Standards Department
County Hall
Hertford SG13 8DE

*Humberside*
Trading Standards Department

Flemingate House
Flemingate
Beverley HU17 0NQ

*Isle of Wight*
Trading Standards Department
County Hall Newport
Isle of Wight PO30 1UD

*Kent*
Trading Standards Department
Springfield
Maidstone ME14 2LS

*Lancashire*
Trading Standards Department
55 Guildhall Street
Preston PR1 3NU

*Leicestershire*
Trading Standards Department
County Hall Glenfield
Leicester LE3 8RN

*Lincolnshire*
Trading Standards Department
County Offices
Newland
Lincoln LN1 1YL

*Norfolk*
Trading Standards Department
County Hall
Martineau Lane
Norwich NR1 2DH

*North Yorkshire*
Consumer Protection
Headquarters
County Hall
Racecourse Lane
Northallerton DL7 8SA

*Northamptonshire*
Trading Standards Department
Wootton Hall Park
Northampton NN4 9BL

*Northumberland*
Trading Standards Department
Southgate House
Morpeth NE61 2DP

*Nottinghamshire*
Trading Standards Department
Trent Bridge House
Fox Road West
Bridgford
Nottingham NG2 BJ

*Oxfordshire*
County Trading Standards
Department
Rewley Road
Oxford OX1 2EH

*Shropshire*
Department of Trading Standards
The Shirehall
Shrewsbury SY2 6ND

*Somerset*
Trading Standards Department
South Street
Taunton TA1 3AN

*Staffordshire*
Trading Standards and Consumer
Protection Department

41a Eastgate Street
Stafford ST16 2LZ

*Suffolk*
County Trading Standards
Department
St Edmund House
Rope Walk
Ipswich IP4 1LZ

*Surrey*
Trading Standards Department
Mount Hill South Street
Epsom KT18 7PT

*Warwickshire*
Trading Standards Department
Budbrooke Road
Warwick CV35 7DP

*West Sussex*
Trading Standards Department
The Tannery
Westgate
Chichester PO19 3HN

*Wiltshire*
Department of Trading Standards
and Consumer Protection
County Hall
Trowbridge BA14 8JE

## Welsh Counties

*Clwyd*
Consumer Protection Department
Shire Hall
Mold CH7 6NT

*Dyfed*
Trading Standards Department
County Hall
Carmarthen SA31 1JP

*Gwent*
Trading Standards Department
County Hall
Cwmbran NP4 2HX

*Gwynedd*
Trading Standards Department
12 High Street
Caernarfon LL55 1RN

*Mid Glamorgan*
Consumer Protection Office
Forest Grove
Treforest
Pontypridd OF37 1UB

*Powys*
Trading Standards Department
County Hall Annexe Southfields

Spa Road East
Llandrindod Wells LD1 SES

*South Glamorgan*
County Trading Standards
Department
Tredegar Street
Cardiff CF1 2FB

*West Glamorgan*
Consumer Protection Department
West Glamorgan County Council
County Hall
Swansea SA1 3SN

## Scottish Regions

*Borders Regional Council*
Consumer Protection Department
County Buildings
Jedburgh TD8 6AR

*Central Regional Council*
Trading Standards Department
Forrest Road
Stirling FK8 1UH

*Dumfries and Galloway Regional
Council*
Consumer Protection Department
1 Newall Terrace
Dumfries DG1 1LN

*Fife Regional Council*
Department of Trading Standards
and Consumer Protection
Fife House North Street
Glenrothes Fife KY7 5LT

*Grampian Regional Council*
Consumer Protection Department
Woodhill House
Ashgrove Road West
Aberdeen AB9 2LU

*Highland Regional Council*
Consumer Protection Department
Regional Buildings
Glenurqhart Road
Inverness IV3 5NX

*Lothian Regional Council*
Consumer Protection Department
1 Parliament Square
Edinburgh EH1 1RF

*Orkney Islands Council*
Department of Trading Standards
and Consumer Protection
Council Offices
Kirkwall
Orkney KW15 1NY

*Shetland Isles Council*
Trading Standards Department
3 Commercial Road
Lerwick
Shetland ZE1 0LX

*Strathclyde Regional Council*
Consumer Protection Department
Strathclyde House
20 India Road
Glasgow G2 4PF

*Tayside Regional Council*
Consumer Protection Department
1 Riverside Drive
Dundee DD1 4DB

*Western Isles Island Council*
Consumer Protection Department
Council Offices
Sandwick Road
Stornoway
Isle of Lewis PA87 2BW

*Northern Ireland*

*Department of Commerce*
Trading Standards Branch
176 Newtownbreda Road
Belfast BT8 4QS

# Appendix 6

# List of Official Publications on the Consumer Credit Act

The publications listed below, and a detailed descriptive list of the official guides on consumer credit published by the Office of Fair Trading, can be obtained free of charge from that Office at Field House, Room 310c, 15–25 Bream's Buildings, Chancery Lane, London EC4A 1PR. Publications marked * are leaflets; the remainder are booklets varying in length from 8 to 40 pages.

*OFT Guides for Traders*

*Licensing* (CCP 22)
*Fees* (CCP 18C)*
*Responsibilities of a licensee* (CCP 3)
*The Consumer Credit Public Register* (CCP 9)*
*Are you a credit broker? A limitation on fees* (CCP 12)*
*Credit references: you and your customer* (CCP 11)*
*Guidance for credit reference agencies* (CCP 6)
*Extortionate credit* (CCP 8)
*Regulated and exempt agreements* (CCP 10)
*Advertisements and quotations regulations* (CCP 23)
*Credit charges* (CCP 24)
*A guide to the consumer credit tables* (CCP 14)*
*Equal liability* (CCP 21)

In addition, a set of four free booklets, available separately, gives official guidance on documentation and consumers' rights and duties. These are respectively entitled *Hire agreements*, *Cancellable agreements*, *Non-cancellable agreements*, and *Matters arising during the lifetime of an agreement*. A slide-tape kit *Would you credit it?* shows how the Advertisements Regulations affect the High Street trader.

The following publications are available free of charge from the Department of Trade and Industry, CCC Division, Millbank Tower, Millbank, London SW1P 4QU (01–211 3000).

*Counting the cost of credit*

*Guide on appeals from licensing determinations of the Director General of Fair Trading*
*Exemption of certain Consumer Credit Agreements under Section 16(1)*
*A Computer Based solution to the Problem of Calculating the Annual Percentage Rate of Charge*

The Act itself and the Regulations and Orders made under it are on sale at the following Government Bookshops:

49 High Holborn, London WC1V 6HB
13a Castle Street, Edinburgh EH2 3AR
9–21 Princess Street, Manchester M60 8AS
Southey House, Wine Street, Bristol BS1 2BQ
258 Broad Street, Birmingham B1 2HE
80 Chichester Street, Belfast BT1 4JY

The following publications on *sex discrimination* in the provision of consumer credit facilities are available free of charge from Equal Opportunities Commission, Overseas House, Quay Street, Manchester M3 3HN.

*Credit where credit's due*
*Credit for women*
*Sex equality and credit scoring*

# Appendix 7

# Guide to Commencement Dates, Repeals etc

*Commencement Dates of the Consumer Credit Act 1974*

This table indicates the provisions of the Act which were in operation on 6 October 1980. The symbols in the extreme right hand column indicate the authority for commencement dates shown, and have the following meaning:

A = Note at the head of Schedule 3 to the Act;

B = Banking Act 1979, s 38, and Banking Act 1979 (Commencement No 1) Order 1979 (SI 1979 No 938);

1 = Consumer Credit Act 1974 (Commencement No 1) Order 1975 (SI 1975 No 2123);

2 = Consumer Credit Act 1974 (Commencement No 2) Order 1977 (SI 1977 No 325);

3 = Consumer Credit Act 1974 (Commencement No 3) Order 1977 (SI 1977 No 802);

4 = Consumer Credit Act 1974 (Commencement No 4) Order 1977 (SI 1977 No 2163).

6= Consumer Credit Act 1974 (Commencement No 6) Order 1980 (SI 1980 No 50.

8 = Consumer Credit Act 1974 (Commencement No 8) Order 1983 (SI 1983 No 1551).

9 = Consumer Credit Act 1974 (Commencement No 9) Order 1984 (SI 1984 No 436).

| Section(s) | Subject-matter | Commencement date | Remarks | Authority |
|---|---|---|---|---|
| 1–7 | Functions of Director General of Fair Trading | 31.7.74 | | A |
| 8–20 | Definitions of principal terms | 31.7.74 | (1) Definition of 'regulated agreement' in ss 8(3) and 15(2) became operative on 1.4.77 | A |
| | | | (2) s 19(3) (deferment of linked transactions) not yet operative | — |
| 21 | (1) Need for a licence (consumer credit business not limited to credit of £30 or less) | 1.10.77 | | 2 |
| | (2) Need for a licence (consumer credit business limited to credit of £30 or less) | Not yet appointed | | — |
| | (3) Need for a licence (consumer hire business) | 1.10.77 | | 2 |
| | (4) Need for a licence (credit brokerage business not limited to introductions for credit of £30 or less) | 1.7.78 | s 21 as applied by s 147(1) | 4 |
| | (5) Need for a licence (credit brokerage business limited to introductions for credit of £30 or less) | Not yet appointed | s 21 as applied by s 147(1) | — |
| | (6) Need for a licence (credit reference agency) | 3.8.76 | s 21 as applied by s 147(1) | 4 |

| Section(s) | Subject-matter | Commencement date | Remarks | Authority |
|---|---|---|---|---|
| | (7) Need for a licence (debt adjusting, debt counselling, debt collecting) | | | |
| 22–34 | Mechanics of licensing system | 3.8.76 | s 21 as applied by s 147(1) | 4 |
| 35, 36 | Consumer Credit Public Register | 31.7.74 | | A |
| 37, 38 | Termination of licence on death, bankruptcy etc | 2.2.76 | | 1 |
| 39 | Licensing offences | 31.7.74 | | A |
| 40 | Agreement by unlicensed credit or hire trader enforceable only on Director's order | 31.7.74 | Applies only to agreements made after relevant commencement date of s 21 | A |
| 41, 42 | Licensing appeals | Various (see remarks column) | | 2 |
| 43–47 | Control of advertising | 31.7.74 | | A |
| 48 | Definition of canvassing off trade premises (regulated agreements) | 6.10.80 | | 6 |
| 49 | Prohibition of canvassing debtor-creditor agreements off trade premises | 31.7.74 | | A |
| 50 | Prohibition of circulars to minors | 1.10.77 | | 3 |
| 51 | Prohibition of unsolicited credit-tokens | 1.7.77 | | 3 |
| 52–54 | Regulations as to quotations, display of information and conduct of business | 1.7.77 | It is not proposed to make regulations under ss 53–54 | 3 |
| 55 | Regulations as to pre-contract information | 31.7.74 | It is not proposed to make regulations under s 55 | A |
| 56 | Negotiators as agents | 31.7.74 | | A |
| 57, 58 | Withdrawal from prospective agreement | 16.5.77 | | 2 |
| | | 19.5.85 | | 8 |

| Section(s) | Subject-matter | Commencement date | Remarks | Authority |
|---|---|---|---|---|
| 59 | Agreement to enter future agreement void | 19.5.85 | | 8 |
| 60 | Regulations as to form and content of agreements | 31.7.74 | It is not proposed to make regulations under s 64(3) | A |
| 61–65 | Documentation requirements on making agreements | 19.5.85 | | 8 |
| 66 | Liability of credit-token holder | 19.5.85 | | 8 |
| 67–73 | Cancellation of agreements | 19.5.85 | | 8 |
| 74(1)–(3) | Exclusion of certain agreements from ss 55–73 | 31.7.74 | | A |
| 74(3A) | Exclusion of certain agreements from ss 55–73 | 1.10.79 | | B |
| 74(4) | Exclusion of certain agreements from ss 55–73 | 31.7.74 | | A |
| 75 | Connected-lender liability | 1.7.77 | Only in relation to regulated agreements made on or after 1.7.77 | 3 |
| 76 | Duty to give notice before taking certain action | 19.5.85 | | 8 |
| 77–80 | Duty to give certain information | 19.5.85 | | 8 |
| 81 | Appropriation of payments | Not yet appointed | | 8 |
| 82 | Variation of agreements | 1.4.77 | | 2 |
| 83, 84 | Misuse of credit facilities | 19.5.85 | | 8 |
| 85 | Duty on issue of new credit-tokens | 19.5.85 | | 8 |
| 86 | Death of debtor or hirer | 19.5.85 | | 8 |

| Section(s) | Subject-matter | Commencement date | Remarks | Authority |
|---|---|---|---|---|
| 87–93 | Default of debtor or hirer | 19.5.85 | | 8 |
| 94–97 | Early payment by debtor | 19.5.85 | | 8 |
| 98–104 | Termination of agreements | 19.5.85 | | 8 |
| 105 | Form and content of securities | 19.5.85 | | 8 |
| 106 | Ineffective securities | 31.7.74 | | A |
| 107–111 | Duty to give information about security | 19.5.85 | | 8 |
| 112 | Regulations as to realisation of securities | 31.7.74 | No regulations yet made | A |
| 113 | Act not to be evaded by use of security | 31.7.74 | | A |
| 114–122 | Pledges | 19.5.85 | | 8 |
| 123–125 | Negotiable instruments | 19.5.85 | | 9 |
| 126 | Enforcement of land mortgages | 19.5.85 | | 8 |
| 127–136 | Judicial control | 19.5.85 | | 8 |
| 137–140 | Extortionate credit bargains | 16.5.77 | | 2 |
| 141–144 | Further judicial provisions | 19.5.85 | | 8 |
| 145, 146 | Definition of ancillary credit business | 31.7.74 | | 8 |
| 147(1) | Licensing of ancillary credit business | See under s 21 (paras (4)–(7) ) | | A |
| 147(2) | Regulations as to credit reference agencies | 31.7.74 | No regulations yet made | 4 |
| 148 | Agreements for services of unlicensed ancillary credit traders | Various | Applies only to agreements made after relevant commencement date of s 21 | A |
| 149 | Regulated agreements made on introductons by unlicensed credit-broker | Various | Applies only to introductions after relevant commencement date of s 21 | 4 |

| Section(s) | Subject-matter | Commencement date | Remarks | Authority |
|---|---|---|---|---|
| 150 | Licensing appeals by ancillary credit traders | 31.7.74 | | A |
| 151 | Advertising by credit-brokers, debt counsellors and debt adjusters | 6.10.80 | | 6 |
| 152 | Regulations as to conduct of business by credit-brokers, debt counsellors and debt adjusters | 31.12.74 | It is not proposed to make regulations under s 156 | A |
| 153, 154 | Canvassing by credit-brokers, debt counsellors and debt adjusters | 31.12.74 | | A |
| 155 | Limit on brokerage fees | 31.12.74 | So far as it relates to regulated agreements, not effective before 1.4.77 | A |
| 156 | Regulations as to agreements made by credit-brokers, debt counsellors and debt adjusters | 31.12.74 | It is not proposed to make regulations under s 179 | A |
| 157–160 | Information on credit reference agency files | 16.5.77 | | 2 |
| 161–173 | Enforcement of Act | 31.7.74 | | A |
| 174–193 | Supplement provisions | 31.7.74 | s 185(2) (c) inserted by Banking Act 1979, s 38(3) | A |

*Appendix 7 contd*

*Commencement dates of Repeals to UK Acts*
*(Schedule 4)*

**(1) Amendment effective on 30.3.77:**
County Courts Act 1959, s 192(2) (*Para 19 of Sched 4*)

(*Consumer Credit Act 1974 (Commencement No 2) Order 1977, Sched 2, Pt I*)

**(2) Amendment effective on 1.4.77:**
Trade Descriptions Act 1968, s 28 (*Para 28 of Sched 4*)

(*Consumer Credit Act 1974 (Commencement No 2) Order 1977, Sched 2, Pt I*)

**(3) Amendments effective on 6.10.80:**
Trading Stamps Act 1964, s 2(1) (Para 24 of Sched 4)
Trading Stamps Act 1964, s 3(4) (Para 25 of Sched 4)
Trading Stamps Act 1964, s 10(1) (Para 26 of Sched 4)

(*Consumer Credit Act 1974 (Commencement No 6) Order 1980, art 4*)

**(4) Amendments effective on 19.5.85:**
Bills of Sale Act (1878) Amendment Act 1882, s 7A (Para 1 of Sched 4)
Factors Act 1889, s 9 (Para 2 of Sched 4)
Law of Distress Amendment Act 1908, s 4A (Para 5 of Sched 4) (not in relation to consumer hire agreements)
Bankruptcy Act 1914, s 38A (Para 6 of Sched 4)
Compensation (Defence) Act 1939, ss 13 and 17(1) (Paras 7 and 8 of Sched 4)
Liability for War Damage (Miscellaneous Provisions) Act 1950, s 1(3) (Para 9 of Sched 4)
Agriculture (Miscellaneous Provisions) Act 1950, s 1(4) (Para 10 of Sched 4)
Rag Flock and other Filling Materials Act 1951, s 10(7) (Para 11 of Sched 4)
Reserve and Auxiliary Forces (Protection of Civil Interests) Act 1951, ss 4, 10 and 64(1) (Paras 12 to 14 of Sched 4)
Clean Air Act 1956, ss 14 and s 34(1) (Paras 15 and 16 of Sched 4)
Restrictive Trade Practices Act 1956, s 26(3) (repealed and re-enacted in Sched 1 to the Resale Prices Act 1976) (Para 17 of Sched 4)
Housing Act 1957, s 94 (Para 18 of Sched 4)
Consumer Protection Act 1961, ss 2(6) and 5 (Paras 20 and 21 of Sched 4)
Hire Purchase Act 1964, Part III (Para 22 of Sched 4)
Emergency Laws (Re-enactment and Repeals) Act 1964, s 1 (Para 23 of Sched 4)

Housing (Scotland) Act 1966, s 140(2) (Para 27 of Sched 4)
Income and Corporation Taxes Act 1970, s 495(7) (Para 29 of Sched 4)
Administration of Justice Act 1970, ss 38A and 54(6) (Paras 30 and 31 of Sched 4)
Vehicles (Excise) Act 1971, s 38(1) (Para 32 of Sched 4)
Industry Act 1972, s 6(2) (Para 33 of Sched 4)
Supply of Goods (Implied Terms) Act 1973, ss 8–12 and 15 (Paras 35 and 36 of Sched 4)
Fair Trading Act 1973, s 138(5) (Para 37 of Sched 4)

## Commencement dates of Amendments to NI Acts

See Consumer Credit Act 1974 (Commencement No 2) Order 1977, Sched 2, Pt II; Consumer Credit Act 1974 (Commencement No 6) Order 1980, art 4; Consumer Credit Act 1974 (Commencement No 8) Order 1983, Sched 1, Pt II.

## Commencement dates of Repeals to UK Acts (Schedule 5)

**(1) Repeals effective on 16.5.77 (except in relation to agreements made before that date which are not personal credit agreements):**
Moneylenders Act 1900, s 1.
Moneylenders Act 1927, s 10 and in s 13(2) the words 'Without prejudice to the powers of a court under section one of the Moneylenders Act, 1900'

*(Consumer Credit Act 1974 (Commencement No 2) Order 1977, Sched 3)*

**(2) Repeals effective on 1.7.77:**
Betting and Loans (Infants) Act 1892, ss 2 to 4, s 6 except so far as it extends to Northern Ireland, in s 7 the definitions of 'indictment' and 'summary conviction'.
Moneylenders Act 1900, s 5

*(Consumer Credit Act 1974 (Commencement No 3) Order 1977, Sched)*

**(3) Repeals effective on 1.8.77:**
Pawnbrokers Act 1872, ss 37 to 44, in s 52 the words 'or by the refusal of a certificate for a licence', and Sched 6
Local Government Act 1894, s 27(1)(b)
Moneylenders Act 1927, ss 1 to 3, s 4(1), in s 4(2) the words 'the provisions of the last foregoing section and of', and s 18(a) to (c)
Finance Act 1949, s 15(1) to (3) and (6) to (8A)
Customs and Excise Act 1952, in s 313(1) the words 'or section 15 of the Finance Act 1949'

Finance Act 1961, s 11(1) from 'or section 15 of the Finance Act 1949' onwards

Administration of Justice Act 1964, s 9(3)(*b*)

Local Government Act 1966, in Sched 3, Pt II, the entries relating to s 37 of the Pawnbrokers Act 1872 and s 1(1) of the Moneylenders Act 1927

Local Government (Scotland) Act 1966, in Sched 4, Pt II, the entries relating to s 37 of the Pawnbrokers Act 1872 and s 1(1) of the Moneylenders Act 1927

Theft Act 1968, in Sched 2, Pt III, the entry relating to the Pawnbrokers Act 1872

Courts Act 1971, in Sched 9, Pt I, the entry relating to the Moneylenders Act 1927

Local Government Act 1972, s 213(1)(*a*) and (*b*) and (3).

Local Government (Scotland) Act 1973, in Sched 27, para 96, and in Sched 29 the entry relating to the Finance Act 1949

(*Consumer Credit Act 1974 (Commencement No 2) Order 1977, Sched 3*)

**(4) Repeal effective on 1.10.77 (except in relation to moneylending transactions made before that date):**
Moneylenders Act 1927, s 5(3)

(*Consumer Credit Act 1974 (Commencement No 3) Order 1977, Sched*)

**(5) Repeals effective on 27.1.80 (except in relation to transactions before that date and to Consumer Credit agreements):**
Moneylenders Act 1927, ss 6 to 8, 11 to 14, 15(2), 16 and Sched 1

(*Consumer Credit Act 1974 (Commencement No 5) Order 1979, Art 2(1) and Sched, Pt I*)

**(6) Repeals effective on 27.1.80 (except in relation to moneylending transactions made before that date):**
Moneylenders Act 1927, s 5(1), (2), (4) and (6)

(*Consumer Credit Act 1974 (Commencement No 5) Order 1979, Art 2(2) and Sched, Pt II*)

**(7) Other repeals effective on 27.1.80:**
Moneylenders Act 1927, ss 4(2), 5(5) and 9

(*Consumer Credit Act 1974 (Commencement No 5) Order 1979, Art 2(2) and Sched, Pt II*).

**(8) Repeals effective on 6.10.80:**
Pawnbrokers Act 1872, s 13
Moneylenders Act 1900, s 13
Moneylenders Act 1927, s 4(3)
Trading Stamps Act 1964, in s 10(1) the definition of 'purchase'

Advertisement (Hire Purchase) Act 1967

(*Consumer Credit Act 1974 (Commencement No 6) Order 1980 Sched, Pt I*)

**(9) Repeals effective on 30.3.81:**
Moneylenders Act 1927 in s 14(1) (*a*) the words 'and the rate of interest charged shall not exceed the rate of twenty per cent, per annum'.

(*Consumer Credit Act 1974 (Commencement No 7) Order 1981, Art 2 and Sched*)

**(10) Repeals effective on 19.5.85 (subject to savings set out in Consumer Credit Act 1974 (Commencement No 8) Order 1983, art 6):**
Statutory Declarations Act 1835, s 12
Metropolitan Police Act, 1835, s 50
Police Courts (Metropolis) Act 1839, in s 27 the words 'pawned or pledged' and the words 'or of any person who shall have advanced money upon the credit of such goods', and in s 28 the words 'pawned, pledged or' (in each place)
Commissioners for Oaths Act 1891, in s 1 the words 'or the Pawnbrokers Act 1872'
Burgh Police (Scotland) Act 1892, in s 453 the words 'and all offences committed against the provisions of the Pawnbrokers Act 1872'
Police (Property) Act 1897, in s 1(1) the words 'or s 34 of the Pawnbrokers Act 1872'
Moneylenders Act 1900
Law of Distress Amendment Act 1908, in s 4(1) the words 'bill of sale, hire'
Moneylenders Act 1927
Children and Young Persons Act 1933, s 8
Children and Young Persons (Scotland) Act 1937, s 19
Compensation (Defence) Act 1939, in s 18(1) the words from the expression 'hire purchase agreement' to 'omitted'
Liability for War Damage (Miscellaneous Provisions) Act 1939, ss 4 and 6(*b*)
Law Reform (Miscellaneous Provisions) (Scotland) Act 1940, s 4(2)(*b*) and (*c*)
Limitation (Enemies and War Prisoners) Act 1945, in s 2 the words 'Section 13(1) of the Moneylenders Act 1927'; in s 4 the words 'Section 13(1) of the Moneylenders Act 1927'
Pawnbrokers Act 1960
Hire Purchase Act 1964 (except Pt III and s 37)
Emergency Laws (Re-enactment and Repeals) Act 1964, s 1(4)
Hire Purchase Act 1965
Hire Purchase (Scotland) Act 1965
Companies Act 1967, ss 123–125
Decimal Currency Act 1969, in Sched 2, para 2
Post Office Act 1969, in Sched 4, para 31

Courts Act 1971, in Sched 9, Pt I, the entry relating to the Pawnbrokers Act 1972

(*Consumer Credit Act 1974 (Commencement No 8) Order 1983, Sched 2, Pt I*)


## Commencement dates of Repeals to NI Acts

See Consumer Credit Act 1974 (Commencement No 2) Order 1977, Sched 3, Pt II; Consumer Credit Act 1974 (Commencement No 3) Order 1977, Sched, Pt II; Consumer Credit Act 1974 (Commencement No 5) Order 1979, Arts 2 and 3 and Sched, Pts III and IV; Consumer Credit Act 1974 (Commencement No 6) Order 1980, Sched, Pt II; Consumer Credit Act 1974 (Commencement No 7) Order 1981, Art 2 and Sched; Consumer Credit Act 1974 (Commencement No 8) Order 1983, Sched 2, Pt II.

# Index